Lock, Stock & Barrel
A POLITICAL BIOGRAPHY OF
Mike Ahern

Paul Reynolds is an Associate Professor in Political Science at the University of Queensland, specialising in Queensland politics, political sociology, and electoral behaviour. He is the author of *The Democratic Labor Party* (Jacaranda, 1974) and *Political Sociology: An Australian Perspective* (Longman Cheshire, 1990), and has written over sixty articles, papers, monographs, and chapters — most dealing with federal and state politics. Since 1993, Paul has been Chair of the Queensland Chapter of the Australasian Study of Parliament Group, and was National Chair from 1999–2000. He has also been a media commentator on Queensland and federal politics for over thirty years.

Lock, Stock & Barrel

A POLITICAL BIOGRAPHY OF

Mike Ahern

Paul Reynolds

University of Queensland Press

First published 2002 by University of Queensland Press
Box 6042, St Lucia, Queensland 4067 Australia

www.uqp.uq.edu.au

Typeset by University of Queensland Press
Printed in Australia by McPherson's Printing Group

Distributed in the USA and Canada by
International Specialized Book Services, Inc.,
5824 N.E. Hassalo Street, Portland, Oregon 97213–3640

Queensland Government
Arts Queensland

Sponsored by the Queensland Office of Arts and Cultural Development.

Cataloguing in Publication Data
National Library of Australia

Reynolds, P. L. (Paul L.).
Lock, stock and barrel!

1. Ahern, M. J. (Michael John), 1942– . 2. Politicians — Queensland — Biography. 3. Premiers — Queensland — Biography. 4. Queensland — Politics and government — 20th century. I. Title.

Bibliography.
Includes index.

324.2092

ISBN 0 7022 3294 7

Contents

TO DAMON

Introduction

A political biography of Mike Ahern, former Premier of Queensland, is sorely needed. He has been substantially underrated, perhaps because of the overwhelming personality and machiavellian actions of his predecessor, Sir Joh Bjelke-Petersen, the last premier to be covered in the standard reference book, *The Premiers of Queensland* (Murphy, Joyce and Cribb 1990). This gap in the literature is made all the more surprising by the existence of a biography of his first Labor successor, Wayne Goss, and several books about the 1989 election which brought the Goss Government to power.

The significance of Mike Ahern's government, and indeed the significance of his contribution to Queensland's political history, is greater than his length of office as premier (December 1987 to September 1989) might suggest. In this political biography I argue that his career in public life is unique in the recent annals of Queensland politics. He began his political career after being politically socialised by two formidable mentors, his father and Sir Francis Nicklin. Despite this promising beginning, his parliamentary career was one of constant struggle as he battled powerful forces antipathetic to him from within his own party. After twelve years he virtually had to force his way into Cabinet. Seven years later he again had to adopt similar tactics to become leader. He was never fully accepted by all sections of his party; and his departure from public life can, at best, be described as low key.

Was Ahern then an enigma? Was he another flawed leader? Or was he a man ahead of his time? All three questions are simultaneously both profound and trite. They are profound because they address the essence of the man, his personality, his style and the political circumstances that nurtured, produced and shaped him. They are trite because they are posed too easily and invite a glib response.

His youth, education and religious persuasion certainly meant that he was enigmatic, in his first decade of parliamentary life, to many of his older colleagues. His dedication to comprehensive political, economic and social reform brought forth this response from many of his newer colleagues during his second parliamentary decade. This feeling increased, exponentially, when he became Premier.

As to the proposition of a flawed leader: when writing political biography, one wonders whether all leaders are not in one sense or another flawed. Not being in possession of psychoanalytic skills, I cannot make any competent judgment on this matter at the level of personality analysis. As Premier, he certainly performed strongly under pressure, maintaining his own agenda while facing an array of forces with which few leaders have been confronted in the recent times. It is for the reader to assess how well he coped with a party in disarray, a legacy of corruption which was the work of others, a resurgent Labor Party, and the ever-present media, sections of which were constantly skeptical as to his leadership credentials, if not overtly hostile towards him.

When discussing this project with numerous friends, colleagues, knowledgeable others and parliamentary identities, I was constantly told, "I had nothing against Mike Ahern" or, alternatively, "I rather liked [or admired] Mike Ahern". His difficulty appears to have been that, whether people liked, admired, or simply did not resent him, few seemingly translated these sentiments to unswerving support or lasting loyalty.

Perhaps closer to the truth is the argument that Ahern was ahead of his time. While this begs the question of when exactly his time would be, such a judgment is perpetually delivered against the reformist politician who seeks to abandon the status quo and move his/her colleagues to a different political terrain. Indeed, does such a reformer's time ever come?

Ahern was neither a closet Liberal nor covertly Labor. He remained firmly committed to his party, both to its provenance and to the interests it represented. However, when he accurately described himself as "a small 'n' National", he was in danger of becoming, in Sir David Lange's wonderful quip about Sir Robert Muldoon, "an embattled minority of one". It was not that he was resented by his party (though in some quarters he was) nor that, for the Nationals, he represented a novelty (though many doubtless thus viewed him), but rather that his passions and concerns went unrecognised by many of his colleagues.

The Queensland Nationals are a largely pragmatic party, possessed of a protean, even atavistic ideology. They frequently define themselves by that which they oppose, rather than by any visions they may espouse. If someone aspiring to implement a reform agenda appears among them, s/he is likely to be confronted with bemusement, possibly ridicule and, in time, distrust bordering on resentment. In the end this fate seems to have overtaken Ahern, albeit that he and his government's indecisiveness over the aborted referendum and daylight saving trial persuaded sufficient of his colleagues to return to the false security of authoritarian, pragmatic leadership. For most of the Parliamentary National Party, experimentation and reform were all very well, but they could never imagine making such orientations a habit.

This account, then, represents the life and times of Michael John Ahern. It is neither his personal story nor is it, or could it, be his authorised biography. As a political scientist at The University of Queensland, I had the opportunity to observe, lecture and comment upon many of the events discussed herein. I did not meet my subject until January 1989 at, of all places, the Ashmolean Museum in Oxford. I did not consider this project until he had left public life. He has generously afforded me all the cooperation I have requested. He read early drafts, restricting his comments to factual matters. When I once suggested that he might care to react to my analysis and interpretation he said, with typical modesty, "Oh no, Paul, you are telling the story".

Inevitably this is both his story and mine. It is for the reader to decide its veracity or otherwise. I have commented upon, analysed and interpreted the relevant events and assessed their significance. Mike Ahern remains central to this account because he is its subject. Queensland's recent past would necessarily take on a different colouration if written from the perspective of his contemporaries, Joh Bjelke-Petersen, Wayne Goss or Angus Innes. The texture of this biography derives from its *raison d'être*, Ahern himself.

I take this opportunity to thank those who were generous to me, by giving of their time, opinions, recollections and thoughts. In particular I mention the valued insights of the late Margaret Cribb, the late Don Lane, Brian Austin, David Ford, Hon. David Hamill and Terry White. Also consulted for assistance were Dr Gary Chittick, Bill Hewitt, Bob Katter MHR, Ted Newton, Brian Stephenson and Dr Rae Wear. Thanks are also due to my two research assistants, Simon Kelly and Ross Mensforth, who very ably worked on much of the primary source materials; and finally to Barbara McKenzie for her extremely helpful editorial work.

I have enjoyed skilled secretarial and technical assistance from the staff of the Government Department, especially from Linda Buckham, Tony Bunney, Rachel Eadie, Karen La Rocca and Ros Nicol. My colleagues have networked with me and willingly allowed me to test my views against their knowledge. My daughter, Gretel, always supplied a dose of healthy scepticism as to my chronicling the past. Claire Welshe (nee Ahern), whom I had the privilege of teaching, initially kindled my interest in telling her "Dad's story".

Finally, Mike Ahern's career as backbencher, Minister and Premier was marked by controversy. This may well be the fate of his biography. If such should occur, I suspect that both of us would be well satisfied.

Paul Reynolds
Brisbane
2002

CHAPTER 1
Political beginnings

Political inheritance

Almost two years after Mike Ahern's overthrow as Premier and National Party leader, and one year after he had left Parliament, a research student asked him, "What made you decide to enter politics?" He replied, "I was born to it. My family was always directly involved in politics and my father was State President of the Country Party." She then asked, "Did Sir Frank Nicklin have any influence over you?" Ahern responded, "Yes. Frank Nicklin was a close friend of my father's. That's how we worked it up." (Bennett 1991, Appendix A, p. 1). His acknowledgment of these two influences on his early life suggests that, at an early age, he had decided on a parliamentary career in what was then the Country Party.

It has often been observed that political activists are disproportionately likely to produce offspring who themselves become politically active. Mike's father,[1] Jack Ahern, was a highly successful dairy farmer who, early in his farming career, had applied scientific principles (including artificial insemination) to dairying, thereby establishing an enviable reputation for his Jersey stud. Later, when Mike had entered Parliament, Ahern Snr turned from dairy farming to the less labour-intensive pursuit of beef farming, again emulating his earlier success, on this occasion with a stud of Poll Herefords.

The older Ahern once ran for the Senate, but he does not seem to have harboured ongoing parliamentary ambitions. His political resumé is nonetheless typical of those who from the 1930s to the 1970s were Country Party members involved in an array of political activities. While many of his contemporaries satisfied their political ambitions in shire politics, Jack chose involvement in rural producer groups, in his case the Gympie District Council of the Queensland Dairy Organisation (QDO) over which he presided for three years. From his Gympie base, he graduated to membership of the QDO State Council which, according to his biographer, "put him in touch with the Queensland political scene of the time". (Shannon 1991, p. 45).[2]

His involvement with the QDO both paralleled and complemented his Country Party membership by extending his involvement to an adjacent, albeit cognate organisation.[3] But for Jack Ahern producer group politics were no substitute for active involvement in the Country Party. He chaired his local Country Party branch (Maleny) in the 1940s, and the 1950s opened with him chairing the Landsborough Electorate Council. He then worked his way through the upper echelons of the Country Party's state organisation until, in 1964, he capped his organisational career with a three-year term as Queensland Country Party state president.

Mike Ahern was born in 1942 and was thus eight years old when his father took the chair of the Landsborough Electorate Council. Among other involvements this position made Ahern Snr the campaign manager for the local member and future Premier, Frank Nicklin. Ahern Jnr was twenty-two when his father commenced his term as state president, concluding his term twelve months before Mike was preselected, by plebiscite, to succeed Nicklin.

Mike Ahern's recollection to Bennett that Nicklin and his father were close friends is supported by Shannon, who notes that these two "had a long and harmonious relationship" (Shannon 1991, p. 45), a friendship which dated at least from the 1939 redistribution which created Landsborough, with Nicklin becoming its first member.[4] Mike thus possessed two high-profile political mentors in his father and Sir Frank Nicklin. The former rose to head Queensland's Country Party organisation, while the latter was to serve eleven years as Queensland Premier. Mike was fifteen in 1957 when Nicklin became Premier after the Labor split and the fall of the Gair Government.[5]

In their long and deep friendship, Nicklin and Jack Ahern epitomised the close intimacy and harmonious cooperation that then existed between the Country Party's organisational and political wings. Nicklin would frequently confer with Ahern Snr on parliamentary business and on any issue of general concern to the Parliamentary Country Party. When president, the latter was often asked by Nicklin to attend Parliament, to consult with, and address, Country Party MPs on matters sensitive to the party's operations.

Jack Ahern, then, had become president of his party as it concluded its first decade in coalition government. Both Premier and President had shared a quarter of a century in the political wilderness as, between 1932 and 1957, elections routinely returned successive ALP governments. Both men, however, reached the zenith of their respective party careers during the first of the Country Party's more than three decades in office. Ironically Mike Ahern's parliamentary career peaked at the close of this era. If his mentors enjoyed the fruits of victory, his was the responsibility to strive frantically, and ultimately unsuccessfully, to stave off defeat.

Political socialisation gave Mike two role models who were firmly placed in the lineage of the traditional Country Party. Both were men of probity whose personal reputations meant much to them. In 1980, four months after becoming Primary Industries Minister, Mike, in an interview with *Queensland Country Life*, described Nicklin thus:

> He was a visionary, a man of impeccable honesty and integrity who always did what he considered was right for Queensland. I hope I can aspire to follow his principles and would be honoured if I could achieve the reputation as a Nicklin of the 1980s. (4 December 1980)

Although successful men of the land, Ahern Snr and Nicklin were not exceptionally wealthy. This was the prerogative of the graziers and/or those, represented by Bjelke-Petersen and Russell Hinze, who advanced the ethos of "development at all costs". Unlike these two latter politicians, neither Premier nor president had turned from farming to either agribusiness or land development. Indeed, it would never have occurred to them to do so. Both were prosperous yeomen farmers possessed of personal and political values to match their economic achievements. That Ahern was Catholic and Nicklin Methodist, in a party which was overwhelmingly Protestant with strong Masonic overtones, says much about the depth and quality of their relationship. Their ecumenical friendship was the more remarkable in the 1950s, a time when their ALP opponents were vilifying each other over any number of issues, not least of which was anti-Catholic, anti-Protestant sectarianism (Hogan 1987, pp. 243–55).

Initially Mike Ahern chose to make his political mark in the youth wing of the Country Party. In this decision he emulated his father by concentrating on organisational politics, but differed from him by showing no marked interest in producer group politics. To have followed this path would, in all probability, have meant delaying his parliamentary career, because these organisations were dominated by men of his father's generation, most of whom had virtually retired from active farming and were devoting their semi-retirement to group politics. The situation was much the same in the shire councils. Those who graduated to state (or federal) politics from rural local government were invariably older men, busying themselves with parliamentary politics in their last decade or so of public life (Reynolds 1994).

In Queensland, Mike Ahern was the first representative of a new political type which emerged in Western politics during the 1960s. They were still overwhelmingly males, yet younger at the point of entry to Parliament than were previous generations. They generally possessed higher educational qualifications than had earlier age cohorts. As younger recruits aiming for long, high-achieving parliamentary careers, they positioned themselves appropriately, often bypassing the hitherto normal political apprenticeships of local government, producer group or, in Labor's case, trade union politics (Reynolds 1994, pp. 12–20). Ahern gave recognition to this generation gap in an interview with the *Sunday Sun*, conducted four months before he became Premier. He reflected:

> I've seen an entire Labor Party come and go. Of the Liberals only Knox, Lickiss and Lee remain and in our party, Joh and Hinze.

This fact caused the interviewer, David Bentley, to write:

> In a quiet, logical, disarmingly reasonable manner, [he] proceeded to outwit and outlast just about everyone else in parliament (9 August 1987).

Ahern had been educated at Downlands (Toowoomba) and graduated Bachelor of Agricultural Science from The University of Queensland. He became involved in the Country Party at a time when virtually all their politicians had progressed no further than the Junior Certificate, with many not attaining even that modest level of secondary education. He dates his joining the Young Country Party (YCP) in 1963, then aged twenty-one (Bennett 1991). After four years of active membership he was elected to three prominent positions. In 1967 he became YCP state president and also commenced a two-year term as YCP federal president. The following year (1968) he was elected Junior Vice President of the Country Party in Queensland. Thus, while Jack was serving out the final year of his state presidency (1967), Mike was both state and national president of the youth wing. Shannon described this as "a unique family dual achievement" (1991, p. 45); it also immeasurably advanced the younger Ahern's parliamentary ambitions.

Nicklin's close friendship with Jack Ahern, together with Mike's growing political expertise, exemplified by his rise to prominence in the Country Party organisation from a power base in the YCP, pointed to his being a strong candidate to follow the Premier in Landsborough. After winning the 1966 election, Nicklin wished to retire, leaving the task of the 1969 election to his successor, Jack Pizzey. Ahern has since alluded to this arrangement, telling Bennett, "That's how we worked it up." While "it" doubtless refers to the Landsborough nomination, it should not be inferred that Mike Ahern enjoyed an automatic ride to preselection. He claimed that pre-selection for Landsborough was "tight" (interview 8 September 1993). That he was not necessarily seen by others as the pre-ordained candidate is shown by his being opposed by two high-profile local party stalwarts. The first was Walter Burnett (later Sir Walter and for many years chair of the Royal National Association); the second was Councillor J.L. Beausang, then chair of the Landsborough Shire Council. They ran, respectively, second and third.

This was preselection by plebiscite. When the returning officer, Colonel Nev Hatton, made the membership lists available, Ahern wrote to, and then visited, every local party member to press his claims. Such campaign tactics seem to have been a novelty then in Queensland Country Party pre-selections. Ahern attributed his victory to "shoe leather" (interview 8 September 1993) and, less certainly, to his youth (both of the other candidates were old enough to be his father) and to his educational qualifications. However, while the Landsborough by-election was a memorable event for Ahern, its significance was far wider as Landsborough became the harbinger for future, and worsening, Coalition relations.

Background to the Landsborough by-election

The twenty-six years of coalition government can be divided in two. For the first fifteen years (from the mid-1950s to the 1972 election) there was harmony between the Country and Liberal parties. Thereafter intra-coalition relations steadily deteriorated until the final breach in 1983. The only difficulty in the first period was over preferential voting, which the Liberals insisted on introducing for the 1963 election, but this dispute had evaporated by 1966. This resolution had been assisted by the Queensland Labor Party (QLP; later Democratic Labor Party, DLP). This was an indication that, following the introduction of preferential voting, QLD/DLP would play a more active role in state politics, thereby maximising the new electoral laws to pursue its political tactics, aimed at punishing the ALP for its role in the 1957 split (Reynolds 1974, pp. 48–71). After 1963 Country Party fears were allayed because, outside a handful of seats, preferential voting exerted no discernible influence on the final result (Hughes 1969). Country Party forebodings that preferential voting would alter the state political landscape against its political and electoral interests were thus shown to be groundless.

After the 1963 election, Cabinet was enlarged from eleven to thirteen, by including one additional Liberal (Dr Peter Delamothe) and another Country Party minister (Joh Bjelke-Petersen). While the July 1963 Country Party conference routinely rejected yet another Liberal call for amalgamation (something interminably discussed by the two parties since the formation of the Country Party after World War I), some disquiet surfaced among the rank and file following reports that the Liberals were establishing local branches in Country Party seats, particularly targeting the Gold Coast.[6]

Then, in March 1964, a small group of Parliamentary Liberal Party backbenchers, the so-called "Ginger Group" led by John Murray (Clayfield), publicly criticised the Government's land policy and its excessive domination of parliamentary business. Hughes was thus moved to comment:

> For the first time there appeared a small rift in the Government's ranks, turning mainly on electoral competition between the coalition partners, but involving also a few policy issues and appropriate style of parliamentary government. (1969, p. 15)

Insofar as it is possible to date the beginnings of intra-coalition strife, this "small rift" was precursor to a train of events that culminated, nineteen years later, in the dramatic collapse of the Coalition. Murray's group set a precedent for future backbench Liberals, should they so desire, to play at being mavericks *vis-à-vis* the Ministry.

However, two years later, the 1966 election reinforced the 1963 electoral pattern. The Country Party won twenty-seven seats (gain of one), the Liberals 20 (no change), the ALP twenty-six while there were four Independents and one QLP Member. The Coalition, with a combined vote of 44.5 per cent, had won 61 per cent of the seats, thereby easily retaining control over the Parliament. Nicklin could now contemplate retirement, secure in the knowledge not only that, after a decade, was his Government entrenched in office but also that the zonal system (adapted by him in 1958) ensured that the Country Party led the Coalition, a situation further demonstrated by the seat-to-vote ratio. The Country Party, with 18.9 per cent of the vote, secured 35 per cent of the seats; the Liberals, with 25.6 per cent of the vote, gained 26 per cent of the seats; while Labor, by contrast, achieved 43.8 per cent of the vote yet won only one-third of the seats.

However, the very adoption of preferential voting necessarily raised the possibility of three-cornered contests, and the spectre of direct competition between Country and Liberal Party candidates for both conservative and marginal ALP electorates. Such confrontations could occur when either type of seat had been vacated by death, retirement or, more provocatively and in the absence of any electoral pact, by either party nominating against a sitting Coalition colleague. With the advent of preferential voting, the Country Party proclaimed itself resolutely opposed to three-cornered contests. After all, they had the better of the Coalition arrangement owing to the zonal system maximising their (rural) vote-to-seat relationship (see table 1). Moreover, they could point to the 1966 result to show that it was the ALP, rather than the Liberals (with one-quarter of both votes and seats), that was disadvantaged by the zonal system. After 1958 the brutal reality of the zonal vote weightage system's operation was that Labor under-representation produced Country Party over-representation. This situation persisted until the 1991 Electoral and Administrative Review Commission (EARC) supervised redistribution.

Necessarily, however, the Liberals perceived the issue differently. For the first three elections of the 1960s they were prepared to accept the terms of their electoral pact with the Country Party, which effectively reserved the city seats to them and rural electorates to their allies (Reynolds 1990, p. 38, footnote 2). While first-past-the-post voting prevailed they had no alternative, but the coming of preferential voting posed a further set of problems because the pact, together with the zonal system, all but ensured perpetual Country Party dominance of the Coalition.

Table 1: Seats won at the 1966 Queensland state election: by zone and by party

Party	Metropolitan	Provincial city	Country	Total
Country	–	–	27	27
Liberal	17	1	2	20
ALP	11	9	6	26
Other	–	2	3	5
Total	28 (36%)	12 (15%)	38 (49%)	78 (100%)

In the mid-1960s, 49 per cent of seats were in the Country Zone, 68 per cent of which were won by the Country Party, constituting the entirety of its parliamentary representation. By contrast, just over one-third of the seats were in the Metropolitan Zone, 60 per cent of which were held by the Liberals (after 1963 most on QLP preferences). By winning a higher proportion of seats in their heartland than did the

Liberals in their bailiwick, the Country Party thus dominated the coalition owing both to the vote-to-seat ratio and to the margin between Country and Metropolitan Zone seats.[7]

The 1966 results highlight two further unresolved problems concerning the Coalition electoral pact. The first related to the Provincial Cities Zone. These seats were not particularly vital to the Government, as 75 per cent were Labor held. Consequently the decision as to which Coalition party would, and did, contest them was made on an arbitrary, even random basis. In 1966 the Liberals were the conservative contestant in seven, the Country Party in three, while two were ignored because they were occupied by Independent (anti-ALP) incumbents. Lack of any specific intra-coalition electoral agreement had the potential to turn provincial city seats into a series of semi-autonomous electoral battlegrounds.

Of more proximate concern, however, was that arc of Country Zone seats which surrounded Brisbane, extending north to south from the Sunshine Coast to the Gold Coast. From the mid-1960s these electorates began to experience urban overspill, inevitably commencing the erosion of their rural characteristics. For both Government parties the future of these seats was problematical. The new demographic trends, as they accelerated, would inevitably force their reclassification and consequent removal from the Country Zone. In that event, the political issue was whether the Country Party would follow these seats into the Metropolitan Zone or would surrender them to the Liberals. The corollary question was whether the Liberals would await this development or instead, by anticipating future demographics, establish an organisational, and hence electoral presence, while these electorates remained in the Country Zone.[8]

At the time of the 1968 Landsborough by-election neither party had systematically addressed these matters and, as they had failed to debate them internally, neither were they in any position to engage in cross party negotiations. In reality, as the by-election campaign was to make abundantly clear, while the Country Party maintained its public opposition to all three-cornered contests the Liberals were divided.

Broadly speaking, the Liberal organisation, whose charter it was to secure the long-term interests of its party by advancing its electoral fortunes at every possible opportunity, favoured a pragmatic and selective use of three-cornered contests. However, the leaders of the Parliamentary Liberal Party were opposed to such electoral opportunism, focused as they were on the tasks of government, which included avoidance of disputes with the Country Party. The Landsborough by-election then was the first among many contests that brought these intra-coalition tensions to the surface.

Senator R.D. Sherrington, Liberal President from 1964 until his sudden death in 1966, had broken with the past by adopting a hard line in dealing with the Country Party.[9] This trend was continued by his successor, Dr A.W. Hartwig. At the 1966 Liberal Party annual convention, its state council was empowered to establish a special committee to consider problems associated with three-cornered contests. The following year, a further special committee was given a wider remit to review the party's constitution to consider territorial (i.e. electoral) expansion (Hughes 1980, p. 38). But before either committee could report, their deliberations were overtaken by Nicklin's resignation and the necessity for a by-election in his seat of Landsborough.

Landsborough was a Country Zone electorate. In 1966 a straight fight with Labor yielded Nicklin a vote of 71.3 per cent. The seat was, by Queensland standards, large: 620 square miles in area and containing 10 385 electors (Hughes 1969, p. 347). However, it was one in that arc of seats that encircled the outskirts of Brisbane. Urban growth, emanating from both Brisbane and Sunshine Coast towns, was expected to influence its future demographic composition making it, in the view of some Liberal hopefuls, increasingly Liberal-oriented. More pragmatically, the Premier's resignation had rendered it vacant; thus, for such Liberals, precipitating a three-cornered contest in Landsborough would not violate any supposed rule preventing challenges either to sitting Members or to Coalition Ministers. After all, the Country Party had done precisely this in Toowoomba East in 1966. However, despite these considerations, intra-Liberal tensions showed how ill-equipped the Liberal state executive was to grapple with this challenge. The totality of Liberal disarray was amply demonstrated by the chain of events leading to the by-election.

On 16 January 1968, Hartwig announced that the state executive had decided not to contest the by-election but that he personally opposed this decision. Such an extraordinary admission simultaneously exposed the depths of his party's division and laid its executive open to internal attack, which quickly came from Charles Porter (Toowong), a former Liberal state secretary and member of Murray's "Ginger Group". Porter charged that the state executive's decision was, "flabby, craven and lacking confidence in our purpose." (Barclay 1968, p. 258). The Young Liberal Movement, in the person of its outgoing president, Don Cameron MHR (Griffith), also urged the executive to reconsider.

On 6 February the Landsborough Liberal Electorate Committee, taking its lead from these quarters, defied its state executive by declaring that it would preselect a candidate. Twelve days later it activated this decision by endorsing its secretary, Dr Peter Nelson-Gracie. The dispute now escalated as the Liberal Party president and his parliamentary leader adopted opposing positions. Hartwig announced that he would support Nelson-Gracie in his private capacity because, given the state executive's position, he could not do so as Liberal president. In contrast, Parliamentary Liberal Party Leader and Deputy Premier, Sir Gordon Chalk, said that he would support whomsoever the Country Party chose because this person would be "the official Government candidate" (Barclay ibid.). For good measure, Chalk went on to accuse Hartwig of creating dissension in both party and Government. The president's reply to Chalk went to the heart of the issue. Hartwig, in contradistinction to Chalk's parliamentary perspective, unambiguously stated the organisation's position, claiming that it was politically dishonest for the Liberal Party to recruit members and then deny them the right to contest the seats they lived in; the Landsborough Liberals, therefore, were acting legitimately by seeking to advance the Liberal cause. He added that, to forestall them now, was not in the Liberals' long-term interests.

Murray and Porter said that, if asked, they would campaign for Nelson-Gracie and they went with Bill Lickiss (Mt Coot-tha) to Landsborough on 28 February to attend the opening of his campaign. Meanwhile the Country Party sought to distance itself from the dispute. Jack Ahern's successor as president, E.J.S. Roberts, referred to the problem as "a row in the Liberal Party" (Barclay, ibid.), and the following day (20 February) the Country Party duly preselected Mike Ahern. Jack, still chair of the Landsborough Electorate Council, thus became his son's campaign manager. Interestingly, three years before his preselection, Ahern had publicly rebuked the Liberal Party on the very issue of three-cornered contests. In April 1965 he criticised Sherrington's announcement that there would be selective three cornered contests at the 1966 election, warning that the Liberals were "prepared to wreck not only the coalition but the future of Queensland as well" (Fitzgerald 1984, p. 236) — surely an act of bravado by the yet electorally unblooded rising star of the Country Party.

When Nelson-Gracie launched his campaign, Chalk again declared for the Country Party, with Ahern enthusiastically stating that Chalk was motivated by "the best interests of the Parliamentary Liberal Party and of the people of Queensland". (Barclay, ibid.) Chalk duly visited Landsborough and campaigned for Ahern against Nelson-Gracie, who was perforce running as an Independent Liberal. Twelve years later, in an interview with *Thursday* magazine, Ahern reflected on Chalk's stance:

> We had the strange situation of Gordon Chalk coming up here to speak at a meeting for me and being heckled by members of the Coast's Liberal Party.

Trevor Hocking, the reporter, wrote that Ahern "savoured the irony" (1 May 1980).

During the campaign, Labor tried to sow further dissension in Coalition ranks by directing its preferences to the Liberals. Meanwhile, in a press release, Country Party headquarters declared that should Nelson-Gracie be elected he would not be admitted to the ranks of Parliamentary Liberal Party. As Hughes observed, this was "a statement which was not disputed by Chalk or the Liberal state executive" (Hughes 1980, p. 39). Hence the Liberal Parliamentary leadership, in the midst of a successful attempt to engineer Hartwig's expulsion from the presidency, was apparently prepared to go to all possible lengths to appease the Country Party, even to the extent of allowing its coalition partner to dictate who would or would not be included in the membership of the Parliamentary Liberal Party. Fortunately for Chalk's leadership, and the cohesion of his party, this explosive issue was never tested, for Ahern won on first preferences. Nelson-Gracie collected a fifth of the vote, causing Porter's face-saving claim that the result could be "viewed with satisfaction and pride" (Barclay 1968, p. 259). The last word, however, went to Country Party president Roberts who observed with masterly understatement that if the Landsborough decision was persisted with for the 1969 election, and was extended to Gold Coast seats, it "could cause some friction in the coalition" (Barclay, ibid.).

Ahern had now won his place in Parliament. He had followed his non-familial mentor and inherited what Hughes was later to describe as "one of the safest Country Party seats in the state" (Hughes 1980, p. 39). The Liberal challenge had been disposed of with comparative ease, and thereafter in Landsborough the Liberals caused Ahern no serious electoral concern (Hamill and Reynolds 1983, pp. 46–47). The price the Government paid for this example of Liberal Party electoral adventurism was a dangerous bout of Liberal political instability provoked by a contentious electoral problem, namely three-cornered contests. This issue proved to be beyond the Coalition's ability to resolve. As a consequence, the quantum of electoral disharmony within Government ranks grew at each subsequent election, being particularly exacerbated by each successive redistribution.

However, Mike Ahern had now become both the newest and youngest member of the Queensland Parliament. He was about to turn twenty-six, a rather self-conscious product of his generation who saw himself as "a small 'n' National ... " who "always thought because I was pretty close to Frank Nicklin that it [becoming leader] might be a nice thing to do" (Bennett 1991, Appendix A, p.1).

Notes

1. This account of Jack Ahern's background and political involvement is drawn from Shannon (1991). I am indebted to the late M.N.B. Cribb for this source.
2. Unfortunately no dates are indicated.
3. Until 1944 most primary producer organisations were affiliated to the Country Party. See Overacker (1968, p. 266).
4. Mike Ahern was its second. When he resigned in 1990, the sometime Liberal leader Joan Sheldon won it at the ensuing by-election. The 1991

(EARC) redistribution abolished Landsborough, dividing it between Caloundra and Nicklin (Kelly and Reynolds 1992, pp. 19, 66).

5. The Labor Party split in Queensland. This cost it government for the next thirty-two years, as chronicled in R. Murray, *The Split: Australian Labor in The Fifties*, Cheshire, Melbourne, 1970, chapter 19, and D. Murphy, R. Joyce and M. Cribb (eds), *The Premiers of Queensland*, 2nd edn, University of Queensland Press, Brisbane, 1990, chapter 16.
6. There were then three such electorates, all Country Party held: Logan, Albert and South Coast. All were in the Country Zone with an average enrolment of 10 554, indicating that in the 1960s all were still predominantly rural in character (see Hughes 1969).
7. The difference was ten seats, a Country to Metropolitan Zone margin of 13 per cent.
8. In 1966 there were eight three-cornered contests. In Cairns and Port Curtis the Liberals nominated for the first time in safe ALP Provincial Cities Zone seats. In Toowoomba East, the Country Party nominated for the first time in a Provincial Cities Zone seat vacated by the Liberals (Labor won it). In the remaining five cases the Liberals nominated for the first time in Country Party-held Country Zone seats which lay adjacent to Brisbane: Albert, Logan, Murrumba, Redcliffe and South Coast.
9. Sherrington seems to have been responsible for initiating the five near-Brisbane three-cornered contests of 1966 referred to in note 8 above. As an urban Liberal (from Indooroopilly) he apparently had little truck with the Country Party. His death was remembered in the Liberal Party for a number of years by the Sherrington Memorial Lecture delivered to Liberal Party faithful.

CHAPTER 2

On the backbench

Introduction to Parliament

The Parliament Mike Ahern entered consisted of seventy-eight Members: twenty-seven Country Party, nineteen Liberal (plus one Independent Liberal), twenty-six Labor, three Independent, one North Queensland Labor Party (Tom Aitkens) and one QLP. Premier Jack Pizzey died suddenly on 31 July 1968, fourteen weeks later, whereupon Joh Bjelke-Petersen was elected leader and Premier by the Parliamentary Country Party. Apart from the Premier, there were twelve Ministers, seven of whom were Country Party and five Liberal including Sir Gordon Chalk, Liberal leader, who was Deputy Premier and Treasurer. The Parliament had five committees but only one, Standing Orders, was devoted to non-housekeeping tasks.[1] Ahern took his seat on 20 March 1968, four days after his election, and made his maiden speech a fortnight later (3 April) on the second reading of the Beach Protection Bill. In the course of this he paid a generous and fulsome tribute to his predecessor and political mentor, Sir Francis Nicklin (*QPD* vol. 248, pp. 2772–5).

In retrospect, the 1968 Parliament was a legislature in transition. The Coalition had completed a decade in office while Labor was slowly recovering from the 1957 split. In the late 1960s, all but one QLP Member had been eliminated from Parliament,[2] but the ALP remained dominated by older men, who either were from Trades Hall unions or owed their political careers to the patronage of the Labor machine controlled by Trades Hall leader Jack Egerton (Swan 1983, 105–110).

When interviewed in 1993, Ahern recalled that he met Labor identities for the first time during the Landsborough by-election. Until then they had inhabited separate political worlds. He mentioned Jack Stanaway, Ted Harris (Wynnum) with whom he shared an interest in orchid growing, Fred Newton (Belmont), Percy Tucker (Townsville West), Jack Houston (Bulimba) and Jack Duggan (Toowoomba East), then Leader of the Opposition and the only Minister who had refused to support Gair. In fact Ahern had a further connection with Duggan as he and his sister were at school with, respectively, Duggan's son and daughter. While an admirer of Duggan's highly regarded oratorical prowess, he summed up the rest of the Labor Members as "not bad blokes but very pedestrian" (interview 8 September 1993). Given the iron-fisted control wielded by the Egerton machine over ALP pre-selections, this was a widely held view inside and outside the labour movement (Swan, ibid.).

The composition of the Queensland Parliament had been decisively altered by the events of 1957, but thereafter compositional changes occurred incrementally. The Chamber Ahern joined was characterised by longevity of service, informal procedures and, generally, easy friendly relations between Members irrespective of party allegiance. He spoke of "the great sense of camaraderie in the Parliament which evaporated after Pizzey's death" (interview 8 September 1993).

The size of the House, its masculine ethos, the "clubbiness" of its operations and the fact that, interstate, Brisbane was still regarded as "the largest country town in Australia" influenced the distinctive approach Members brought to their parliamentary tasks. The Federal Coalition was secure in power, having in 1966 won its greatest victory since 1949. The ALP's federal resurgence under Gough Whitlam's leadership had scarcely begun, the zonal system continued to protect the Queensland Coalition Government and Liberal–Country Party relations were generally harmonious. The divisive politics of the 1970s were two elections away.

Ahern's memories of parliamentary arrangements in this period reflect the relaxed features of parliamentary political life. In 1968 there were no Whips' lists to organise either Dorothy Dixers (prearranged questions from Government backbenchers to Ministers) for Question Time or speakers for legislative debates. Members were free to choose their topic areas, decide the frequency or otherwise of their contributions and make their own speaking arrangements. In common with others, Ahern honed his topics and developed his fields of expertise. An analysis of the subjects he chose to discuss, at Question Time, in legislative debates, on Matters of Public Interest and Estimates debates during his twelve years on the backbench reveal his interests. His major preoccupations were agricultural subjects (30 per cent of speeches), social issues (10 per cent), industrial questions (10 per cent), local government (9 per cent), educational and financial matters (7 per cent each), parliamentary affairs (6 per cent) and justice (5 per cent). Otherwise he busied himself with matters as they arose.

In part, this pattern was typical of Country Party Members of his era. As they represented rural seats, all had a vested interest in agricultural politics. Similarly, much of the legislation that came before Parliament concerned some aspect of rural politics. The close link in the shires between agriculture and local government meant that Country Party Members were always sensitive to the latter, not least because the shire councils were administered by either their supporters or their rivals within the local party machine. In addition rural local authorities were traditionally responsible for the provision and maintenance of much regional employment and infrastructure.

The concerns of a typical Country Party MP, then, accounted for about two-fifths of Ahern's speechmaking; his atypical background can be gauged from the remainder of his contributions. His interest in education was unusual but reflects the fact that, after Pizzey's death and until 1983, he was his parliamentary party's only graduate. His colleagues appear to have accepted his specialisation in this area. Education, together with a concern for social issues, established his political persona, as did his increasing concern over the reform of parliamentary procedures in the face of Bjelke-Petersen's ever-tightening authoritarian control over Parliament. This latter trend was accompanied by the Premier's obdurate refusal to accord any recognition to either the Opposition or Government backbench.[3] Finally, Ahern's speeches on industrial affairs were largely concerned with the need to provide government assistance to small business enterprises, a staple and long-standing bipartisan feature of Queensland politics.

The House the Members built

If the Whips adopted a laissez-faire approach to Members, this approach was typical of the Government as a whole. It was not until 1975 that a Minister was designated Leader of the House, a task initially given to Max Hodges, then Minister for Police. Hodges and Bjelke-Petersen subsequently fell out over the administration of the police portfolio. Bjelke-Petersen overruled Commissioner Whitrod's order for an inquiry when a police officer batoned to the ground a young female student during a street march; he also ignored Whitrod's advice that Terry Lewis not be promoted to Assistant Commissioner. When Whitrod then resigned, Hodges and Tom Newbery were given each other's portfolios, and the latter became the second Leader of the House. Thereafter the position of Leader of the House and the task of managing Government business both were routinely bestowed upon a senior Minister.

Until the Government appointed a Leader of the House, there was no ministerial chain of command devoted to the ordering and prioritisation of Government business. When interviewed in 1993, Ahern recounted an amusing pattern of events which he claimed was typical of the way Parliament operated. Each sitting day, which began at 11.00 am, Chalk decided the order of Government business, and, after Question Time, communicated this to the House. Just before the luncheon adjournment, the Premier would enter the House, read the Order Paper and invariably alter Chalk's arrangements. At 2.30 pm, after the luncheon adjournment and none too happy, Chalk would move restoration of the original order of business, thereby frequently prompting further disputes between them. When this occurred, and if Bjelke-Petersen later absented himself, at 4.00 pm an angry Chalk would have the House adjourned.

Such reliance on "Rafferty's rules" both reflected and gave scope to the growing animus between Chalk and Bjelke-Petersen, in direct contrast to Chalk's generally harmonious relationships with both Nicklin and Pizzey. But such incidents also reflected the traditional in-house atmospherics of the Parliament. There was no need to systematise proceedings because Parliament was accorded neither a high priority by Government (as much attributable to twenty-five years of Labor rule as to Bjelke-Petersen's attitudes) nor a creative, meaningful role in the legislative process.

One further instance of the game-playing that characterised those days was the relationship between the Government and Opposition. Government Whip Vince Jones (Callide) was described by Ahern as "a survivor" who lost no parliamentary votes while holding office (interview 8 September 1993). While this suggests Jones was competent, of greater interest are his interactions with a member of the Opposition. Labor's Whip was Horrie Davies (Maryborough) but Merv Thackeray (Rockhampton North) "was on the outer with the ALP, partly because he was a left-wing meat worker and partly because he was hopeless" (interview 8 September 1993). If Labor planned a surprise division, Thackeray would go privately to Jones's office to indicate ALP tactics by a pre-arranged signal. Thus forewarned, Jones had time to organise his Members for the apparently unexpected division. Such dealings scarcely suggest an Opposition unrelenting in its hostility to Government, nor a Government in any real danger from the Opposition's tactical ingenuity. Indeed, during this period, an absence of the political "killer instinct" seems to have characterised all sides of Parliament. The Liberals, for example, had not bothered to appoint a Whip, being content to leave the management of Government front-bench and backbench relations to their Coalition partner.

The Country Party leadership

Ahern then brought three attributes to Parliament: youthfulness, idealism and an intense admiration for Sir Francis Nicklin. He mentioned, when interviewed, that he began his parliamentary career believing in the application of high standards so that a politician "could do things for others". He attributed this attitude of service to Nicklin's influence but he partly qualified, or perhaps defended, this stance by adding that it derived "from a conservative perspective". He asserted that the former Premier "had shown the way as an ideal leader who commanded wide respect from the Parliament and the community" (interview 8 September 1993). In Chapter 1, Ahern is quoted as invoking Nicklin when he (Ahern) became a Minister. If he articulated such an attachment then, there can be no doubt that he felt the linkage even more intensely twelve years earlier. Not only had he entered Parliament as a neophyte backbencher steeped in Nicklin's ways, but he had also assumed his mentor's seat.

As Ahern himself recognised, his political inspiration derived from the twin sources of his father, who personified the Country Party organisation, and Nicklin, the embodiment of the Parliamentary National Party. However, with the advent of Bjelke-Petersen's premiership in 1968 and the commencement in 1970 of Sir Robert Sparkes' twenty-year term as National Party president, new forces began to work their way through the party. The days of the old-style Country Party were numbered, as Sparkes sought to widen the party's base by turning it into an aggressive conservative party relying on modern administrative methods and campaigning techniques. Ahern's role models were being superseded, and he could not give his total loyalty to the new regime. Paradoxically, as the youngest member of the parliamentary party he continued to identify with the traditionalist model.

Initially the new Premier and party president appeared to be an ideal and powerful combination. Both belonged to the same generation. Both were successful men of the land who had served in shire politics. Both were intensely ambitious but, for most of their respective political careers, neither sought to usurp the intra-party influence of the other. Below the surface, however, there were crucial differences of background, style and focus.

Sparkes was a pastoralist, firmly in the tradition of wealthy graziers, thereby personifying the squattocracy with its old money. Bjelke-Petersen was an arable farmer who had begun his working life with virtually no financial support (his father an impoverished Lutheran pastor). He could never have derived his later wealth from peanut farming alone and, to make his fortune, branched into agribusiness. If Sparkes was the patrician pastoralist, Bjelke-Petersen was the self-made man of the land who worshipped his creator.

Sparkes's obsession was the future of the Country Party. He devoted all his strategic thinking to this end, "operating by extensive planning, working through tactics and then applying these to be ahead of the play" (Cribb, interview 24 March 1993). Bjelke-Petersen, lacking any ability for such forward planning, concentrated on his power base. He strove to retain his pre-eminence by surrounding himself with people he trusted, and/or could manipulate, playing patron to those who would neither challenge nor undermine him. Thus Sparkes was the backroom operator, the strategic planner who used his long-time deputy president Charles Holm as "his confidant and hatchet man" (Cribb, ibid.). Bjelke-Petersen, the confrontationalist, was briefed and advised by both the ambitious and the sycophantic, with whom he surrounded himself. Successfully projecting an uncompromisingly populist appeal to the electorate, Bjelke-Petersen was made politically indispensable both to his party and its organisation by Allen Callaghan, his press secretary. As long as the political agendas of both Premier and party president coincided, harmony reigned between the political and organisational wings. When their ambitions and styles later began to diverge (especially after 1986), the rift between them became as acrimonious and public as it was irrevocable (Cribb 1991b).

Ahern and Bjelke-Petersen

If Sparkes and Bjelke-Petersen forged an alliance of convenience, there was never the remotest chance that a similar Bjelke-Petersen–Ahern axis could or would develop. Ahern described the two of them as "being out of separate moulds" (interview 8 September 1993; see also Bennett 1991, Appendix A). There was neither a time nor an incident that caused them to become antagonists, because they were antipathetic from the beginning, rivals from the day Ahern was elected. To Bjelke-Petersen, Ahern was a political paradox. His provenance, youth and education clearly marked him as a rising star within the Country Party. It was, after all, inconceivable that a twenty-five-year-old graduate, entering a governing party in 1968 dominated by men a generation and more older than himself, would be content with a parliamentary career confined to the Government backbench. Some parliamentary leaders might have welcomed such a recruit, seeking out this talented new Member to groom him for an important future. He might have been recognised as a successor to the leadership in the longer term, and given encouragement as befits one who could move the party in new directions attuned to future requirements. While this scenario may possibly have been in harmony with Sparkes's wider strategies, there were any number of reasons to prevent Bjelke-Petersen adopting this view of Ahern.

Generationally, while Ahern represented the "wave of the future", he maintained strong links with traditional Country Party politics of the type that owed very little to either Bjelke-Petersen or Sparkes. After all, Ahern's two role models predated Bjelke-Petersen and Sparkes's rise to power. Consciously or otherwise, Ahern represented a different style of Country Party politics, rural without being populist, developmental without being rapacious and strongly emphasising personal probity in political life (Cribb 1991b, p.116).

Bjelke-Petersen, as the dark horse in a field of three candidates, had become deputy leader of the Country Party on Nicklin's retirement. When, at the end of July 1968, the leadership suddenly became vacant as the result of Pizzey's death, Bjelke-Petersen frantically called in all the political debts he had accumulated when administering the Police and Works portfolios. He won, but for the next four years was preoccupied in establishing his control over the leadership, the Ministry and the Coalition. Ahern, at this stage, was simultaneously the newest recruit and a younger manifestation of the Nicklin–Pizzey era in Country Party politics. As the latter he could never be Bjelke-Petersen's ally. Further, as Bjelke-Petersen became politically more domineering and increasingly ready to impose his authoritarian style an both the Government and society, suspicion and hostility between them mounted.

While Ahern obviously entered Parliament on a personal learning curve, he nonetheless had firm convictions as to the necessity for parliamentary reform. With Bill Hewitt, and later Terry White,[4] Ahern constantly urged a positive, creative parliamentary role for the Government backbench and, by extension, for the Opposition. He was a strong advocate of parliamentary committees, believing that they were central to any wider reform of parliamentary proceedings. In part, his stance represented youth's impatience with the perceived inadequacies of older and more traditional ways. But more importantly, this orientation was the manifestation of core political beliefs shared with others of his age cohort. Central to these was a commitment to genuine parliamentary democracy in Queensland.

Bjelke-Petersen could not have been more opposed to such views. He entered Parliament, aged thirty-six, in 1947, when Labor had been back in power for fifteen years. Under Labor, Parliament and the Government benches were controlled by a series of autocratic Premiers who treated their own backbench as lobby and electoral fodder, and gave their opponents no quarter. For the Opposition, opportunities, facilities, political recognition and the perquisites of office ranged from minimal to non-existent. Moreover, when the Government changed in 1957, Bjelke-Petersen was destined to spend another six years on the backbench, being promoted by Nicklin only five years before the latter's retirement. Doubtless this constituted yet another reason to dislike and distrust Nicklin's successor, especially one who so willingly demonstrated his closeness to a leader who had been tardy in advancing Bjelke-Petersen's own political career. Ever possessed of a vengeful personality, Pizzey's new successor was as determined to repay Labor in its own pre-1957 coinage as he was to sideline Nicklin's young protégé.

It was now Bjelke-Petersen's turn to marginalise the Opposition by continuing the devaluation of Parliament.. If this also meant some short-term deprivation for his own and Chalk's backbenchers, it was a price he had no trouble in paying. In any case, the Government backbench could be kept quiescent, secure in the knowledge that in both Coalition parties elevation to Cabinet was by seniority. This gave the necessary incentive to Government Members to endure a relatively obscure apprenticeship, knowing that they all occupied places in a queue which was moving, however incrementally, toward Cabinet. Mavericks, including those who became outriders over issues such as parliamentary reform, or any other type of political or electoral reform, not only disturbed this orderly succession but also gave fuel to the Opposition. Hence it was appropriate that such people forfeited their places in the line for preferment.

The final reason Bjelke-Petersen and his supporters distrusted Ahern concerned religion. This was a sensitive subject, and one never raised in public; nevertheless, it is mentioned widely by participants and observers who monitored these events. To place the religious factor in perspective one needs to consider what was occurring in, and to, the Country Party during the 1970s. Under Sparkes's presidency, his party was attempting to transform itself from an essentially sectional and rural force into Queensland's dominant and mainstream conservative party. This process was highlighted at the 1974 annual state conference held in The University of Queensland's then-new Mayne Hall. This venue was chosen to symbolise the Country Party "coming to town". At this conference the party decided to change its name to the National Country Party (with subsequent deletion of "Country") and to amalgamate with the remnants of the Democratic Labor Party, formerly the QLP, which wound itself up after the 1974 federal election. This gave the Nationals something of an urban organisational presence to facilitate contesting Labor-held Brisbane federal and state seats; in Sparkes's words, to "maximise the anti-Labor vote" (Reynolds 1988). Sparkes's aim was to augment the rural vote with conservative urban voters won, necessarily, from the Liberals.

While these initiatives, masterminded by Sparkes, were designed to reorient the traditional Country Party in Queensland, they could never totally eliminate its rural base. The party's electoral and organisational core inescapably remained rural Queensland, epitomised by shire politicians and rural branch members whose political world view was shaped by the ethos of "countrymindedness" (Aitkin 1982). According to Tom Aitken (an Independent who founded his own North Queensland Labor Party), "countrymindedness" when compared with patterns of urban political behaviour, was characterised by support for authority symbols such as the monarchy, by a higher frequency of church attendance, and by the holding of traditional religious belief systems.

Reflecting on this period, Margaret Cribb remarked that the Country/National Party was:

> a very Protestant party with many MPs having attended Anglican and other Protestant schools prior to returning to the land. Very few Roman Catholics were in the Country Party, and even fewer had power or influence within it (interview 24 March 1993).

Terry White, himself a Catholic, entered Cabinet in 1980 at the same time as Ahern. He claimed that Bjelke-Petersen "had a pathological hatred of Mike Ahern and that religion was of fundamental importance to his [Bjelke-Petersen's] views". He further claimed that anti-Catholicism was rampant through the senior ranks of the National Party "and was not confined to the Premier" (interview 15 October 1993).

These opinions offer strong circumstantial evidence that religion played a vital role in the intense animosity all agree existed between Ahern and Bjelke-Petersen. However, then as now, it is virtually impossible to quantify religion's influence in such matters, both because of its interplay with the other factors discussed above and because of the covert nature of religious prejudice. In religiously pluralist societies, religious bigotry will invariably operate at subterranean social and psychological levels. Furthermore, its existence would almost certainly be strenuously denied by those accused of practising it.

Ahern's youth, his graduate status and his religion all contributed to making him an oddity in the Parliamentary Country Party of the late 1960s and early 1970s. His father's close friendship with Nicklin could never have prepared him for any future display of religiously generated antagonism emanating from the upper echelons of his party's parliamentary or organisational wings. However, his remark to Bennett concerning his education may also be coded for religion. In answer to one of her questions about his graduate status, Ahern responded, "Certainly he [Bjelke-Petersen] was really big into anti-intellectualism. He wasn't the original anti-intellectual, but he was high on the scale" (Bennett 1991, Appendix A, p. 2).[5]

The leadership spirit

The first manifestation of hostility between the Premier and his new backbencher occurred two years after Ahern's election and centred on an attempted leadership spill. In 1970 a group of senior ministers, apparently led by Russell Hinze, were increasingly concerned about Bjelke-Petersen's inadequate communication skills, his inability to tolerate criticism and his indifferent leadership performance. They therefore decided to bring on a leadership spill, but gave him twenty-four hours warning of their plan (Walter 1990, pp. 500–501).

It needs to be remembered that this event was unprecedented. Within the Queensland State Parliamentary Country Party no one had ever challenged an incumbent — not even Nicklin, who had led the Country Party to no less than five successive electoral defeats before 1957. Thus the party possessed neither rules nor procedures to deal with such an occurrence. The plotters had foolishly given Bjelke-Petersen a day's notice of their intentions. So, in a rerun of his tactics when contesting the leadership two years before, he spent the next evening on the phone rounding up his votes. He then called a meeting of the Parliamentary Country Party for 10.00 am, one hour before Parliament was to sit.

The Premier assumed that the vote would be by show of hands; however, Ahern moved for a secret ballot, a motion to which Bjelke-Petersen "angrily agreed" (interview 8 September 1993). The meeting appointed Ahern as one of the two tellers, although it was no secret to anyone in the room that Ahern would be voting against the Premier. When the tellers declared a hung ballot, Bjelke-Petersen plucked two pieces of paper from his pocket and threw them down on the table, asserting that they were proxy votes he held for the two absent Country Party Members. No one had a chance to verify this claim as the bells were now ringing to summon Members to the Chamber. Bjelke-Petersen scooped up the papers and marched triumphantly from the room, leaving Ministers and backbenchers alike to file into Parliament and vote confidence in the Government. As none of the parliamentary party was prepared to initiate a Country Party version of the 1957 ALP split, and divide the party on the floor of Parliament, all rallied to the Premier. Appalled by such a turn of events, Sparkes, then newly installed as president, threatened any Member who plotted another leadership spill with instant deselection. Thus he reminded Members that their political futures were controlled by the organisation. In retrospect, while Ahern did not belong to the inner circle of malcontents, he was widely identified with their cause within Country Party ranks. Bjelke-Petersen neither forgot nor forgave Ahern for his stance. Ahead lay a decade of intense political struggle before Ahern finally ascended to the Ministry.

Ahern the backbencher

After Bjelke-Petersen and Sparkes had turned this drama into a display of solidarity between Premier and party president, Ahern busied himself with a round of backbench tasks. He concentrated on his electorate, successfully consolidating his personal position in a seat which was subject to continual demographic expansion. He opened new branches, built up a strong financial and organisational base and, again using his father as a role model, once more plunged into organisational politics.

An indication of such organisational activity occurred at the landmark 1974 annual conference.[6] Among the many initiatives undertaken by Sparkes in his quest to harness the future to National Party ends, was an attempt that would colour Ahern's future relations with the president. Perhaps as a result of the abortive leadership spill four years earlier, Sparkes decided to tighten the organisation's grip on the Parliamentary National Party. To this end he proposed an amendment to the party's constitution which would bind Members to state conference decisions. The conference was largely orchestrated by Sparkes and his nephew-in-law, then state secretary, Mike Evans. However, to bring about such constitutional change required the support of two-thirds of the delegates. Ahern lobbied very hard against this move. He strongly believed that the parliamentary party should be free from outside (i.e. organisational) interference, so that it could demonstrate independence concerning its own decision-making procedures. Ironically, the charge of outside domination was one the conservative parties habitually levelled at the ALP, most dramatically eleven years earlier in Menzies' "faceless men" campaign for the 1963 federal election.[7]

Ahern's persistence succeeded. Conference rejected the amendment by a wide margin, thus inflicting possibly the only defeat that Sparkes, as president, ever suffered at the hands of his normally docile conference. When he recalled these events, Ahern recounted an observation made by an old party stalwart, Sir William Allen, to his father Jack (who in all probability assisted his son in this endeavour): "Young Mike may have had a victory today, but he will never gain a Ministry while Sparkes is president" (interview 8 September 1993). While this was inaccurate as prophecy, it well illustrates the essential antipathy between Sparkes and Ahern, which culminated three months before the 1989 election in Sparkes's support for Russell Cooper's second and successful attempt to wrest the National Party leadership from Ahern.

Ahern as Government Whip

One significant reason for Ahern's 1974 conference success was his accession, in 1972, to two parliamentary jobs: Secretary to the Parliamentary Country Party and Government Whip. In 1972 Government Whip Vince Jones died suddenly. Ahern, in a career move, decided to nominate because he wanted "to get myself an office upstairs" (interview 8 March 1993). In the event he was narrowly beaten by Claude Wharton (Burnett), who, having been elected in 1960, was both eight years his senior in parliamentary experience and undoubtedly the Premier's preferred, if not nominated, candidate. However Wharton, once elected, had second thoughts about taking the job; according to Ahern (interview 8 March 1993), Wharton "had a number of directorships around town". At all events, Wharton resigned the position twenty-four hours later and Ahern, in the absence of another nominee, was returned unopposed in a reconvened ballot.

In a Westminster Parliament the Whip has a twofold task. S/he is responsible for negotiations with the party's political opponents on parliamentary matters while simultaneously promoting and nurturing intra-party cohesion. With reference to the second of these roles, Ahern observed that the Whip was in a position to know a good deal about his/her colleagues because, sooner or later, all roads lead to the Whip's office. Thus, to perform effectively, the Whip has to maintain lines of communication with all colleagues. The Government Whip must ensure the Government wins all divisions, and necessarily knows all Members' haunts and movements, proclivities and foibles. A Parliament as small as Queensland's enhances the intimacy of contact and close relations among Members. In occupying this position, the Whip becomes the major conduit between frontbench and backbench, functioning as the party's internal manager. Ahern felt that this aspect of the job required him to obtain a thorough grasp of parliamentary procedures in order "to bring to bear a creative managerial role" (interview 8 March 1993). Until Max Hodges was appointed Leader of the House in 1975 Ahern, as Whip, tended to assume responsibility for organising Government business in Parliament.

The institutionalisation of the Whip's position demonstrates that both sides of the Parliament have a mutual and vested interest in its operations. It is expedient for all Members to know what business is planned and how it is to be timetabled. Governments generally prefer to minimise the necessity for overriding parliamentary procedures and standing orders with resort to gag and guillotine. But because the Government and the Opposition are essentially adversaries, negotiations between the two are delicate, constantly requiring skill, tact and diplomacy. When confronted with this aspect of the job, Ahern quickly found that he had inherited a snake pit.

For his first two years, until 1974, Ahern had to deal with the Labor Whip, Doug Sherrington (Salisbury). Sherrington, however, was used to dealing with Bjelke-Petersen who, in Ahern's words, "never honoured any deals". Not only was the Opposition uncooperative after its relatively strong showing at the 1972 elections; it was also markedly hostile towards the Government on a day-to-day basis. When Ahern was elected Whip, Sherrington was initially suspicious, regarding him as being tarred with the Bjelke-Petersen brush. Before long, however, Ahern felt that they had developed a "reasonably friendly working relationship", which he attributed to always telling Sherrington the truth and guaranteeing that all deals struck would be duly honoured (interview 8 March 1993).

The Queensland Parliament was now beginning to move from an informal to a more systematic approach to its business. The regularisation of Government–Opposition relations via the Whips' offices was one manifestation of these changes, while another was the Liberals' decision to appoint their own Whip. Whatever their motive, this event represented a small step in their quest to gain a parliamentary identity that was more distinct from that of the Nationals. Initially, in an early attempt at party assertiveness, they chose Geoff Chinchin (Mt Gravatt), one of the "Ginger Group" of occasional rebels on the Liberal backbench; later they turned to Bob Moore (Windsor). Ahern considers that he had good relations with both Labor and Liberal Whips despite Moore's "rough attitude to life".[8]

In contrast to Jones, his predecessor, who had never given a Whip's report to meetings of the Parliamentary National Party, Ahern instituted these on a regular basis. He also systematised the Whip's task by writing a procedural manual for himself and for his successors. As a result of Bjelke-Petersen's ongoing exclusion of him from the Ministry he spent a total of eight years as Whip, covering the time when Labor's electoral fortunes plummeted (1974) and then partially recovered (1977), and when the Liberals experienced an electoral false dawn (1974–77), convincing themselves that they were on the threshold of senior party status within the Coalition. With these events as a political backdrop, Ahern moved among his backbench colleagues, developing his interpersonal skills and gaining managerial experience.

As discussed above, promotion through National Party parliamentary ranks was by seniority. When a ministerial vacancy occurred, usually (but not invariably) after an election, the most senior backbencher was selected by the Premier. After each election between 1972 and 1980 construction of the Coalition Cabinet was characterised by bitter wrangling between the National and Liberal party leaderships and organisations; but until Ahern's case, promotions within the National Party had been uncontroversial.

After the 1974 election (which reduced Labor to eleven seats), two National Party Cabinet vacancies occurred. Had the seniority precedent been followed, Ahern would have automatically been appointed to one of these, irrespective of any additional claims he might have advanced concerning his innate ability and/or experience as Whip. Instead, early in 1975, Bjelke-Petersen promoted Wharton but bypassed Ahern in favour of Val Bird (Burdekin). Four years later, when Bjelke-Petersen had his next chance to reshuffle Cabinet before the 1980 election, Ahern was again overlooked when the Premier promoted Ivan Gibbs (Albert) and Tom Newbery (Mirani). Thus on two separate occasions Ahern was given a clear message. Unless he forced a confrontation with Bjelke-Petersen on his (Ahern's) terms, he would never enter Cabinet while Bjelke-Petersen was Premier. Typically the Premier felt no need either to explain or to justify his behaviour to Ahern or anyone else.

Ahern and the select committee

By 1979 Bjelke-Petersen's treatment of Ahern was the subject of critical speculation and unfavourable comment. Cribb, voicing wider sentiments, perhaps within National ranks, wrote: "Ahern was passed over [in 1979] for the Ministry despite being Government Whip and the Chairman of the successful Parliamentary Select Committee on Education" (Cribb & Boyce 1980, p. 105). This select committee was the Government's attempt to regain the initiative in a political row which had begun to spin out of its control. By the decade's end, Ahern's public profile had been largely shaped by his chairing the said select committee — something of a personal coup which afforded him sufficient recognition to set him apart from his colleagues on the Government backbench. That his political star was now reckoned to be in the ascendant can largely be attributed to the Premier's ineptitude.

Bird, the first beneficiary of Bjelke-Petersen's obdurate hostility towards Ahern's Cabinet ambitions, had been made Minister of Education. Normally an uncontroversial Ministry, it had a history of being administered by senior Nationals including Pizzey (before he became Premier) and Sir Alan Fletcher (Cunningham). As a signal that Education lacked any priority for Bjelke-Petersen, he gave this portfolio to the most junior of his Ministers.

Apart from the occasional industrial relations dispute, the only potential area for controversy within Education concerned curriculum content. It was Bird's singular misfortune that, within two years, he became embroiled in the worst such dispute for twenty years. This row, as it escalated, raised many symbolic issues including what should be taught in schools and by whom, plus a plethora of moral and religious matters never far from the surface during this period in Queensland politics. It also revealed the Government's lack of expertise when grappling, over a lengthy period, with political controversy mounted and sustained by well-organised yet opposing lobby groups.

This imbroglio began when Bjelke-Petersen, in a characteristically arbitrary decision, banned two educational resource kits, "Man — A Course of Study" (MACOS) and the "Social Education Materials Project" (SEMP). He did so at the behest of Mrs Rona Joyner, who claimed to be the spokesperson for two pressure groups, Society To Outlaw Pornography (STOP) and the Committee Against Regressive Education (CARE).[9] His unilateral action was taken without reference to Cabinet, the Minister or the Education Department, let alone any consultation with teachers, parent representatives, educationalists or any other stakeholders. As these events occurred over the 1977–78 summer holidays, Bjelke-Petersen probably calculated that the vociferous protests would die down when the state returned to work, and other less inflammatory issues emerged. However, the Queensland Teachers' Union (QTU) and the Combined State Schools Organisation (CSSO) were not to be placated. Their stance was reinforced when the Catholic Education Office announced that it both approved of, and would use, MACOS and SEMP. More ominously for the protesters, Bill Knox (Nundah), then Liberal leader and Deputy Premier, told a Liberal Party area conference that the Government would strip policy-making responsibilities from the Education Department and return these to "Parliament" (i.e. to Cabinet).

For all the bravado emanating from Knox and Bjelke-Petersen, the controversy refused to abate. By February 1978 the Government became defensive as the media initiated a highly critical campaign, demanding to know how Joyner and her fundamentalist-inclined followers enjoyed apparently limitless and exclusive access to the Premier on such sensitive questions. Bjelke-Petersen and Knox were now forced into damage-limitation mode, announcing that a Parliamentary Select Committee, with broad terms of reference, would be established to investigate this issue. Clothed with full parliamentary powers, its brief would be to conduct a wide-ranging investigation into Queensland's education system. This committee was to be "advised" by a panel of educational experts (naturally those acceptable to the Government), to monitor its activity and to ensure that its recommendations would be congruent with Government policy. Importantly, however, there would be no time limit on its deliberations. Hence, the longer the committee sat, and the wider and more complex its investigations, the less central MACOS and SEMP would be to its considerations. Thus immediate pressure would be taken off the Government. SEMP and MACOS would be overshadowed by other and broader concerns which, in turn, would lead the Parliamentary Select Committee into probing more complex educational matters. Meanwhile the "offensive" education materials would remained banned.

Despite the antipathy between Ahern and Bjelke-Petersen, several factors pointed to the Whip as the obvious choice to chair the select committee. On the Government side he and Bill Hewitt, then a prominent small "l" Liberal backbencher, were the only notable backbenchers to advocate the establishment of parliamentary committees, having co-authored a forceful report on this matter for the Goverment's joint party room. Additionally Ahern had visited Ottawa in 1976. Impressed by the Canadian federal parliamentary committee system he had, made a strong speech to Parliament on his return, urging the Queensland Parliament to adopt a similar system.

Paradoxically, and despite his implacable opposition both to parliamentary committees and to Ahern and Hewitt, Bjelke-Petersen sent them on an interstate trip to study parliamentary committee systems in other Australian jurisdictions. On their return they wrote a report for Cabinet recommending a Public Accounts Committee, a Public Works Committee, a Subordinate Legislation Committee and a Parliamentary Privileges Committee. The Premier, and hence Cabinet, would accept only the last two, which were duly established, with Ahern appointed to chair the Privileges Committee. While others did not know why Ahern had been given the chair of the Select Committee on Education, his own theory was that Knox and Callaghan (by then Bjelke-Petersen's chief political adviser) urged Ahern's appointment "to give him something to do and to keep him out of [Bjelke-Petersen's] way" (interview 8 September 1993). There can be little doubt that, by their calculations, any odium that the committee might attract would adhere to the chairperson, and not to Cabinet or the Premier.

Bjelke-Petersen was, however, too astute a political operator to give Ahern carte blanche. If Ahern was to have the chair, Hewitt was the other obvious choice from the Government backbench. Col Miller (Ithaca) was the second Liberal while Lin Powell (Isis), a former primary school teacher, was the second National. It was no secret that Ahern and Powell detested each other; herein lay the hand of the

Premier.[10] Both Ahern and Hewitt, in separate interviews, claimed that Powell was Bjelke-Petersen's "plant" on the select committee, put there to sabotage both its work and Ahern; Cribb agreed. Hewitt further emphasised that he immediately decided that his role was to give Ahern maximum support. The Labor appointee was Eric Shaw (Wynnum), a Brisbane City Council alderman and former plumbing inspector. Ahern found him to be useful owing to his links with the QTU, particularly as their strident and ongoing protests had done much to bring about the establishment of this committee.

As indicated by its press release, the Government insisted that the Committee be advised by a panel of so-called educational experts. However, in reality Cabinet had no idea who should constitute this panel, apart from Dr Rupert Goodman, then Reader in Education in the Division of External Studies at The University of Queensland. Goodman, an extreme conservative, was the only educationalist, academic or otherwise, to give public support to the Government's banning of MACOS and SEMP. Ahern, on assuming the chair, appointed people he felt would balance Goodman's influence. He nominated Kevin O'Connor, formerly Principal of Wavell State High School and then a high school inspector, Mrs Jan Herron, a parents' representative whose husband was a surgeon and subsequently a prominent Liberal Party politician, and Peter Krebs, the recently retired Principal of St Paul's (Anglican) School, Bald Hills. Ahern later observed that, as Goodman was sufficiently professional and open in his approach to all issues raised, he was prepared to consider reasoned argument and discussion (interview 8 September 1993).

The parliamentary debate on the establishment of the select committee was wide-ranging, attracting many more contributors than was usual in most legislative debates. The issue was controversial, and Members gave full vent to their feelings, emotions and prejudices. The debate also provided a chance to comment upon parliamentary procedures, and in particular how these could be reformed, given the infrequent recourse the Parliament then made to either select or standing committees. Some MPs, such as Bill Gunn (Somerset), a future Education Minister, and Bob Katter (Flinders), provided rambling confused contributions barely above the level of ranting. By contrast Ahern and Hewitt (who seconded the motion), made insightful speeches based on the circumstances surrounding the establishment of the committee, its wider significance and what was expected to emerge from it. The Premier did not speak.

Ahern's speech (*QPD* vol. 274, 4 April 1978), for the first time aired details of the backroom manoeuvrings that had led to the committee's establishment. Bjelke-Petersen's preferred option was for an ad hoc committee of four MPs and three educationalists. However, this proposal failed because Crown Law doubted its legality. To meet these objections, Cabinet then decided upon a select committee. Ahern, presumably in his capacity as Whip, was now asked to liaise with the Premier's Office. In his speech, he claimed to have been "closely involved in drafting the terms of reference,[11] and the details of these terms of reference were not altered by Cabinet". He assured the House that the wide terms of reference were designed to prevent the committee from being limited solely to investigations into SEMP and MACOS. The committee would have at its disposal the full range of powers possessed by the Parliament and would consult as widely as possible with all interested individuals and community groups. He praised the qualifications of the panellists, implied that Goodman was well counterbalanced, and concluded by observing that the prevailing controversy would serve a useful purpose if it produced worthwhile solutions to current educational problems.

For his part, Hewitt agreed with Ahern that more use should be made of select committees. He warned Cabinet not to "colour" any subsequent recommendations and, by way of background, noted that there had been sustained agitation in the joint party room for a broad-based inquiry into education in Queensland. In the previous Parliament the Education Minister's Government Members' Committee had attempted a similar task, but soon abandoned it for lack of resources. In conclusion, Hewitt added:

> I commend [the Government] warmly also for the choice of chairman. I have worked in close harness with Mr Ahern since he came into this Parliament. I hold him in very high personal regard ... it should be acknowledged that he is a disciplined person, an organised person and a reasonable person, and the success of this committee will be attributable,

in no small measure, to his firm guiding hand on its deliberations. (*QPD* vol. 274, p. 114)

Thus was their alliance publicly paraded.

The Opposition, in the person of its leader Jack Houston (Bulimba) was both supportive of the committee yet skeptical about it. In his speech Houston made two valid points. First, if, as Hewitt claimed, there had been such great pressure on the Government from within its ranks, why had it refused to allow the Education Department's estimates to be debated the previous year?[12] Second, if the select committee was to be properly balanced, Labor was entitled to two representatives, not one. He finished by correctly observing that, had Crown Law's opinion not prevailed, Labor would have been denied any representation. Eric Shaw used this debate to make his maiden speech, traditionally heard in silence, which revealed him to be a cautious progressive.

The select committee held its last meeting on 31 January 1980 and tabled its final report on 11 March, almost two years after its establishment. A year earlier, and in the midst of its deliberations, Cribb noted that it had received over 4000 written submissions, hearing evidence from more than 100 individuals and groups (Cribb 1979). The final report of the select committee is comprehensive yet comparatively succinct, being only forty-three pages in length. By then the committee had produced six interim reports: *Composition and Functions of the Board of Secondary School Studies and Secondary School Assessment*; *The Aims of our Schools and the Future of Social Education*; *Literacy and Numeracy*; *Human Relationships*; *Isolated Children and Isolated Schools*; and *Post-Secondary Education*. The final *Report* consolidated these in twenty-five major recommendations (*Report of the Select Committee on Education in Queensland* 1980, p. 8).

The only politically sour note in the whole proceedings concerned the *Interim Report on Human Relationships*. In an interview (24 March 1993), Cribb asserted that Ahern had surprised many by being very strongly supportive of sex education. She felt that he had been "on a learning curve [and] his Roman Catholicism had not inhibited him". Ahern not only advocated sex education but fought tenaciously for it, and at a time when the Government was extremely hostile to any such suggestion. Cribb considered that Ahern's stance "owed a lot to his concept of himself as the father of a young family and [to] his horror of discovery that sex education was done behind the bikeshed, and was wrong".

Predictably, Bjelke-Petersen was furious with this particular interim report, especially as it was well received both by the media and by educational opinion leaders. He urged Powell (who scarcely needed convincing) to bring down a minority report opposing the Human Relationships recommendations (*Report* 1980, pp. 41–43), thereby providing the Government with its requisite, albeit extremely flimsy excuse, to reject this particular set of recommendations.[13] All Bjelke-Petersen would permit was a team of volunteers, led by a failed National Party parliamentary candidate, the Rev. Allan Male,[14] going into schools after hours to teach sex education to those pupils who had received parental permission to attend. The result was that most of those who would have profited from this educational initiative were precluded from experiencing it.

Later, Ahern delighted in recounting how he steered the final *Report* through the 1980 National Party Bundaberg Conference where it was adopted by three hundred votes to thirty. In his opinion, it was, "a well received and well applied report"; "a constructive two years on the job" (interview 8 September 1993).

One contemporary writer (Hughes 1980) saw the SEMP and MACOS controversies as indicative of two wider problems concerning Queensland education in the 1970s. These were "that basic skills and traditional standards were being eroded by new teaching methods ... [and] that students were being exposed to 'unsuitable' materials in schools" (Hughes 1980, p. 289). The *Report* squarely addressed these issues and detailed the concerns which flowed from them.

Politically, the Government was fortunate that the MACOS and SEMP controversies exploded immediately after the 1977 election, and that its final report was brought down well before the 1980 election. The fact that education was defused as an electoral issue can be attributed to the committee's comprehensive recommendations, the wide consideration it afforded to the views of all interested parties and the support it engendered, within both the QTU and the Education

Department, for its approach, operational methods and recommendations. The final report set a benchmark in educational administration for the 1980s and beyond. While never totally free from controversy, education policy had not, at the time of writing, again erupted to do political damage to the government of the day.

By 1980 Ahern's public profile had been largely shaped by chairing the select committee — something of a personal coup which had set him apart from his colleagues on the Government backbench. His heightened political profile was, ironically, brought about by the Premier.

The road into the Ministry

If the select committee had settled education's political future it singularly failed to perform this same function for Ahern. If Bjelke-Petersen and his advisers had bestowed the job of chairing the select committee upon Ahern "to give him something to do", they had succeeded; but if they had hoped that Ahern would become politically damaged in the process, they were to be disappointed. In fact the reverse occurred, as Ahern emerged from this two-year period with an enhanced reputation. He was widely seen as a progressive, sensible, if rather careful reformer who had prevented education from being captured by political and social reactionaries who, in making education their political plaything, would have subjected it to their whims. Moreover, apart from the never-to-be-conciliated Powell, he had both forged and maintained a strong tripartite consensus as to the future direction of education in Queensland — no mean feat given the political circumstances that gave rise to his select committee. Throughout the whole exercise Ahern acquired a solid political and public reputation for the quality of his own and his committee's work. For these reasons he stood out in a party steeped in agrarian conservatism and led by an authoritarian fundamentalist.

By the latter half of 1979, the select committee had generated a political momentum for Ahern. He was "on a roll" and was determined to sustain this impetus after the select committee had ceased its work. But by year's end not only had he again been denied a Cabinet position; he had also learned that the next vacancy (expected after the 1980 election) would go to Vicki Kippin (Mourilyan) who had been elected only six years earlier.[15] It was now abundantly clear to all, and especially to Ahern, that there was nothing he could do to persuade Bjelke-Petersen to promote him. Indeed, if anything, his very success in chairing the select committee was held against him in that quarter. His progressive approach to the issues dealt with by the committee was anathema to Bjelke-Petersen. The very media plaudits he received no doubt confirmed him in the Premier's eyes as the upstart pretender — the leadership rival in exile.

Ahern's chance came when the National Party's deputy leader, Ron Camm (Whitsunday), announced that he would retire at the 1980 election, thereby creating the Cabinet vacancy targeted for Kippin. Ahern quickly let it be known that he would be a candidate for the deputy leadership. His aim was to rally the backbench in response to Sparkes's call (at the 1978 National Party conference) for older Ministers to stand aside to allow new talent to be recruited into Cabinet. In a limited reshuffle the following year, Bjelke-Petersen had partly addressed this by promoting Gibbs[16] and Newbery, but this only fuelled the widely articulated belief among commentators, the media and the Government backbench that Ahern, who possessed the strongest claim of all to promotion, was again being victimised.

Ahern, nevertheless, was gathering his numbers. He reasoned that, if he were to be elected as the deputy leader, Bjelke-Petersen would be forced to admit him to Cabinet. While Members in all three parliamentary parties discerned his tactics, they also recognised that Ahern was in a strong position to attain his goal since, apart from the leader, the Whip is the one normally owed most favours. The dynamics of this situation explain why Hinze, one of Ahern's potential rivals for the leadership, approached Bjelke-Petersen and informed the Premier that Ahern would in all probability win the ballot.

Hinze's motives were entirely pragmatic. Although not a natural Bjelke-Petersen supporter (he had, after all, been credited with orchestrating the abortive 1970 leadership challenge), they were Cabinet allies. Hinze publicly supported the Premier, who in response gave Hinze the high-profile, multi-patronage portfolios he craved.[17] To Bjelke-Petersen Hinze then stressed the worst-case scenario, that

Ahern, after winning the deputy's position, would thereupon force his way into Cabinet. Owing nothing to Bjelke-Petersen for his position, Ahern would begin to destabilise the Premier by working his Cabinet and backbench numbers until he was in a position to make a successful lunge for the leadership.

Hinze extended his line of argument by urging upon Bjelke-Petersen the better option, namely to buy Ahern off with a portfolio. By adopting this strategem, the Premier could run his own candidate for deputy, thereby denying Ahern the leverage he enjoyed as Whip. Ahern would be locked in and, by accepting the Cabinet doctrine of collective responsibility, would thus have to display loyalty to the Premier. Inside Cabinet, any manouvreings Ahern might signal against Bjelke-Petersen's leadership could be monitored, with appropriate steps taken to foil him.[18] All such moves, however, had to await the outcome of the 1980 election, the last until 1995 to be fought by the Coalition, and characterised by an ever-rising wave of bitterness now sweeping over Liberal–National relations, augmented as it was by a secret deal struck between the Nationals and the ALP.[19]

The National–Labor pact

Labor had won only eleven seats in 1974, but had made some headway in 1977, winning a total of twenty-three seats. However, in 1980 it was again wracked by dissension. Trapped in the political labyrinth of federal intervention, close to bankrupt and apparently irretrievably disunited, Labor found itself in a replay of the events of the 1957 split, again in danger of disintegrating into warring factions. Before the 1980 campaign, a National backbencher, the late John Goleby (Redlands) approached Bill D'Arcy (Woodridge), then deputy Labor leader, to ask whether Bjelke-Petersen had contacted him. When told by D'Arcy that the Premier had not, Goleby enigmatically replied, "The Premier has something to show you" (D'Arcy interview, 13 September 1993). Shortly thereafter, and responding to a phone call, D'Arcy went to Bjelke-Petersen's office and was shown private copies of opinion polls commissioned by the National Party, which charted a decline in voting support for both Labor and Nationals, while displaying a commensu-rate rise in the Liberal vote. It was put to D'Arcy that, since Labor and

Nationals were both in danger of losing to the Liberals, they should conclude a deal.

D'Arcy then took this proposition to the late Dr Denis Murphy (ALP president and leader of forces in favour of federal intervention). Because Labor could not afford its own polling, Murphy had spot checks done on the National-funded polls, which verified their findings. The Labor leadership then fully discussed the proposed deal. They concluded that, since the Nationals and Liberals were now so bitterly embroiled in three-cornered contests, the Coalition allies were now effectively rivals. The Government parties were now hardly tolerating each other, and the Coalition faced imminent collapse. According to Labor's reasoning, should this occur, Labor stood to be the sole beneficiary. Consequently Labor's leaders decided to negotiate an agreement to maximise intra-Coalition disharmony. Electorally Labor was desperate to avoid a repetition of 1974, hoping to build upon its modest 1977 gains. The Nationals were determined to retain their position as senior Coalition party, secure in the knowledge that the Liberals had no other option but to stay with them.

At this stage D'Arcy turned the negotiations over to Murphy, but the latter would not deal directly with Bjelke-Petersen. A complex three-part deal was struck between Murphy and one of the Premier's advisers.[20] The provisions, according to D'Arcy, were that:

- the Nationals would run bogus candidates in selected seats who would direct their preferences to Labor
- ALP preferences in Surfers Paradise and Southport would be switched to the Nationals to defeat, respectively, Bruce Bishop and Peter White, two anti-Bjelke-Petersen Liberal backbenchers (Thus the Nationals would eliminate two of their more vociferous Liberal backbench critics and win a further two seats at their Coalition partner's expense.)
- the National Party would approach certain of its corporate donors to make funds available to Labor for the campaign, thus preventing any money directly passing from the Nationals to the ALP.

This agreement remained absolutely secret, confined to a small cabal of the leadership of both parties. The Liberals were of course kept in total ignorance. However, the striking of this deal helps explain why, seven years later, Bjelke-Petersen approached Peter Beattie (then ALP state secretary) in a desperate eleventh-hour attempt, to stave off Ahern's leadership challenge (Beattie 1990). One must also remember that in 1980, despite Malcolm Fraser's remonstrances, the Queensland Liberal organisation broke their joint Senate ticket agreement with the Nationals with the result that, to the Liberals' chagrin, Lady Florence Bjelke-Petersen was elected at the expense of one of the Liberal Senators. Three-cornered contests had also exponentially increased at every election after 1972. And in yet another desperate move, the state Parliamentary Liberal Party had unceremoniously dumped their former leader, Sir William Knox, in favour of Sir Llew Edwards (Ipswich) in the (vain) hope that the latter would be more publicly assertive when dealing with Bjelke-Petersen.

During the 1980 campaign, the Premier may have felt embattled on all sides, but the Labor–National pact held. Labor made some incremental gains (ironically beating the incumbent National, Kippin, in Mourilyan); Peter White and Bruce Bishop were duly defeated (although in both Southport and Surfers Paradise a third of ALP voters rebelled, giving the second preferences to their respective Liberal incumbent); and the Nationals retained their senior status in the Coalition.[21] Bjelke-Petersen could now turn to the problem posed by Ahern.

Into the Ministry

After the election the Parliamentary National Party met to decide the vacant deputy leadership. Before this meeting commenced, Bjelke-Petersen announced that he had appointed Ahern to Cabinet and was giving him the traditional National Party powerhouse portfolio of Primary Industry. While it was an astute move, Bjelke-Petersen, never given to acknowledging the "justice" of Ahern's claims, had simply responded to a situation forced upon him. The Premier, in working his own numbers, had to eliminate any protest vote in the Parliamentary National Party that might accrue to Ahern as a result of sympathy for his long and arbitrary exclusion from Cabinet. The Premier now threw his considerable political support and prestige for deputy premier behind Vic Sullivan (Condamine), whom Don Lane once described as "a lazy yes man" (interview 2 April 1993).

Sullivan, in a show of unity (although the figures were never released), was duly elected deputy leader, thereby saving Bjelke-Petersen from the ignominy of having Ahern as his second-in-command. At this time Cribb observed that Ahern "was a known behind-the-scenes critic of the Premier on a number of issues, while Sullivan was a close supporter of Mr Bjelke-Petersen" (Cribb 1981, p. 72). Ahern's opinion, admittedly offered with hindsight, is somewhat different. He maintains that although Sullivan "was not strictly in Joh's camp, he [Bjelke-Petersen] thought he could control him" (interview 8 September 1993).

Ahern was thirty-eight when he entered Cabinet and, while not winning his party's Deputy Leadership, had forced Bjelke-Petersen to terminate his long backbench apprenticeship. He was now both the newest and youngest National Party Minister, and the one most observers were watching. His chairing of the select committee and his ploy to obtain a portfolio both signalled that he was finally on his way to the realisation of his long-term leadership ambitions.

Notes

1. The others were: Library, Parliamentary Buildings, Printing and Refreshment Rooms.
2. He was Les Diplock (Aubigney), Minister for Education in the Gair government. His seat was abolished in the 1971 redistribution, thus preparing for his retirement at the 1972 election.
3. Brian Austin (interview 7 July 1993) dates Bjelke-Petersen's authoritarian parliamentary behaviour (for instance forbidding Government MLAs from dining or drinking with their ALP counterparts) from 1980. Margaret Cribb (interview 24 March 1993) noted that Ahern entered Parliament committed to parliamentary reform and "pushed this behind the scenes, especially after becoming Whip [in 1972]. In doing so he further soured his relationship with the Premier." It seems that Austin, after 1980, observed the public and more extreme manifestation of a phenomenon which had hitherto been largely kept within Country Party parliamentary ranks.
4. Hewitt had entered Parliament in 1966; White at the Redcliffe by-election in 1979.
5. The motif of religion runs through the observations of Cribb, White and Ahern himself. Ahern told Bennett (1991), in answer to a question on religion, "I don't know about that and I've never commented on it" (Appendix A, p. 2). He goes on to observe that there were any number of other difficulties between himself and Bjelke-Petersen. The pattern of this

answer suggests that he was concerned to distance himself from the religious factor, perhaps because the suggestion that this was at the root of the problem, although having merit, was personally distasteful to him.

6. Arguably the most important development that dated from this conference was the growth of three-cornered contests. See Hamill and Reynolds (1983) for an analysis at state level and Reynolds (1988) for discussion of this in Queensland federal electoral contests.
7. In the 1963 federal election campaign Sir Robert Menzies had used, to devastating effect, a press photograph showing ALP Leader Arthur Calwell and deputy leader Gough Whitlam waiting outside a conference of the ALP federal executive who were debating Labor policy on US bases in Australia. The Liberals charged that Labor was run by "faceless men", and this would be the country's fate should Labor be elected.
8. Don Lane, in conversation, recalled how Moore told Liberal Member Rosemary Kyburz (Salisbury 1974–83), when she demanded to speak on women's issues in the House, that there were no women, only Members, and that a women's place was pregnant and barefoot at the clothesline with a mouthful of pegs. Moore was one of the few tradespeople (an electrician) the Liberals ever elected. He was a typical anti-Labor trade unionist and male working class Tory of his generation. See McKenzie and Silver (1968) and Nordlinger (1967).
9. The details and analysis of this issue are well covered by Gowers and Scott (1979), and Scott and Scott (1980). The matter is discussed here insofar as it impinged on Ahern, his political ambitions and career. While Joyner claimed 1000 members for each of these groups (Hughes 1980, p. 289), this claim should be treated with the utmost scepticism.
10. On hearing about research for this book, a parliamentary attendant remarked that, if Ahern had claimed that the colour of the parliamentary lawn known as Speaker's Green was green, Powell would have insisted it was blue.
11. Seven were broad, though targeted, while the eighth was a final "catch-all" term of reference.
12. Under Bjelke-Petersen Cabinet decided, after the Budget had been brought down, which departments would have their estimates debated.
13. Powell, when at a later date, he himself became Minister of Education, "distinguished" himself by ordering that "Creation Science" (sic) be taught in high schools whenever Evolution was taught. He was a member of the same Government that ordered police on to university campuses at midnight to rip condom vending machines from student toilets.
14. Murrumba, 1977. He subsequently became Director-General of the Department of Family Services under the Borbidge Government, and had his contract terminated in 1998 by the Beattie Government.

15. Ahern had six year's seniority over Kippin. As it happened, she was defeated in the 1980 election by Bill Eaton, a future Minister in the Goss government of 1989–92. The only other woman then in the ranks of the Government was Kyburz (see note 8) who won another term in 1980 before being defeated in 1983 by Wayne Goss.
16. Gibbs, the owner of used car yards in the Gold Coast hinterland, was made Minister of Conservation. In the press interview following his promotion, he vouchsafed that he was very concerned about conservation issues as he had planted "a lot of fauna" (sic) around his car yards. Thus did the failure to promote Ahern expose the Government to increasing derision.
17. In 1979–80 Hinze was Minister of Local Government and Main Roads. Thereafter he added Police to his portfolio responsibilities and was dubbed by the media "Minister for Everything".
18. These machinations irresistibly provoke an analogy with the observation attributed to former US President the late Lyndon B. Johnson, who replied, when asked why he tolerated a political rival in a powerful position, "I would rather have him in the tent pissing out, than out of the tent pissing in." While it is hard to imagine Bjelke-Petersen knowing this quotation, let alone using it, with Hinze both knowledge and usage are highly plausible.
19. The following account is based on an interview with Bill D'Arcy (Woodridge), 13 September 1993. It is included not because Ahern was in any way implicated, nor because, either directly or indirectly, this impinged upon him or his career. Rather it is recorded because until now it has not been publicly revealed. Had it been known at the time, it would have caused a political sensation. The fact that it occurred at all illustrates the tenor of state politics in the late 1970s.
20. Research has failed to identify the person definitely, but Wendy Armstrong has been mentioned.
21. At the 1980 election the Nationals won 27.9 per cent of the vote (+1.0 per cent) and 35 seats; Labor won 41.5 per cent (–1.3 per cent) and 25 seats; while the Liberals polled 26.9 per cent (+1.5 per cent) for 22 seats.

CHAPTER 3
Minister for Primary Industries

Mike Ahern's appointment to Cabinet in 1980 coincided with two countervailing political tendencies. On the one hand Bjelke-Petersen was approaching the zenith of his power as an autocratic Premier. For as long as he maintained a correct, and perhaps even close, working relationship with Sparkes the National Party appeared invincible. On the other hand, the Coalition had commenced its steep and rapid descent into oblivion. Irrespective of these trends, Ahern had, through a long and carefully prepared campaign, purposefully moved towards the Ministry, adding the final touches by making it too politically risky for the Premier to continue his exclusion. As Ahern was later to observe:

> Almost everyone in Parliament believed it was my turn to be included in the Ministry. I had been passed over and it was just his [Bjelke-Petersen's] animosity which was holding me out, so I ran for the deputy leadership … and he was told quite bluntly by Hinze that if I wasn't appointed, then I would be elected deputy leader. (Bennett 1991, Appendix A, p. 2)

Nonetheless, at the time of Ahern's translation to Cabinet there were relatively few changes among the Nationals' line-up. Camm's retirement had enabled Sullivan, as the new National Party deputy leader, to move up to the third-ranking ministerial position (behind Liberal leader Dr Llew Edwards, who was Deputy Premier and Treasurer), and to acquire Camm's former portfolio of Mines and Energy. Sullivan's former Ministry, Primary Industries, went to Ahern. Bjelke-Petersen gave Camm's other responsibility, Police, to Hinze, thus continuing the Nationals' domination of law and order in Queensland. Cabinet was further increased to eighteen, now comprising ten Nationals and eight Liberals. Ahern had entered as the tenth National, occupying a somewhat anomalous position by being the most junior-ranked Minister, yet administering what in any Queensland Government was one of the broadest and most diverse portfolios. Within this last Coalition Cabinet until 1996, the National Ministers continued to be predominantly older males representing rural electorates. Before the 1980 election, only two Cabinet Ministers had held seats with any significant urban population: Gibbs in Albert and Max Hooper in Townsville West. However, in 1980 Hooper was defeated at the polls by Geoff Smith who, nine years later, became a Minister in the first two Goss Governments.

Apart from the manoeuvrings over Mike Ahern's promotion, it was the Liberal leader who radically restructured Cabinet. Charles Porter had retired as Minister for Aboriginal and Islander Affairs, thereby creating one vacancy. After the election, Edwards sacked Norm Lee (Yeronga) from Industry and Administrative Services, Bill Lickiss (Mt Coot-tha) from Justice and Attorney-General, and John Greenwood QC (Ashgrove) from Survey and Valuation. In their places Hewitt (Greenslopes) was finally promoted to Employment, Valuation and Administrative Services, Don Lane (Merthyr) to Transport, Brian Austin (Wavell) to Health, and Terry White (Redcliffe) to Welfare Services. Edwards had thereby given the Liberals a "night of the long knives", and the impact of these changes in ministerial personnel upon both the balance of power in Cabinet and intra-coalition relationships, was profound.

An opinion of Ahern at his point of entry to Cabinet was provided in an interview with Terry White. White, who had won the Redcliffe by-election only a year earlier, was given a none-too-subtle message by Hinze and Gunn that Ahern was not fully trusted by them and thus was not in their confidence. As an attempt to keep White and Ahern apart this rather clumsy ploy failed; White almost inevitably identified with Ahern, seeing him as another "contemporary conservative". White felt that he and Ahern shared similar views on matters of "conservative ideology", in White's words. White also recognised and appreciated that Ahern was "attempting to move the National Party out of the backwoods" (interview 7 May 1993).

The origin of this overture from Hinze and Gunn is uncertain, but it is likely that they were articulating a general concern as to their party's succession. By 1979 Ahern had been in the Parliament eleven years, seven as National Party, and hence Government, Whip. Thus he had possessed ample time and opportunity to evaluate his colleagues and, in turn, to be appraised by them. Hinze's attitude to Ahern, and his motivation in advising Bjelke-Petersen to admit Ahern to Cabinet, have already been discussed. Ahern's own attitude to the leadership ambitions of Hinze and Gunn was: "Nobody could tolerate Hinze; he was not in serious contention and Bill Gunn was considered [only] because they figured that he would be most like Bjelke-Petersen." (Bennett 1991, Appendix A, p. 3)

Further to the Gunn question, Lane claimed that both he and Mike Ahern, after they had entered Cabinet, "were contemptuous of Gunn". According to Lane, "Gunn set traps for Mike Ahern in Cabinet and incited Joh against Ahern". He suggested that the basis of this antipathy was the "Mason–Roman Catholic divide" (interview 2 April 1993). This theory was also supported by White (interview 15 October 1993) who claimed that, when in 1983 he challenged Edwards for the leadership (just before the collapse of the Coalition), Gunn lobbied Liberal MPs for Edwards, claiming that White should not be supported because he was a Roman Catholic. With these currents flowing around his elevation to the Ministry, Ahern was certainly correct when he observed that the National Party did not groom him for the leadership, but that he groomed himself and "gathered support from the community ... business ... and in the Parliament" (Bennett 1991, Appendix A).

Ahern as Minister

The Primary Industries portfolio covers every conceivable aspect of Queensland rural life. Given the decentralised character of Queensland, the traditional prominence of primary production in the state's economy, the ongoing salience of the industry for the future economic growth of the state, together with the wide array of farming enterprises and the comparatively slender and under-resourced manufacturing and finance sectors, the administration of this Ministry, with both its client groups and its rural electoral base, was of crucial importance to the Government's fortunes. Ahern's was a task that ensured he was under thorough and continuous scrutiny from his colleagues. As virtually all National Members came from rural backgrounds and at this time represented rural electorates, there were as many views as there were Members on how his department should be administered.

It may be that Bjelke-Petersen was replicating the tactics he used when Cabinet established the Select Committee on Education. He may have deliberately set Ahern a difficult political task, hoping that it would prove too great for him to handle. If that indeed was the Premier's secret agenda it was singularly unrealistic, because Ahern possessed two strong qualifications for this particular Ministry. First, he had impeccable rural credentials deriving from both his family background and his representing Landsborough which, as late as 1991, could be described thus:

> Cultivation of tropical fruits including bananas and pineapples is the main agricultural pursuit. Beef, dairying and vegetable production are also significant. On the coast, tourism and related service industries are of major importance. (*Queensland Parliamentary Handbook*, 1991, p. 140)

Second, his university studies stood him in good stead. As he remarked, when he was appointed he did not know a lot of the detail of the portfolio because there were then sixty-five statutes to be administered. He did, however, feel that he possessed a sound intellectual knowledge of the industry and had "a solid grasp of the technology behind the issues" (interview 7 April 1994). In addition, he had networks from his undergraduate days, having studied with ten or twelve officers in the Department of Primary Industries (DPI). He was, then, familiar with much of the technical information associated with the administration of his portfolio and, more importantly, knew the additional sources he would need to tap.

Ahern was Minister for Primary Industries for three years and four months. In this time he initiated and presided over the passage of forty-four pieces of legislation, made many ministerial statements and answered innumerable parliamentary questions. All previous National

Party incumbents in this portfolio had been farmers who, while being familiar with those areas personally associated with their own rural experience, lacked expertise in the totality of its administrative activities. They tended to leave much of the routine administration of this usually uncontroversial ministry to the Director-General and his senior departmental staff. Since Ahern understood the technical information that drove many of the policy decisions, his administration of DPI represented a decisive break with his predecessors' administrative styles. Ahern, Austin and White also imported a new, technocratic approach to Cabinet business, then a novelty in Queensland politics and, before Ahern entered Cabinet, totally unknown in the Parliamentary National Party.

An indication of the range of activities that preoccupied him can be gained from an examination of the Committee of the Whole debate on his Estimates-in-Chief, which took place on 12 November 1981. As noted earlier, under Bjelke-Petersen Cabinet decided, after the Budget was brought down, which Estimates would be debated. DPI was debated only once while Ahern was the Minister, after he had held the portfolio for only eighteen months. He had therefore not had much time to make his reputation in a department previously administered by Vic Sullivan, who was a popular Minister with the National rural backbench despite Lane's jaundiced opinion that Sullivan "never did anything for them" (Lane interview 2 April 1993).

On this occasion the DPI Estimates were debated for a total of nine hours and ten minutes. As is typical of Estimates debates, all speeches except those of the Minister were limited to ten minutes. Twenty-one Members rose in this debate, including thirteen Government backbenchers (twelve Nationals, one Liberal) and eight from the Labor frontbench and backbench. Ahern spoke at some length, for twenty minutes in introducing his Estimates and forty-five minutes in reply. In a wide-ranging discussion, eight major themes recurred:

- concern over the sale of agricultural land to foreign owners, focusing on the National Party organisation's resolution to have a register of foreign land ownership, but blocked in Cabinet by Bjelke-Petersen's obdurate hostility;
- the current state of the fishing industry, which had not been included

in Ahern's portfolio when he took it over but which Bjelke-Petersen, despite Ahern's protestations, had off-loaded on him;

- the future of dairying, especially from fellow Sunshine Coast MPs, given that this industry then faced an uncertain future;
- soil erosion problems, exacerbated by the cessation of Commonwealth money for a state–federal program to investigate and combat this serious and ongoing rural and environmental issue;
- the future of sugar (over 90 per cent of which was and is grown in Queensland), which was then facing the rise of a European (and subsidised) sugar beet industry and the decision of the West Australian Government to commence its own sugar industry as part of the Ord River scheme;
- the desirability, and risks, of bringing new areas into grain production;
- the announced review of all fruit and vegetable legislation, including the City of Brisbane Market Act; and
- ongoing problems for drought-ravaged shires, together with the Minister's announced review of drought-relief procedures.

Coincidental with these major concerns, and necessarily linked to them, were the inevitable and innumerable parochial matters raised by rural National backbenchers and provincial ALP Members. Such contributors ventilated matters of particular concern to their locality and constituents (*QPD* vol. 286, 12 November 1981, pp. 3453–3526.)

Ahern later acknowledged that DPI's broad brief made it all too easy for the Minister to be overwhelmed by the sheer bulk of the work (interview 7 April 1994). He set himself a series of goals when he took over the portfolio: to rebuild the Fisherman's Island terminal, to rewrite the honey legislation, to rebuild the tick fence from Cloncurry to Charters Towers, and to revise the grains legislation. Such concerns clearly illustrate the agenda that inevitably preoccupies a Minister, in any Australasian jurisdiction, who is responsible for the major agricultural portfolio.

For much of his tenure, his major preoccupation was the crisis-ridden state of the fishing industry. Max Hooper had previously been Minister for Maritime Services (effectively Fisheries). In Ahern's opinion, Hooper lost his seat of Townsville West in 1980 because, against the wishes of most in the fishing industry, he proceeded towards a comprehensive restructuring, beginning with the abolition of the Fish

Board. At the 1980 election the industry successfully campaigned against him. Ahern was therefore under no illusion about the political risks that could flow to him from any lack of dexterity over fishing matters. Although it was unlikely that he would be defeated on this issue in Landsborough, it could have a profound effect on his political career, given the Premiers' attitude towards him.

His short-term problem was simple: the Fish Board was insolvent. As he explained to Parliament (*QPD* vol. 286, pp. 3521–3), its "outstanding debts, including the overdraft accommodation and contingent liabilities … totalled more than $6 million". The first plan was:

> to [ask] Treasury to write off the debts … but that request was refused … Of all the other opinions that were available, the one that appeared most attractive, and which had been recommended by many people who were advising the industry, including the fishermen, was that the Board's assets should be realised to cover the outstanding debts. (*QPD* vol. 286, p. 3521)

This meant a rationalisation of operations, cost cutting and the industry's withdrawal from several east coast ports. All this produced a degree of *angst* from those MLAs (from both sides) whose electorates incorporated fishing centres. Ahern massaged them by stating that:

> … private enterprise is not enough for the fisherman of Queensland; they must have some other outlet for their produce when private enterprize is unwilling or unable to cope in a particular situation. Those outlets can be provided through fish board depots, agencies or co-operatives and … the Government has promised to provide them. (*QPD* p. 3522)

He concluded by promising extensive reform in the guise of, "two major pieces of legislation … [to] be presented to the Chamber this session [and] … further amendments later this year".

His longer-term aim, after extensive consultation, was to restructure the industry completely. He aimed to induce them to accept the need for self-regulation rather than relying, as before, on Government regulation. The eventual outcome of these initiatives was the establishment of the Fish Management Authority which Ahern still regarded years later as "a significant achievement" (interview 7 April 1994). The record shows the complexity of this process. Between 1981 and 1983 he steered five major pieces of legislation through Parliament to implement the fishing industry policy. Eleven years later the Goss Government had to undertake another extensive inquiry into the needs of the fishing industry, suggesting that this industry needs fairly constant surveillance and review, with a view to reassessment.

Ahern's ministerial style involved being open and available both to the plethora of interests and to the complex networks which revolved around the DPI. By Queensland standards his was a large department which had forged innumerable contacts within the rural sector. A successful Primary Industries Minister was one who, in addition to his routine administrative duties, was mindful of the need to cultivate all such interests. In the multifaceted rural industry, the DPI bureaucracy interacted with a wide array of pressure groups, all of which expected to be included in "their" sector's decision-making processes. Ahern, as Minister, addressed this obligation by attending as many producer groups' annual general meetings as possible, and ensuring that he was on first-name terms with their major office holders. One of the short cuts he utilised was to make extensive use of his committee of backbenchers, frequently convening meetings with them.[1] He claimed that doing this was:

> ... vital given the range of interests within the portfolio, and because "bushfires" could occur on the backbench given the number and variety of Members representing rural seats (interview 7 April 1994).

Should such outbreaks occur, Ahern continued, these MPs "could be pressured [by their constituents] to run to Joh, or other ministers".

Lane's version was more ominous. He maintained that these backbenchers:

> ... could run to Sparkes, who was encouraged by sections of the Parliamentary National Party to believe Mike Ahern was promoting division [in the Parliamentary National Party] by promoting himself against Joh. (Lane, interview 2 April 1993)

As an extension of this ongoing consultative process, Ahern's portfolio encompassed a number of intergovernmental councils. He singled out the Australian Agricultural Council, Australian Fish Council and Rural Adjustment Council, all of which meet regularly, either in a succession of state capitals or in Canberra (interview 7 April 1994). In reply to his Estimates-in-Chief debate, Ahern also mentioned further ad hoc consultations involving other jurisdictions, including the attempt to gain Australia-wide agreement on "a uniform approach to the sale of foreign land [sic]", "management of the Australian Fishing Zone", and discussions with the West Australian Premier, the WA Minister of Agriculture and Bjelke-Petersen over the establishment of the Ord River sugar industry (*QPD* vol. 286, pp. 3521–3).

Relations between Bjelke-Petersen and Mike Ahern were rarely trouble-free, notwithstanding Ahern's elevation to the Ministry and consequential preoccupation with a busy and wide-ranging portfolio. Yet another example (also in 1981) of the continuing bad blood that persisted between them arose over the Great Barrier Reef Marine Park Authority (GBRMPA). The Premier had appointed Ahern to the Great Barrier Reef Ministerial Council, which had been established in 1979. It consisted of the relevant state and federal ministers, presided over by Prime Minister Malcolm Fraser (whom Ahern described in the interview cited above as "an eminently logical and intelligent person").

During the 1970s, Bjelke-Petersen had frequently threatened to approve exploratory drilling for oil on sections of the Reef. To forestall such environmental vandalism the Whitlam Government had passed the *Great Barrier Reef Marine Park Act 1975*, but progress in proclaiming the park under the GBRMPA was slow. After six years only 2.4 per cent of the reef had been incorporated in the park. Then, in November 1981, the ministerial council meeting declared the incorporation of the so-called Cairns Section, thereby adding a further 8 per cent of the reef to the park.

Ahern had attended this meeting accompanied by the Queensland Coordinator-General, Sir Sidney Schubert. When the decision was made public, the Premier denounced it and protested to Fraser. The Prime Minister replied that Ahern, on behalf of the Queensland Government, had agreed to the proclamation. Bjelke-Petersen thereupon "carpeted" Ahern for agreeing to this, but was informed by Ahern that he had checked with Schubert who advised that the Government "did not have a problem with the proposal" (interview 7 April 1994). Bjelke-Petersen retorted that Schubert could not possibly have given Ahern this advice, whereupon Ahern invited Bjelke-Petersen to phone

Schubert to verify his account. When the Premier did so, and Schubert confirmed Ahern's version, Bjelke-Petersen immediately sacked Ahern from the GBRMPA ministerial council and appointed himself. According to one account, the Premier took this action "to resist further federal threats to the state's control over Queensland coastal waters, asserting that, 'We are determined to keep our coastline free' " (Fitzgerald 1984, p. 375).

The Premier's show of bravado was entirely for public consumption, however. As Ahern observed, at the next council meeting — the first one Bjelke-Petersen attended — "the Cairns section of the park was confirmed with Bjelke-Petersen in favour" (Ahern, interview 7 April 1994).

Assessment of Ahern's tenure at Primary Industries

When interviewed, those who were Ahern's Cabinet colleagues offered a qualified assessment of his performance as Minister for Primary Industries. Before discussing their opinions, however, one should note the view of the late Margaret Cribb. From her vantage point as a senior academic who carried out extensive research into the National Party, Cribb judged Ahern at this stage to be "better and more competent than most of his National Party colleagues" (Cribb, interview 24 March 1993). Terry White, who suggested that Ahern had entered Cabinet with "the wholehearted support of Mike Evans[2] and, to some extent, of Robert Sparkes also" was of the opinion that the Nationals had no choice but to promote Ahern if they were serious about developing an urban base (White, interview 7 May 1993). However, in White's view, Ahern was indecisive at DPI, being driven by his department. White saw him as tending to give industry lobbyists what they wanted, when they asked for it. He cited by way of an example his own opposition to:

> ... the erection of a sugar storage facility on the river by the fish market. It was a prime piece of real estate which the Liberals wanted for parkland, ... but Mike Ahern bowed to industry pressure and authorised construction. (White, interview 7 May 1993)

Lane's assessment was harsher. While acknowledging Ahern as

"highly intelligent, with a good memory", he did not see Ahern as an "initiator", but as one who "was good at carrying out others' orders". He further claimed that Ahern "did not tell his department what to do ... the Director General ran the department" (Lane, interview 2 April 1993). Austin concurred, stating:

> Mike never made a decision when Primary Industry Minister. Any hard decisions were always sent to a committee, which explains why Neil Turner [Warrego] had a tough time following Ahern, as many of these committees were then reporting and often recommending findings contrary to National Party policy. (Austin, interview 7 July 1993)

Ministers inevitably compete with each other. In Cabinet, all are conscious of their respective positions in the seniority and status stakes. Attaining a ministry satisfies one's prior ambition but also pushes one forward towards future preferment, if necessary at the expense of one's colleagues, despite any close personal ties that might exist among them. Additionally, none of these sources is unbiased. White had been outplayed by Bjelke-Petersen and the Nationals in the 1983 Coalition crisis;[3] after the 1983 election Lane and Austin deserted the Liberals for the Nationals and, in the aftermath of the Fitzgerald Inquiry, were imprisoned for dishonestly dealing with their ministerial expenses. Lane, in particular, continued to exhibit great bitterness toward Ahern, because one of Ahern's first actions as Premier was to stand Lane aside from the Ministry, on the grounds that he had been adversely mentioned before the Fitzgerald Inquiry. Lane frankly admitted that from this point onwards he worked to destabilise Ahern (interview 2 April 1993). Austin, by contrast, gained advancement under Ahern, becoming Minister for Finance, Minister assisting the Premier and Treasurer, and Leader of the House. His fall occurred after the 1989 election.

These somewhat sour reflections as to Ahern's competence in Primary Industries can be set against the acknowledgment he received from several speakers in his Estimates debate in November 1981. For example:

> Joe Kruger (Labor, Murrumba): "I have quite a respect for the ability of the Minister for Primary Industry." (*QPD* vol. 386, p. 3469)
>
> Len Stephan (National, Gympie): "[the] industry generally has ex-

pressed confidence, as I do, in the Minister's handling of his portfolio." (p. 3470)

Max Menzel (National, Mulgrave): "I pay tribute to the work the Minister has done … in the short time he has occupied the portfolio." (p. 3482)

Peter McKechnie (National, Carnarvon): "I am very pleased to hear even the Opposition commend the able and efficient way in which he [Ahern] is administering the department." (p. 3499)

Members on the government backbench, together with sections of the Labor frontbench, thus praised Ahern's administration, despite his then admittedly short incumbency. No participant in the debate directly or personally denigrated or criticised the Minister. Instead, participants raised factual or opinionated matters based on concerns related to aspects of the DPI Annual Report, which had been tabled before the Budget papers.

Along with his colleagues (apart from the Premier) Ahern was not, of course, able to choose which Ministry he received, nor the length of time he would spend administering it. With over sixty major statutes to oversee, he faced a major administrative crisis when the Sugar Acquisition Act was ruled *ultra vires*, which necessitated the rewriting of all Acquisition Acts. It was inevitable that, under such pressures, the Minister was frequently seen to be reactive rather than proactive.

Additionally Ahern had to deal with a wide range of claims, submissions and requests constantly put before him by the varied industries that his portfolio ecompassed. Inevitably there were some (for example White) who failed to have pet issues resolved to their satisfaction. Lane and Austin were activist, some may say ruthless, Ministers who forced the decision-making pace in their portfolios. When interviewed they tended to be generally sceptical, if not contemptuous, of the administrative ability of many of their older National Party colleagues. Superimposed upon their behaviour was Bjelke-Petersen's own political style. In Cabinet there was no doubt that, when challenged, his will prevailed. Any opposition to him was brutually crushed. As the Premier set the standard, inevitably many Ministers emulated his approach. Ahern was not autocratic by nature, nor did he take his cue from the Premier. By the same token he was not the "ball boy" for

DPI or its Director-General. There is no evidence, during his tenure at DPI (or in any other portfolio), that he played Jim Hacker to his Director-General's Sir Humphrey Appleby.[4] Some may see his establishment of committees to which he could refer contentious issues, together with a commitment to political and administrative networking, as evidence of chronic indecision and a desire to escape from the responsibilities of decision-making. An alternative perspective, however, suggests an orientation towards consultation and the ability to take advice, together with a prudent recognition that it was necessary (on all important matters) to cultivate a wide circle of opinion.

When appointed, all Ministers have to engage in on-the-job learning. Ahern had waited longer than nearly all his peers for promotion. As a junior Minister who had to administer a large and complex department, his learning curve was inevitably steeper than most. He was, after all, given no soft landing when promoted to a position at the Cabinet table.

Additionally, while Bjelke-Petersen was widely perceived to be in firm control, his leadership style did not guarantee stability or smoothness in either the administration of Government or the flow of decision-making. Cribb captured the character of this period (from the mid-1970s to the mid-1980s) when she reflected on her attendance at National Party annual conferences.

> When Bjelke-Petersen and Flo [sic] arrived, it was as though the Queen and Prince Philip had turned up. Adulation and almost knee bowing were the order of the day ... There was a limit to the number of times Mike Ahern (or anyone else) could stand up to Bjelke-Petersen in Cabinet. If Ministers seriously took Bjelke-Petersen on, they faced instant dismissal from Cabinet and nobody in the Parliamentary National Party would support them. (Cribb, interview 24 March 1993)

Terry White referred to the chronic instability that characterised Cabinet meetings as a result of Bjelke-Petersen's authoritarian behaviour. White particularly remembered the machinations, just after his promotion, concerning the appointment of Chief Justice.[5] This dispute reinforced and further exacerbated the barely latent and persistent tensions between the Coalition partners. White blamed what he termed the National Party "old guard" for the constant and self-serving leaking of Cabinet submissions and discussions to the media and to sectional groups. He also blamed them for the increasing sycophancy that many National and some Liberal Ministers, together with certain officials, cultivated towards the Premier, and for the almost total absence of a consensual decision-making style, both among Ministers and between them and the Premier (White, interview 7 May 1993).

The judicial appointments controversy

Controversy over the appointment of Chief Justice was precipitated toward the end of November 1981 when Sir Charles Wanstall CJ announced his retirement, and Bjelke-Petersen asserted that Wanstall's successor could be "anyone on the Bench" (Cribb 1982, p. 97). He was publicly reproved for this by Sam Doumany (Kurilpa), the Liberal Attorney-General, who insisted that the customary seniority rule, which would favour Justice Douglas SPJ, must prevail. He went further, claiming that, unless this occurred, the future of the Coalition was at stake.

White maintained that Bjelke-Petersen, Sir Edward Lyons ("Top Level Ted") and Sir Terence Lewis, the Police Commissioner, had already conspired to elevate Justice Dormer Andrews, then a junior judge who, in a move unusual within the Queensland judiciary, had earlier been promoted to the Supreme Court from the District Court. At the 21 December 1981 Cabinet meeting, Bjelke-Petersen rejected Doumany's nomination of Douglas for Chief Justice and ruled that the decision would be deferred until 12 January 1982, the first Cabinet of the new year.

According to White, the Liberals thought they could win on this issue because, in Cabinet, Sullivan, Ahern and Tomkins often sided with them while Lane frequently allied himself with Bjelke-Petersen's supporters. White asserted that the Premier "heavily" lobbied these three National ministers in the lead-up to 12 January. At this first Cabinet meeting he went around the table, pointing to each Minister in turn to demand an answer. All the Nationals lined up behind him and, while the Liberals supported Doumany, "Lane told Bjelke-Petersen that, while he would have to support the Liberals, he was really with the Premier" (White, interview 7 May 1993). After further acrimonious debate, the Liberals had a partial victory. Bjelke-Petersen was forced to accept Campbell J as the compromise candidate for Chief Justice. However the Premier struck back, using the Nationals' numbers in Cabinet to force the appointment of Andrews J as Senior Puisne Judge.

The minute recommending the appointments of Campbell and Andrews was then "rushed to the Governor" (Cribb 1982, p. 425), but only after the seven Liberal Ministers had signed a notation to the minute recording their opposition to Andrews's promotion. They also despatched Llew Edwards to Government House to explain to the Governor their opposition both to the decision and to the way it was taken. Despite these desperate efforts to retain some political credibility, the Governor, Sir James Ramsey, bound as he was by constitutional convention to heed the advice of the Premier and a majority of Cabinet, signed the minute. His action provoked a humiliating Liberal backdown. Doumany withdrew his resignation, the Liberals announced that they would, after all, remain in the Coalition, and the Queensland Liberal Party state executive passed a pusillanimous face-saving motion. It stated:

> This executive gives notice to the executive of the National Party that it will not tolerate the National Party using its numbers in Cabinet to implement its views against the total and expressed opposition of Liberal Ministers. Should any further breach of the agreement or principles occur, the Liberal Party will regard the [coalition] agreement as having been terminated by the National Party. (Cribb 1982)

This was the version that remained on the public record. According to Terry White, however, the situation in its entirety was more complex. After the December Cabinet meeting, he travelled to Edwards's home in Ipswich and argued strongly that the Liberals should take a principled stand on the issue of maintaining judicial independence from political interference. Should the Nationals refuse to concede this principle, and continue the plan for Douglas's elevation, the Liberals must then seize the occasion to leave the Coalition. White, who had been at Nudgee College with the late Dr Denis Murphy, then ALP state president, further informed Edwards that he understood Labor was prepared to offer conditional support to a minority Liberal government.[6]

According to White, Edwards, when appraised of this situation, authorised White to negotiate with Murphy. White subsequently met with both Murphy and Peter Beattie, then ALP state secretary. Murphy and Beattie excluded the leader of the Parliamentary Labor Party, Keith Wright (Rockhampton), from the meeting, however; according to White, this was because they did not trust Wright.[7] White related that an agreement was, in principle, reached between them (White, interview 7 May 1993). They decided:

- The Liberals would govern as a minority government with support from the Parliamentary Labor Party.[8]
- The minority government would introduce, and both parties would sponsor, a one vote:one value redistribution before the next election (scheduled for 1983).
- The Liberals would not bring down any anti-trade-union legislation.[9]

Murphy and Beattie assured White that they could carry both the Parliamentary Labor Party and the ALP organisation with them.

As the Cabinet meeting of 12 January concluded, Edwards announced that he accepted the Campbell compromise. He intimated that, before Cabinet met, he and the Premier had discussed this option, both agreeing as to its desirability. Although Edwards was the only Minister who knew of White's negotiations with Murphy and Beattie, he had neglected to inform White of this conversation with Bjelke-Petersen. Edwards's statement left White deeply distressed. Feeling an acute sense of betrayal, while repaired to Hewitt's office, where they held a long and intense discussion as to whether to resign from Parliament. As well as being close political friends and allies they represented the small "l" Liberal wing of their party, and were strongly opposed to any erosion of the separation of powers between the executive and legislature on the one hand and the judiciary on the other. Both, however, hesitated as theirs was the classic political dilemma: whether to continue the work for reform from within Government, or to quit, thereby signalling that while Bjelke-Petersen remained in power any chance for reform was doomed. White felt, in retrospect, "I should have resigned as my political career was all but over from this point and my critics could not have abused me for taking a stand on this issue." (interview 7 May 1993; cf. Miller and Koch 1983, pp. 157–8).

Resign is precisely what he and his supporters did eighteen months later when they crossed the floor (Hewitt leaving the Chamber rather than casting a vote), over whether Parliament should suspend standing orders to debate the establishment of a Public Accounts Committee. Ironically White had no idea that, three years earlier, the Nationals had forged a secret electoral pact with the ALP (see chapter 2) to deny the Liberals the chance for majority status within the Coalition. Labor was taking every opportunity to sow tares in the wheatfield of Government. For the record, White's opinion was that the appointment of Chief Justice was the occasion when "Mike Ahern effectively made the decision to compromise on an issue of principle for the future of his career". Nor, White added, should Ahern "be condemned for this in the light of future events" (interview 7 May 1993). White did not appreciate, as events in 1983 escalated beyond his control, that he would have been on stronger political ground had he challenged the Nationals over these judicial appointments rather than over the establishment of a Public Accounts Committee. As events transpired, the 1983 election rendered the Liberals politically irrelevant in Queensland for the next twelve years.

Notes

1. In Queensland it is the practice for Ministers to convene a committee of Government backbenchers with whom they consult (on matters including proposed legislation) as to the administration of their portfolios. At this time, and in the absence of a comprehensive parliamentary committee system, this was the only way some Members could make any input into executive decision-making. It remained for individual Ministers to decide how frequently and systematically they utilised these committees. Ahern's testimony is that he took his backbench committee seriously and used it extensively.
2. Then state director (formerly state secretary) of the Queensland National Party.
3. See Miller and Koch (1983), passim.
4. These were characters from two very popular British television series, "Yes Minister" and "Yes Prime Minister". Hacker was the Minister/Prime Minister, Appleby the senior public servant.
5. These appointments are by Governor-in-Council on Cabinet's recom-

mendation. Under Bjelke-Petersen, such appointments increasingly depended on whether Cabinet could be coerced by the Premier after he had reached agreement with his political confidants, none of whom was a Minister. See White (in Miller and Koch 1983, p. 157).

6. Labor had, by then, largely recovered from the trauma of federal intervention (see chapter 2) and, having reconstructed its organisation, was anxious to re-enter the political state arena as a revitalised player.
7. Wright subsequently moved to federal politics as the Member for Capricornia.
8. The current state of parties in the Chamber was: Liberals 22; Nationals 35; Labor 25. Labor would then no longer have been recognised as the Opposition, because the Nationals would have become the larger of the non-Government parties. With Labor supporting the Liberals on the floor of Parliament (47:35) the Liberals were assured of winning confidence motions and passing Supply, the two constitutional tests for any Government in a Westminster system.
9. Murphy, a Reader in History at The University of Queensland was the pre-eminent Labor historian in Queensland. His reputation still stands. He thus possessed an acute sense of Labor's historical and then contemporary position in Queensland political history.

CHAPTER 4

A change of pace

As discussed above, Mike Ahern was Minister for Primary Industries for almost three and a half years. By his own account he enjoyed his time administering this large, multifaceted department, the activities of which were central to the economic and political concerns of the National Party. Despite his rural background, Ahern was unusual among National Party politicians of the time in not having devoted himself to a long period of farming. His agricultural science degree, too, placed him at one remove from virtually all his colleagues who both owned and managed their properties.

In one sense, because the National Party was dominated by farmers and farming interests, DPI was something of a "dream" portfolio for a National Party minister. During the twenty-six years of Coalition Government, Primary Industries was never occupied by a Liberal, and was typically held by older former farmers and/or graziers nearing the end of their political careers. Ahern represented a break from this pattern. Nevertheless, when he was moved, the portfolio went to Neil Turner (Warrego), then a 50-year-old grazier from western Queensland.[1]

Ahern and the end of the Coalition Government

While the timing of ministerial reshuffles was generally unpredictable, under successive Bjelke-Petersen Governments they often turned upon the need either to clear the decks before an election, or to recommence the governing process after one. During the 1970s, controversy invariably attended post-election reshuffles as the two Coalition partners relentlessly squabbled over the numbers each was entitled to have in Cabinet, and the occupancy of various portfolios. The final Coalition Ministry was a typical case in point, comprising ten Nationals and eight Liberals. Those portfolios particularly relevant to the rural sector, and/or involving opportunities to target patronage at electorally relevant special interests, were kept firmly in the Nationals' orbit. Such ministries were Primary Industries (Ahern); Local Government, Main Roads, Police and Racing (Hinze); Northern Development and Maritime Services (Bird); Works and Housing (Wharton); Mines and Energy (Gibbs); Lands and Forestry (Glasson); and Water Resources (Goleby).

By contrast, the Liberals administered departments which were typically managed according to orthodox public service practices and managerial styles, or which dealt with urban policy matters, lacking significant opportunities for the distribution of political largesse. Thus the junior partner ran Treasury (Edwards), Justice and Attorney-General (Doumany), Employment and Labour Relations (Knox), Environment, Administrative Services and Valuation (Hewitt), Transport (Lane), Health (Austin) and Welfare Services (White).

In chapter 2 attention focused on Ahern's arduous route to a Cabinet post. Once in the Ministry, he could be displaced only if there was a major scandal involving an issue of administrative incompetence, or if the Government was defeated at the polls. The Nationals' system of zonal vote weightage (popularly known as the gerrymander), regularly recrafted at each redistribution, was specifically designed to minimise the possibility of electoral defeat. It protected the Nationals both from being beaten by Labor and from being displaced as senior Coalition partner by the Liberals. As to dismissal, Ahern was simply too good an administrator, across the three portfolios he successively occupied, to be derailed by managerial problems. Although this is, of course, a judgment made with hindsight, contemporary commentators also favourably assessed his role as Minister, perceiving him to be a very able performer. Cribb's opinion of him (see Chapter 3) as a forward-looking and innovative thinker was typical.

He enjoyed a similarly favourable reputation among both public servants (David Ford, interview 6 March 1993) and those interest-group representatives with whom he interacted as a Minister of the Crown. Thus, having finally been forced to appoint Ahern, Bjelke-Petersen would have found it politically difficult to sack him.[2] Any such move would have been judged as originating from blatant personal considerations, and would almost certainly have provoked an adverse public reaction. Had Ahern been rusticated to the backbench, he would doubtless have looked to his numbers, reworked his support base and, when politically expedient, engineered a leadership spill.[3]

In this context, his reaction to White's concern about the Chief Justiceship is illuminating. He stated that while he "had numerous arguments with Joh in the past, [he] was now trying to live with him and grapple with the complexities of DPI" (interview 7 July 1994).

They could never be personally close, but after 1981 both Bjelke-Petersen and Ahern gave the public appearance of attempting to live with each other, despite their pursuing radically different, if not diametrically opposed, political agendas.

After the 1980 election, the Coalition was demonstrably being pulled apart on any number of issues. In such a crisis-ridden atmosphere, it is impossible to calculate when the tensions between Ahern and Bjelke-Petersen would have erupted had not the Liberal–National alliance imploded on 4 August 1983. The Coalition's demise, together with the 1983 election campaign and its results will be discussed later and have been thoroughly covered elsewhere.[4] Suffice it to say here that the consequent political realignment impacted upon the political careers of all players, including Ahern.

During this period Ahern was closer to the Parliamentary Liberal Party than any of his Parliamentary National Party colleagues. In addition, he was on better terms with more Liberal Ministers than any other National Minister. For example, he had shared a good relationship with Bill Hewitt from the time they worked together on the Select Committee (see chapter 2). When interviewed in 1994, he specifically identified an ongoing friendship with Norm Lee (Yeronga), sacked from the Ministry in 1980 by Edwards. Moreover he and Terry White were clearly similar in age, background, qualifications and political values. As Ahern put it, he "interacted well with Terry White and the

Liberals". As to the Coalition's collapse, while he personally "regretted its demise" none saw him as an active participant (Ahern, interview 14 September 1994)

When discussing the events in Parliament that precipitated the Coalition's collapse, Ahern claimed that it was well known to both the public and the Parliament that he strongly advocated a parliamentary committee system and, in particular, a Public Accounts Committee. However, neither at the time nor in retrospect did he think that 4 August 1983 was the occasion to realise this goal. Similarly, he did not favour the Liberal rebels' tactics. In view of his marginal role in these events it is pertinent to recall that, when in due course he became Premier, he established both the Public Accounts and the Public Works Committees.

Ahern was undoubtedly correct in claiming to be a strong Coalition supporter. This reputation, among other factors, almost certainly precluded his playing a central role. He rightly observed that he was not one of the "heavy [Cabinet] players" during this terminal period of the Coalition Government's life cycle. Moreover, he cites a vivid example which amply demonstrates his "walk-on" part. After the Parliamentary Liberal Party had elected Terry White and Angus Innes to their respective positions as Liberal Leader and Deputy Leader on 4 August 1983, they proceeded to the Premier's office on the fifteenth floor of the Executive Building to inform Bjelke-Petersen of their new status, and the consequent need to refocus Coalition arrangements. While considering his options, and the tactics available to dispense both with them and with their party, Bjelke-Petersen kept them sitting for an hour outside his office, in full view of both the media and any passers-by. During this time Ahern walked down the corridor, whereupon he was approached by White who asked him, "Is Joh for real?" To this inquiry, Ahern could truthfully reply that he simply had no idea as to the Premier's intentions (Ahern, interview 14 September 1994). It was, after all, inconceivable that in such a charged political atmosphere Mike Ahern, of all people, would be in Bjelke-Petersen's confidence. The Premier, as was typical on such occasions, remained closeted with his closest and most intimate non-ministerial advisers.

The definitive account by Miller and Koch (1983) confirms Ahern's peripheral position. In their 161-page book they make only two references to him. The first mention is of a local government issue in Caloundra, in his seat of Landsborough, which surfaced during the campaign (see pp. 114–15). Their second reference simply places him in the list of Ministers (together with their portfolio designations) who were sworn in after the election. However, by way of augmentation Tony Koch commented later:

> Mike Ahern supported Joh over the White episode. He thought Joh did the right thing in demanding that White be sacked and refusing to serve with him after he [White] became Liberal Leader. (Koch interview 1 September 1994)

Koch's longstanding and enviable reputation as a state political roundsman and chief political reporter for the *Courier-Mail* remains undisputed, but Ahern's personal recollections of this period are not nearly as straightforward. Moreover by 1982, as Koch agreed, in the same interview, despite their personal and political relations Ahern and White were increasingly pursuing different political agendas. By illustration one can return to the Chief Justiceship, a matter central to White's evaluation of this period's politics (see Miller and Koch 1983, pp. 157–8; cf. Terry White, interview 7 May 1993). To counterbalance White's personal and political investment in the question, Ahern saw it as:

> ... just another ball game played by Joh with the heavy players in Cabinet ... [It was] not seen as a bread and butter issue and, had the Liberals consulted [me] as to whether they should break with the Coalition over this matter, [I] would have advised them against doing so ... [I] had known Sir Walter Campbell for years [they shared a school connection in Downlands] and was, in fact, very happy with the [Campbell CJ] compromise. (interview 14 September 1994)

Ahern's words do not suggest any personal rift with White; simply that they were now travelling along separate political paths — neither an uncommon nor surprising development when backbench allies and friends are promoted to Cabinet and must henceforth focus upon their specific and particular ministerial responsibilities.

By refusing to accept the White–Innes Liberal leadership team,

Bjelke-Petersen cancelled Coalition agreements that had endured for twenty-six years.[5] This event was universally welcomed by the National Party backbench because it had one obvious political consequence: to make immediately available to them the eight former Liberal-held portfolios. In moves that further widened the options, Val Bird retired at the 1983 election, while the Premier dropped Tony Elliott (Cunningham) from Cabinet.

Lane and Austin, despite having been re-elected as Liberals, switched within days to the Nationals, giving that party its requisite parliamentary majority. The defectors in turn received their anticipated rewards, having restored to them their former ministries of Transport and Health respectively. Theirs was a calculated gamble, that by deserting the Liberals they could continue their political ambitions.[6] Naturally, what was left of the Parliamentary Liberal Party judged their behaviour to be perfidious, and all the more galling because their actions gave the Nationals the two crucial parliamentary seats they required to govern alone. With Lane and Austin back in the Ministry, only Hinze, Goleby and Gibbs retained the portfolios they had occupied as Ministers in the Coalition Government. Seven former National backbenchers now made their way into Cabinet, and, among other changes, Ahern was moved from Primary Industries to Bill Gunn's former portfolio of Industry and Commerce, with "Commerce" deleted from the title and replaced with "Small Business and Technology".

The (failed) quest for the Deputy Premiership

Ahern, having been ranked tenth in the Coalition Government, and the most junior National Minister, was now promoted to fifth position. Nevertheless it was Gunn's political fortunes rather than those of Ahern that were currently in the ascendant. Nearly twelve months before the end of the Coalition, Sullivan and Tomkins had been sacked for their involvement in the "*Melbidir* affair" (Chittick and Reynolds 1992). Sullivan and Tomkins had taken a trip on the Queensland Government vessel *Melbidir*, allegedly on Government business, to Far North Queensland. From an aircraft a press photographer photographed them fishing from the side of the *Melbidir*. This received wide publicity, together with allegations that they concocted the reason for the trip as an excuse to indulge in a fishing holiday at public expense. As a consequence of their political ineptitude, a bitter power struggle arose over the deputy leadership of the National Party.

Despite some procrastination from the Premier, designed to distance himself from Sparkes's demand that Sullivan be sacked immediately and a new deputy elected, a meeting of the Parliamentary National Party was finally called for 1 December 1982 at which Hinze, Gibbs, Gunn and Ahern all nominated for the vacancy created by Sullivan's enforced resignation. This intra-party event assumed greater significance because of intense speculation over Bjelke-Petersen's possible retirement plans. Contemporary popular wisdom was that he would voluntarily retire at some point between the 1983 and 1986 elections. Hence any contest, late in 1982, for the deputy's position would necessarily involve prospective candidates staking their respective claims to the premiership. None knew then that the Coalition Government would collapse nine months later, allowing the Nationals to realise Sparkes's long-cherished dream of governing alone. A major consequence of the Coalition's cessation was the indefinite postponing of any plans the Premier may have harboured to quit politics.

The two least-supported candidates, Gibbs and Hinze, were eliminated after the first vote; but on the second, Ahern and Gunn tied, each securing seventeen votes. A third ballot was then held, in the course of which one Member deserted Ahern, thereby electing Gunn by eighteen votes to sixteen. (Ahern has confirmed that he still has no idea who changed sides.) The Nationals' deputy leadership had been settled, albeit narrowly, well before the Coalition ended. The 1983 election result therefore elevated Gunn to Deputy Premier and Minister Assisting the Treasurer. Freed at last from the presence of a Liberal Leader who gained Treasury as the price of Coalition agreement, Bjelke-Petersen immediately assumed the Treasury portfolio. (He had for a number of years been the only State Premier who was not also his own Treasurer.)

In 1983, the Nationals finally attained their long-sought-after objective, first publicly adverted to by Sparkes at the landmark 1974 Mayne Hall conference, in which he proclaimed the new urban strategy for the party. They had displaced the Liberals as the pre-eminent urban conservative party in Queensland state (but not federal) electoral politics, by winning five former Brisbane Liberal electorates,[7] to give them their much-coveted urban presence (Reynolds 1986). By this wide-ranging victory, the Nationals had ruined what was widely perceived as Labor's best chance since 1957 to return to government.[8] They were now in a position to embark on their final redrawing of the electoral boundaries, thereby taking their zonal system of vote weightage to its furthest extremity from the principle of one vote, one value. Such unrepentant hubris served to convince them that, thanks to their 1985 creative electoral cartography, they would retain power in perpetuity.

Minister for Industry, Small Business and Technology

Leaving Primary Industries marked a watershed in the advancement of Mike Ahern's political career. He had been a solid performer in this National Party heartland portfolio, but was now more than prepared to move; in short, he needed an alternative administrative focus. To realise his ultimate ambition of becoming the National leader in order to move his party in a progressive direction, he had to make an impression beyond the confines of the rural lobby. He wanted to create other networks, and stamp his concerns on alternative areas of public policy. He had to be exposed to the claims, and appraisals, of a wider and more varied range of economic interest groups. It was crucial, in the now-altered climate of post-Coalition politics, for Ahern to be recognised by Queensland's industrial and commercial leaders as the preferred, indeed the only viable, heir to Sir Johannes Bjelke-Petersen.

The administrative contrast between DPI and Industry, Small Business and Technology was stark indeed. Ahern's new challenge was to preside over a small, recently cobbled together department which had so far exerted no discernible or noteworthy influence on Queensland's economic and commercial development. Beyond the processing of agricultural products, Queensland possessed only a small rudimentary manufacturing base which gave rise to Brisbane's reputation, and self-image, of being a "branch office city" for virtually all large companies in the private sector, as well as those federal government departments and statutory authorities headquartered in Sydney, Melbourne or Canberra.

At DPI Ahern had administered more than sixty statutes; in this new ministry he was responsible for only a handful. Between 1983 and 1986 he piloted a total of five Acts through the Legislative Assembly, three of which addressed what was then a current and controversial issue: retail shop leases (Humble 1984). He made only four ministerial statements. Compared to DPI, his legislative and parliamentary workloads were minimal; his political challenges, however, lay elsewhere.

By the mid-1980s, a consensus of informed opinion began to coalesce around the proposition that Queensland's tripartite economic base of agriculture, mining and tourism was inadequate to sustain current and projected levels of economic activity. Moreover, this base had not the potential to underwrite the exponential economic and demographic expansion predicted for Queensland.[9] The state had not profited to any appreciable extent from Australia's post-war immigration program, as most European, and later Asian, migrant labour gravitated either to New South Wales or Victoria, inevitably attracted by the large manufacturing plants and associated labour-intensive industries housed in those states. However, following Bjelke-Petersen's 1977 initiative to abolish Queensland's death duties, there commenced a strong trend of interstate migration to Queensland.

Initially retirees dominated the population flow, responding to the Government's financial inducement and the inherent attractions of Queensland's climatic conditions. Within the decade this pattern was modified as increasing numbers of workforce-age migrants arrived, thereby commencing a pattern which, although it initially preceded the recession of the late 1980s to early 1990s, was given fresh impetus by it. The economic downturn was characterised by retrenchments, contractions and hence job losses in the manufacturing sectors of New South Wales and Victoria. In Queensland, pressures on the state's infrastructure inevitably flowed from such large-scale and diverse interstate migration, and urgently forced state planning authorities to address strategies aimed at broadening and diversifying Queensland's economic and fiscal base. Large-scale manufacturing was not a viable option, because heavy-industry economies were in recession virtually everywhere in the world (apart from some of the so-called "tiger economies" of East and South-East Asia); in addition, the pattern of decline adversely impacted upon a myriad of associated downstream industries. Hence the only realistic alternative appeared to lie with the computer revolution, and its associated information and high-technology enterprises. As it happened, advisers to both the state (National) and federal (Labor) governments were at one on this matter; and by the 1980s Prime Minister Bob Hawke was urging Australians to forego their self-image as inhabitants of the "Lucky Country" and become members of the "Clever Country".

Ahern, when appointed to this new portfolio, asked the Premier what was meant by the reference to "Technology". The term had not previously appeared in the portfolio descriptions, and Ahern was intrigued as to its provenance. He related, "Joh replied, 'Oh, Mike, you'll know' " (Ahern, interview 14 September 1994). What Ahern did not then appreciate was that the Coordinator-General's staff had been researching the case for a Ministry of Technology. Once the data and arguments had been assembled in a brief, Coordinator-General Sir Sidney Schubert, by then chief public service adviser to Bjelke-Petersen because his department had been merged with that of Premier's, presented these proposals to Bjelke-Petersen. However, as this coincided with the 1983 political crisis, any resolution awaited the outcome of the election. Consequently the old Industry and Commerce Department became restructured, renamed, and then passed to Ahern to become its first Minister.

Had this development occurred during the Coalition's period of office, the new Ministry would probably have gone to the Liberals, unless or until Hinze and/or Bjelke-Petersen discerned that it presented patronage possibilities. Such considerations were apparently not on Ahern's agenda when, in response to the Premier's instruction, he approached Schubert, who responded by producing "a tome ... from the [Coordinator-General's] department" — the brief arguing the rationale for a Department of Technology. Bjelke-Petersen did not fully accept this recommendation, and amalgamated Technology with the existing areas of Small Business and Industry, possibly in a bid to keep Ahern's ministerial activities under the scrutiny of the "heavy Cabinet players". Nonetheless, Ahern enthusiastically embraced the notion of a Technology portfolio and set about establishing it within the parameters he had been given (Ahern, interview 14 September 1994).

While Industry, Small Business and Technology represented a new challenge for Ahern, and was necessarily also being touted by the Government as an exciting initiative for Queensland, the reality was more prosaic. This new department was small, consisting of one of the Government's "Cinderella" departments (Industry and Commerce), a former QANGO (Small Business Development Corporation), and a newly created but neither large nor extensively resourced department (Technology). In his new Ministry, Ahern ran a department with a budget only one-third the size of that for his previous portfolio.[10]

The reshuffle meant that Ahern now had a department to administer largely as he pleased. While he was repeating the ministerial learning curve he had first experienced at DPI, so too were his senior departmental officials, now assembled in a newly created department that confronted them with a new set of responsibilities. In a department such as DPI, a new Minister had to conform to well-established rules and procedures which had been developed over time, to address perennial and ongoing issues. In a new department, the incoming Minister could formulate his own approach in a novel setting, where neither Minister nor portfolio carried baggage from the past. But because nothing in politics, or in public administration, is truly a blank slate, the various components of the new Ministry brought with them past associations and practices.

Industry was undoubtedly the most controversial part of the Ahern inheritance. In a perceptive analysis of contemporary Government–business relations, Charlton (1983) traced the history of Queensland's economic development, arguing that, because manufacturing occupied such a limited role in Queensland, the Industry Department was consequently small and marginalised.[11] He observed:

> At the end of the decade [the 1960s] the number of professionally qualified men and women employed by the then Department of Industrial Development could be counted on the fingers of one hand. Its Director, Sir David Muir, fought magnificent bureaucratic battles for the enlargement of his department and of its professional expertise but it was not until well

into the 1970s that this happened to any marked extent. (Charlton 1983, p. 196)

While the department remained stagnant and underdeveloped, Cabinet was dragged behind the chariot wheels of Bjelke-Petersen's obsessive policy of attracting any and all types of foreign investment. Charlton's acid observation was:

> Under Bjelke-Petersen, Queensland has courted foreign capital with all the discrimination of a tart seeking customers ... Bjelke-Petersen has repeatedly said that he is prepared to welcome ... anyone who is prepared to invest in Queensland. (Charlton 1983, p. 203)

The establishment of the Bjelke-Petersen Foundation in 1979 was crucial in that it provided the political background for this policy, inducing businesses to donate to the National Party as their price for doing business in Queensland. Thus was established a pattern of patronage which, as the Fitzgerald Report demonstrated in 1989, led all too readily to corruption. Charlton cited a series of decisions in support of his conclusion that patronage drove government–business relations: for example the siting of a power station at Tarong instead of Milmerran, purely on the insistence of Bjelke-Petersen who overrode expert departmental advice to the contrary (in 1978). In 1979 the Brisbane Port Authority was overruled when it called tenders for stevedoring rights to the new container terminal, and was threatened with disbandment unless the company favoured by the Government won the contract. Then in 1981 the Winchester South coal contract was awarded to a consortium of BP Australia, Drayton Investments (the family company of longstanding Bjelke-Petersen admirer and financial supporter Sir Leslie Thiess) and Westfield.

All of these decisions, together with their procedures, attracted serious criticism. In all three cases, fair and open tendering practices were varied at the Premier's will, as expert advice and scrutiny was either ignored or bypassed. An under-resourced and understaffed Industry Department was no match for a highly interventionist and erratic Cabinet whose approach was characterised by the Premier's rewriting of the rules whenever he decided the occasion warranted it. Between 1980 and 1983 Ahern had been relatively insulated from these matters, being preoccupied with administering DPI. Now, however, he stepped into an arena where the game plan did not favour a Minister who espoused an independent technocratic approach to decision-making. In Charlton's accurate assessment, the Government's industrial and investment policies were predicated upon the increasingly autocratic behaviour of the Premier, supplemented by the sycophantic approach adopted towards him by virtually the entire Ministry (and, one may add, by many senior bureaucrats).

One major problem with Bjelke-Petersen's style of government was that it was both opaque and unpredictable. The basis (if any) from which Bjelke-Petersen operated was unclear to any who were outside his immediate circle of admirers and advisers. Ahern (interview 7 April 1994) gave an example of this irrationality, which by then had overcome the Premier and those close to him. Before stepping into his new Ministry, Ahern became involved in the Oskar affair. Sirath Oskar, a foreign entrepreneur, had fired Bjelke-Petersen's imagination with the type of grandiose proposition that never failed to seize the Premier's interest. Oskar planned to build a large oilseed-processing plant to cater for what he claimed would become a burgeoning domestic and overseas market. Ahern's department (DPI) had, however, been warned by the Australian High Commission in Singapore that Oskar was under suspicion as an active player in the drug trade. As well, DPI's advice was that there was no chance of an oilseed-crushing plant in Queensland being economically viable. And if criminal suspicion and expert departmental advice were insufficient, a third warning had been issued by the West Australian Government against dealing with Oskar, in view of his intimate involvement with a WA company which had been declared bankrupt. Llew Edwards had received similar briefings from his senior Treasury officials.

Rational decision-making procedures should have ensured that these warnings would immediately cause the Government to terminate any further negotiations. Rationality, however, had nothing to do with Bjelke-Petersen's insistence that Oskar meet with Edwards, Ahern and himself. Ahern recollected that "Oskar wanted a huge Government guarantee and no money [from him] up front", and that "Edwards made all the running at the meeting but eventually stormed out" because the Premier obdurately refused all contrary advice. Bjelke-Petersen apparently saw Edwards and Ahern as representing bureaucratic obstructionism so, when the Treasurer effectively terminated the meeting, the Premier immediately announced to the media that Oskar's proposals would go ahead with full Government support.

Appalled by this turn of events, Ahern then gave the Singapore dossier (which he said had been compiled by one of his senior public servants, Des Lappige) to Bjelke-Petersen, hoping that its contents would persuade the Premier to reverse his decision. Shortly thereafter the file was leaked to the *Courier-Mail*, which immediately broke the story. The controversy which then erupted over the proposal, the proposer, and the manner in which the Government (in the person of Bjelke-Petersen) had supported it, terminated any possibility of an agreement. Not for the first time, Bjelke-Petersen bitterly accused Ahern of instigating a politically motivated leak. While Ahern has denied that he was the source of the leak, he cannot have been surprised when the Premier refused to believe him.

Industry was rapidly falling prey to the Government's version of patronage politics, and there was never any doubt that this had been the ultimate rationale for the Small Business administration. In the 1970s a political focus on small business enterprises had become the "flavour of the month". It was fashionable to assert, in political rhetoric, that small business represented the sector of the economy where fastest economic progress would be made and where economic recovery, together with the largest amount of job creation, would occur. The Queensland Government's response to pressure from the small-business lobby was to create the Small Business Development Corporation (SBDC) under the administration of a former National MLA, Bill Lammond (Wynnum 1974–77). Its charter was vague, there was little by way of concrete precedents for its specific operations and, as a statutory authority, it was neither under ministerial control nor subject to full public service scrutiny. It may be too harsh to dismiss the SBDC as an example of political window-dressing; it nevertheless bore the characteristics of a quick-fix response to a problem which by then, necessitated tangible evidence of governmental attention.

Ahern was aware that small-business policy was patronage driven and almost invariably devised in Bjelke-Petersen's office, with scant reference to Cabinet. When SBDC was subsumed in his new department, he turned to prominent Brisbane businessperson Jim Kennedy.[12] As a result Small Business was restructured and relocated, Ahern's ambition being that it would no longer exist to provide handouts to anyone and everyone who gained access to the Premier. Henceforth its charter was to devise guidelines to assist small entrepreneurs with training, networking, and building a resource base sufficient to combat the high failure rate among small businesses. Ahern was familiar with current New South Wales Corporate Affairs research showing that 80 per cent of all small enterprises failed within the first two years of operation. He therefore wanted to change the image of Small Business from that of a "milch cow" to one of an infrastructure and resource supporter. As can be imagined, this led to innumerable disputes between himself and the Premier, as Ahern asserted that he aimed "to pick winners, not help lame dogs" (interview 7 April 1994).

It was the Technology branch of Ahern's tripartite portfolio that was of most interest to him. It was impossible for him, acting alone, to reverse Queensland's approach to investment policy; instead he aimed to take the state into the era of high technology by researching and implementing an ever-increasing number of such initiatives. In this ambition he was well served by two able senior public servants: his Director-General, Don Young, and Young's deputy, Doug Rowell. Rowell, who was personally close to Ahern, became his confidant rather than merely a senior public servant in a line department. Austin, from Cabinet's perspective, commented that:

> Doug Rowell was Ahern's close adviser on high-tech and managerial matters where he [Ahern] made a name for himself. Mike was not stupid and was prepared to promote anything that might be a goer. (Austin, interview 7 July 1993)

As this Ministry for Technology was a novel concept, Cabinet permitted Ahern to take a three-week trip to North America to investigate the state of these "high-tech" industries. He visited Silicon Valley in California and the research triangle of North Carolina, before proceeding to Boston and a number of Canadian centres. On his return, he "wrote up the bones of a philosophy on technology and what should be its strategic direction in Queensland" (Ahern, interview 7 July 1994). This trip, and its resulting report, gave birth to Queensland's satellite technology and the introduction of Q-Net.

Ahern's tenure at Industry, Small Business and Technology coincided with Australia's entry into the field of satellite technology. He first intimated this, and his Government's approach, in a ministerial statement made to Parliament on 28 March 1985 (*QPD* vol. 298, p. 4562), by informing the House that the Queensland Government had acquired a transponder on Aussat, Australia's first domestic satellite. In doing so, he announced, the Government was moving "to implement a satellite-based telecommunications network — now known as Q-Net", directed at "extend[ing] and enhanc[ing] education, health, emergency and other services". He said he had received advice which confirmed that high-technology industry was the only long-term viable option for Queensland's economic development, and declared that "space age communications [were] absolutely vital in today's world for the sustenance of economic growth".

Six months later, in a further ministerial statement, on 3 September 1985 Ahern announced that Aussat was now in orbit and the Government had decided upon a ten-year telecommunications strategy, preceded by a pilot program for Q-Net. He affirmed his view that "The real focus of satellite developments in Queensland will be on the uses to which they can be put and not on the technology itself" (*QPD* vol. 299, p. 506). He commended to Parliament a paper written by his Chief Executive Officer, Doug Rowell, entitled "The Aussat Satellite and Social and Economic Development in Australia". Effectively Ahern's vision was that Q-Net would provide Government services to all Queenslanders, especially those in remote localities, while being accessed by "other interested parties to utilise what is, in principle, a Government services infrastructure investment". This latter use would allow Government to gain a revenue base to offset Q-Net's capital and operating costs, while providing openings for local government and "self-help organisations". He also instanced its potential for use by commercial TV stations and the ABC. It was typical of Ahern's approach that Q-Net, and associated satellite technology, became a project for investigative research undertaken by senior departmental staff under his personal encouragement and supervision.

Ahern obviously thought Q-Net was "a goer" (to quote Austin), because the research process was followed by evaluation as to commercial applications, both of which were then disclosed to Parliament. He also displayed to the House his hopes and ambitions for this innovation. While Ahern had enthusiastically taken up the technical dimension of his portfolio, doubtless influenced both by his background in applied science and by having Industry included in his responsibilities, he was also well placed to facilitate Q-Net's development from the technical phase to possible commercial applications.

These and other matters concerned with Industry, Small Business and Technology were aired (two years after he assumed the portfolio) in his Estimates debate on 10 October 1985 (*QPD*, vol. 300). The three themes that emerged concerned the Government's decentralisation and regional development policy (or alleged lack thereof), Government tendering policies with reference to computer and other high-technology equipment, and Q-Net. Ahern detailed the tendering policy and process in relation to each of the first two themes making it clear that a satisfactory offset clause was crucial for any tenderer's success. He was pleased that this had been agreed with the transnational computer company Sperry (which had an annual budget larger than that of Queensland); this company was to supply, in a deal worth $500 000, three thousand computers to the Queensland Education Department. The regional development policy consisted largely of subsidising industrial parks around the state. This was done on a sliding scale depending on whether the industrial developments were in rural, provincial or metropolitan localities. Inevitably those (Government) Members who had such estates in their electorates praised the policy, but most Opposition Members were sceptical, pointing to an uneven and ad hoc approach to this apparent decentralisation policy.

Undoubtedly Ahern's priority was Q-Net, as he led on this issue when introducing his estimates. He referred to the pilot program to test the range of services on Aussat 1, while disclosing that forty earth stations would be installed in Queensland. His chief regret seemed to be the lack of constructive debate:

> Few questions have been directed to me in this place on policy issues ... the total number of questions directed to me ... in the last two years has been pitifully few — about half a dozen. (*QPD* vol. 300, p. 1756)

His disappointment was reinforced by the tenor of the Estimates debate. In addition to himself only twenty Members rose (25 per cent of the House), with just five of these mentioning Q-Net, even in passing. He was, however, widely praised on all sides for his handling of his portfolio, for his enthusiasm and availability to Members and others, for driving his slender resources a long way and for his open administrative style.

The two Labor Members who spoke about Q-Net raised concerns, however, revolving around the relationship between Ausset/Q-Net and Telecom. Thus Bill Price (Mt Isa), affirmed an in-principle support for Q-Net, but worried about possible moves to privatise Telecom (hardly a matter within the purview of the Queensland Government, let alone Ahern's department), pointing out that, without cross-subsidisation paid for by long-distance STD profits, 425 000 rural telephone subscribers would pay an extra $200 per year. More directly, he suggested that these profits were threatened by Q-Net, claiming that, as Telecom could provide a satellite communications system more cheaply than Q-Net, developing the latter represented a waste of Government money and resources.

A more detailed probing came from Glen Milliner (Everton), who also proffered general support, but returned to the theme that Telecom could have adequately provided all services offered through Q-Net. He then asked a series of questions: What was the total cost? How many were employed on the "technical aspects" of the project and where were they recruited from? When Q-Net became operational, would it be required to use the Telecom network? If so, to what extent? Had agreement been reached with Telecom? (Ahern interjected that it had.) As Telecom had a parallel service, what was the cost differential between the two? Would user departments have to pay for Q-Net and, if so, what were the cost comparisons between Telecom and Q-Net?

Such was Ahern's close attachment to his policy that he immediately intervened rather than waiting until the last speaker had finished, to answer the matters canvassed by the two Labor Members. He laid to rest the privatisation and cross-subsidy concerns by confirming that Telecom was the common carrier, hence cross-subsidisation by Q-Net did not apply. Domestic satellites had by then a long history of use and, with their increased flexibility, saved money by extending services impossible to provide by land line, microwave and digital concentrator technologies. He claimed that, because Aussat was specifically designed for Australian needs and conditions, it alone represented the Government's correct course. Moreover, as Telecom would interconnect with Aussat, no revenue would be lost to Government.

His department had examined Telecom's Interra program and was convinced that the Aussat/Q-Net approach could fulfil the relevant tasks more cheaply, with some estimates suggesting costs 50 per cent below those of Telecom. The Q-Net program would cost $7 million and would by the end of that year (1985) employ seventeen contract staff from the Queensland Public Service, Papua New Guinea, the private sector, ABC, Aussat and Telecom. Q-Net would be a 50:50 user of both Aussat and Telecom systems, an arrangement acceptable to the latter because it would gain extra revenue. Q-Net despite still being in its pilot stage, was designed to provide many services not currently available from Telecom. Q-Net was already beginning to perform this function and when fully operational would provide these services more securely, and no more expensively, than Telecom. Finally, all user departments would pay. In winding up this part of the debate, Ahern constantly used the term "exciting" to describe all aspects of the Q-Net policy.

His reply effectively closed the debate on Q-Net, and succeeding speakers turned to regional matters and parochial concerns related to business developments. However, in a postscript to the Estimates debate a month later, Ahern made another Ministerial Statement (*QPD* vol. 301, 6 November 1985) in which he announced the publication of a report commissioned by the Government from PA Computers and Telecommunications entitled, *A Review of Current and Possible Future Issues Affecting Queensland Telecommunications Strategy Study*. This he laid on the table, informing the House that he had now made arrangements to brief Opposition Members on Q-Net, "to improve Members' understanding of the reason behind the Government's support for the program". To offer the Opposition a departmental briefing on a matter of important Government policy was, to say the least, unusual in Queensland politics. However, it was typical of Ahern that he would not allow past restrictive political practices to detract from his attempt to gather the widest possible support for his vision of Queensland's technology-based future.

Notes

1. After resignation from Parliament in 1986 for health reasons, Turner was re-elected in 1989 as Member for Nicklin and became Speaker during the Borbidge Government. He lost his seat in 1998 to an Independent, Peter Wellington, whose support returned Labor to Government.
2. Bjelke-Petersen did not actively seek Ahern's overthrow during this period despite their personality problems. In part this seemed to stem from Ahern's competence as an administrator, but also because he was a loyal party supporter who put in "the hard yards during election time" (Ahern, interview 14 September 1994). When Bjelke-Petersen did finally move against Ahern and four other Ministers in November of 1987, he destabilised the Cabinet and precipitated his own political demise.
3. All of which he did in November 1987 (see Chittick and Reynolds 1992; Coaldrake 1989).
4. Miller and Koch (1983), Reynolds (1986).
5. See chapter 2, Footnote 5.
6. Both have emphatically denied that they were offered any inducement by the Nationals to desert, or that there was any collaboration between them before the election. (Austin, interview 7 July 1993; Lane, interview 2 April 1993).
7. These were Mansfield, Greenslopes, Aspley, Mt Gravatt and Toowong. Labor captured a number of Liberal urban marginals.
8. So great was the uncertainty surrounding the outcome of the 1983 election that many thought Labor would win. Indeed Tony Koch has confirmed that the book on the 1983 election, of which he was co-author, was initially given the title *Joh KO'd*. After the declaration of the result, and Lane and Austin's defections, it was hurriedly retitled *Joh's KO*.
9. Figures quoted in the *Sunday Mail* (12 March 1995) showed that, for a five-year period ending in 1992, a total of 872 interstate migrants *per week* came to Queensland. Most settled in the south-east part of the state, from Coolangatta in the south to Noosa in the north, and west to Ipswich.
10. In 1981 Ahern's DPI budget was $169 739 087 (*QPD* vol. 286, p. 3562). In 1985 the budget for Industry, Small Business and Technology was only $53 294 700 (*QPD* vol. 300, p. 1849).

11. Before he became a journalist, Charlton had been employed by the Department of Industry as its first economics graduate.
12. Kennedy had advised the Whitlam Government on the splitting of the Postmaster-General's Department into two statutory authorities, Australia Post and Telecom (later Telstra). He would later advise the Ahern Government, in the person of Russell Cooper, on the establishment of the Corrective Services Commission.

CHAPTER 5

The premiership

By November 1987 Mike Ahern had been in Cabinet for seven years, successively as Minister for Primary Industries, Industry, Small Business and Technology and, since 1 December 1986, as Minister for Health and Environment. He had not put aside his leadership ambitions but had sought to prove his credentials by being a hardworking Minister and not overtly destabilising the leadership. However, by 1987 a crisis was looming for the National Party, despite its seemingly being at the peak of success.

The party had won the 1983 election in its own right, thanks to the defection from the Liberal Party of Brian Austin and Don Lane. After a redistribution in 1985, which took Queensland further from the "one vote, one value" ideal than at any time since 1949 and enlarged Parliament to eighty-nine seats, the Nationals convincingly won the 1986 election with forty-nine seats. Politically, both the Nationals and the Premier were now at their zenith.

In retrospect, however, it can be seen that these electoral successes sowed the seeds of political destruction. Bjelke-Petersen became convinced that he alone was responsible for the successes; and the party organisation had contributed to this hubris by making him the focal point in both campaigns.[1] A varied group of informal advisers flocked to him, led by the so-called "white shoe brigade" of property developers, who urged their own agendas on him by flattering him and sycophantically supporting him. Consequentially Sparkes and the organisational influences were downgraded and marginalised.

That this new court was politically naive and the Premier the victim of his own vaingloriousness was no better illustrated than the "Joh for Canberra"/"Joh for PM" campaign of 1987. Since 1983 Australia had been governed by the Labor Party, with Bob Hawke as a highly successful and very popular Prime Minister. He had called, and won, an early election in 1984, so the next federal election was due in 1987. After Bjelke-Petersen's state electoral triumph in 1986, his so-called advisers urged him to set his sights on Canberra and lead the Coalition to victory, thereby extending his sway to the nation.

In retrospect this proposition appears laughable in its naive stupidity, but so removed from reality had Bjelke-Petersen become that he enthusiastically embraced it and carried both Cabinet and the Parliamentary National Party along with him. Privately Sparkes was aghast, but he had no choice but to endorse the plan and do his best to implement it. The federal National MPs from Queensland withdrew from the Coalition, thereby all but terminating it, to the fury of the then National Party leader, Ian Sinclair, and the Queensland Nationals preselected former Treasury Secretary John Stone to head the Senate ticket. Hawke, sensing disarray in the Opposition ranks, called the election six months early, while Bjelke-Petersen was out of the country and before he had nominated for a federal seat. The result was a rout of the Opposition, with the Nationals losing two seats in Queensland and two in northern New South Wales.[2]

This result sent a shock wave through Queensland political circles. For the first time since 1968 when he became Premier, Bjelke-Petersen had gambled and lost. The party was not electorally invincible after all. However Bjelke-Petersen, rather than reflecting on the political and personal meaning of these results, turned on Sparkes and accused him of taking over the campaign with a view to sabotage. Sparkes's reply was the epitome of disdain. The damage to their relationship was now irreparable and the danger was that this would be followed by a breakdown between the organisation and the Parliamentary National Party.

During his nineteen years as Premier, Bjelke-Petersen had substantially consolidated his power. Thus to stay within his orbit Ministers, party and organisational leaders, together with other allies, effectively faced two choices. One option was to work loyally at their portfolios or within their operational spheres, to keep their distance, and accept whatever the Premier decreed should come their way. The other was to seek to ingratiate themselves with their leader on a regular basis to reinforce his position as a means of advancing their own. Some senior Ministers and longstanding National parliamentarians (such as Ahern) adopted the former stance, but between 1983 and 1987 it became increasingly evident (as Police Commissioner Terry Lewis's diaries revealed) that businesspeople, politicians, judges, senior public servants and high-ranking police officers judged it expedient to gravitate towards Bjelke-Petersen's circle, thereby predicating their continuing political and personal fortunes upon his maintenance of power.

Such developments promoted a schizophrenic governmental style. Routine matters of public administration continued to be handled according to statutes, regulations, established procedures and precedent. By contrast, while the business of Government was generally non-controversial in its routine and administrative tasks, its decision-making apparatus was increasingly influenced by the informal "courtiers" who turned its operations to their own ends. Several examples have been cited above; but it fell to the Fitzgerald Inquiry and subsequent report to document the pervasiveness of this trend, especially in the corruption of Government tendering processes. In Queensland, where Government has always been the largest project builder, infrastructure provider and economic regulator, the final Bjelke-Petersen years were replete with examples of economic decision-making that had long since departed from best practice.

The third and final factor in the shift of forces within the Parliamentary National Party was the issue of corruption. In retrospect, it is evident that the Government was following past practices when it suddenly responded to spectacular allegations of police corruption by announcing a limited inquiry. Since the mid-1960s there had been three previous investigations touching on similar allegations. These, however, were characterised either by impossibly restrictive terms of reference (National Hotel) or by their reports being both suppressed and ignored (Sturgess and Lucas). Initially the Fitzgerald Inquiry also had narrow terms of reference, and was generally expected to sit for six weeks. It is surely relevant that Bjelke-Petersen was absent from Queensland at the time of the inquiry's establishment, but a population grown wearied and cynical by the prevailing political climate was initially unprepared for anything other than a rehearsal of the three previous exercises, best characterised by the sobriquet of "whitewash". The Fitzgerald Report, as a scathing and comprehensive indictment of the excesses of the later Bjelke-Petersen period, has now passed into the folklore of Queensland politics. The proposed remedies, accomplished via Electoral and Administrative Review Committee (EARC) and the Criminal Justice Commission (CJC), were institutionalised and came to dominate the state's political agenda in the 1990s.

These factors were integral to the complex background that surrounded the bid Ahern now made for the leadership. He had to convince his parliamentary colleagues and the National organisation (particularly Sparkes) that a leadership change was now a pressing necessity and that he was the best, indeed the only credible, candidate. Support, albeit with reservations, came from both quarters. In the former case during the latter part of the 1987, Bjelke-Petersen's erratic actions served to convince the waverers, with varying degrees of enthusiasm, that the Premier had to go. The Parliamentary National Party was finally persuaded to force the issue for reasons of political survival. They now knew that they needed both to counter the backlash among conservative voters, (evident in the 1987 federal election results), and to address growing public alarm regarding the damaging revelations now unfolding before the Fitzgerald Inquiry. The longer the inquiry ran, the more relentless was the flow of evidence, from the inquiry's epicentre of corrupt police, prostitutes and illegal gaming operators to the upper echelons of the law enforcement establishment and to the Government itself.

Effectively Ahern was now their only choice. Gunn had certainly served as deputy leader for five years, four of these as Deputy Premier; but, despite any kudos that accrued to him for establishing the Fitzgerald Inquiry, his age and media portrayal (deserved or otherwise) as a "Joh clone" made him neither electorally attractive nor politically viable. Unswerving Bjelke-Petersen supporters such as Lin Powell and Yvonne Chapman (Pine Rivers), while detesting Ahern, were not alternative candidates, nor did they possess the numbers to stop Ahern, even presuming that they had an alternative available. In the event they too were forced to bow to the inevitable.

For Sparkes the situation was more problematic. While his early relations with Ahern had been far from close, additional factors had now come into play. Sparkes was not one to bear long-term or unreasonable grudges. His was the world of "realpolitik". He subordinated all other considerations to his perception of the National Party's future and long-term advancement. Hence he had no hesitation in dealing and working with Bjelke-Petersen while the latter was an electoral and political asset. When this asset became a liability, however, Sparkes cast around for alternatives, with (to put it no more strongly) Ahern necessarily being high on his list.

It is not particularly difficult to see Sparkes's actions as those of a consummate political realist, the pragmatist working towards a well-defined goal while utilising all available means to gain it. It may well be, as Lane has asserted (interview 2 April 1993) that, had he been free to choose, Sparkes would have preferred Austin. However, in November 1987, this luxury of choice was denied him. Indeed it stretches credulity that he would have seriously contemplated it. Austin's lack of rural provenance, his method of entry into the National Party, his "hard-ball" political style and "head-kicking" reputation as a Minister (especially in Health) would surely have excluded him as the preferred candidate to operate in such a fraught political and social atmosphere. Moreover, Austin was also a political realist who, along with Ahern, had also incurred Bjelke-Petersen's wrath in the twilight months of his latter's premiership. Given the manner in which the leadership crisis unfolded, with Austin and Ahern now linked, Austin, by his own testimony (interview 7 July 1993), had little trouble in gravitating to Ahern. In the latter months of 1987, however, it was not a foregone conclusion that Bjelke-Petersen would stand down nor, obviously, that Ahern would be his successor.

Coaldrake (1989, p. 15) notes two additional difficulties for Bjelke-Petersen in August and September 1987. The first concerned opinion polls results, which showed both a drop in support for the Premier and scepticism as to his continuing political abilities. The second was

Sparkes's decision, at the National Party's annual conference in Townsville scheduled for early November, to nominate for another term as president.

The month before the party conference, the Nationals' State Council met in Rockhampton where Bjelke-Petersen suffered a tactical defeat. At Sparkes's urging, the Council resolved that "Ministers be required to step down from their portfolios a reasonable time before their retirement" (Coaldrake 1989, p. 16). The Premier's hostility derived from two suspicions; that the organisation was trying to assert control over the Parliamentary National Party, and that he was the one being targeted by the resolution.

Bjelke-Petersen's rebuff in Rockhampton precipitated a tactical manoeuvre. Immediately after the State Council (8 October) he announced that he would resign the premiership on 8 August 1988, the twentieth anniversary of his accession to the leadership. Publicly the party supported this decision, noting that this would enable him, as Premier, to receive Queen Elizabeth II when she opened Expo 88. However, in reality, the announcement gave him a free hand, for ten months, to reorganise the party. Ahern subsequently laid the serious allegation that, had Bjelke-Petersen remained Premier, he would have terminated the Fitzgerald Inquiry — a distinct possibility when the revelations began to engulf him and those around him. Also, he could easily have purged his critics from Cabinet (which he set out to do after the Townsville conference) and blunted Sparkes's renewed bid for intra-party power by calling a snap election. This would have forced the party behind him, negated any leadership spill, occasioned a replay of 1983 and 1986, and reignited his triumphalism. The 8/8/88 option, then, was no option at all. It was a ploy to buy time to reinvent the political world as he wanted it to be.

Under Sparkes's domination, however, the Townsville conference marginalised Bjelke-Petersen. On policy issues, conference endorsed the introduction of condom vending machines; decided to go some distance in prostitution law reform; provided for sex education in school time; established a foreign land register and refused to give the Iwasaki Company "trusteeship of land proposed as national park near Iwasaki's holiday resort at Yeppoon" (Coaldrake 1989, p. 16). Bjelke-

Petersen had firmly opposed the four former policies and heavily supported the fifth. But, from the Premier's viewpoint, a worse reverse was the re-election of Sparkes with 80 per cent of the delegates' votes. No one was in any doubt about the profound animus between president and Premier, so this result was an unambiguous repudiation of the Premier by the organisation. By now Bjelke-Petersen was simply playing the spoiler. He had no viable candidate to run against Sparkes and could only rail from the sidelines as his party swept past him. The advice given to him by his deputy, Bill Gunn, after the conference said it all: that the Premier should "go fishing, have a rest and do a fair bit of thinking" (Coaldrake 1989, p. 16).

The next fortnight proved to be a time of hiatus in the quest for the leadership. Parliament had returned, and inevitably both Members and the media focused on day-to-day political matters. However, all sides were gathering their players for the next scene; it was not long in coming. Tenders had been called for vacant Queensland Rail land at Brisbane's Central Station. An Interdepartmental Committee (IDC) had recommended the Seymour Group's proposal, which had then gone before Cabinet. Without anyone's prior knowledge, Bjelke-Petersen suddenly introduced a proposal from John Minuzzo, a property developer Ahern described as "one of Bjelke-Petersen's White Shoe Brigade mates", who proposed to build "the world's tallest building" on the site (Ahern, interview 24 February 2000).

These plans, when revealed, created a storm of controversy. Town planning experts showed the shadowing effect the building would have on nearby King George Square, and pointed out that the equivalent of the population of the city of Warwick would be working in the building, with attendant stress on water, sewage, transport and other infrastructure. The Liberal-controlled Brisbane City Council, led by Lord Mayor Sallyanne Atkinson was placed under considerable pressure to reject this grandiose proposal. Bjelke-Petersen simply saw this as another occasion to leave his mark on Brisbane. At the last Parliamentary National Party meeting over which Bjelke-Petersen presided, Hinze recommended to his colleagues that they pass special enabling legislation which would override any BCC objections. Indeed, if the

Bill was passed immediately it would pre-empt BCC considerations entirely and the Council would be bypassed.

Opposition came from a hitherto unexpected quarter. Huan Fraser (Springwood) was an urban National, though a retired grazier who had been a Paroo Shire Councillor. On leaving the land, he had been elected Deputy Mayor of Logan City. As such, he claimed an attachment to local government while feeling no particular allegiance to Bjelke-Petersen, who had not supported his bid to enter Parliament. Fraser had seen three letters, two dated the previous February and a third in March that year (1987), which showed that the Government had committed itself to take twenty-one floors of the "world's tallest building" for public service office space and, further, that it would provide Minuzzo's company with $5 million to cover the outfitting of these floors. After Hinze's speech advocating the legislation, Fraser asked Bjelke-Petersen if these leasing arrangements were correct (Fraser, interview 24 January 2000).

Bjelke-Petersen tersely replied that Fraser did not know what he was talking about and moved to close the meeting. Fraser's response was that, if he did not obtain an answer, he would leave the meeting and "ask the question outside". All in the room knew that reporter Tony Koch (state roundsman for the *Courier-Mail*) was waiting outside the room. Gunn, playing conciliator, thereupon suggested that the meeting break for lunch, and asked Fraser to bring any evidence he had to the reconvened meeting. Fraser then told Gunn of the three letters, and urged him to use the adjournment to retrieve them. Whether Gunn actually obtained them and read them, or was simply made aware of their contents, is unclear, but he verified Fraser's story and told Fraser that all this "would soon blow over" (Fraser, interview 24 January 2000).

The reconvened meeting did not revisit the issue, the contents of the letters were not disclosed and Fraser's evidence was thus neither considered nor debated. According to several sources, meetings of the Parliamentary National Party under Bjelke-Petersen were tame, docile affairs, with few backbenchers daring to criticise or even question Ministers, let alone the Premier. In the interview cited above, Fraser confirmed that a number of his colleagues remonstrated with him for his "effrontery" in openly questioning the Premier.

Ahern, in his account (interview 24 January 2000), added that the promise to take up floor space in "the world's tallest building" was without reference to a committee under the chair of the Director-General of Works to consider the Government's accommodation requirements. In yet another example of autocratic decision-making, Bjelke-Petersen thought that existing legislation pertaining to the office and powers of the Coordinator-General would enable him to act, without the specific enabling legislation to which Hinze had referred. However, this course was not open to him unless he could obtain prior Cabinet approval, so he needed Cabinet colleagues who would not make trouble for him over the issue. This, Ahern suggested, was the reason Bjelke-Petersen then went to the Governor. If Ahern is correct, this explains why Bjelke-Petersen, without warning, commenced the process for the apparently unnecessary and hitherto inexplicable Cabinet reshuffle which was to bring him undone. Fraser observed, with some understatement, "I had just given Mike the ammunition" (Fraser, interview 24 January 2000).

On Monday 23 November Bjelke-Petersen visited the Governor, Sir Walter Campbell QC, with a letter in which he proposed to sack the entire Cabinet, before restructuring it and reducing the number of portfolios from eighteen to some unspecified number. It seems, from the evidence, that Campbell effectively rejected this advice, although he was too clever a jurist to do so forthrightly. After discussing the proposal he suggested the Premier depart, further consider the question, and then return. The following day Bjelke-Petersen made two trips to Government House for further consultations. On the former occasion he proposed to dismiss five Ministers; on the latter, three (Ahern, Austin and Peter McKechnie). The Governor assented to this final proposition, and three backbenchers were duly sworn in, thereby occasioning the remark in a subsequent parliamentary debate (from Keith De Lacy, ALP, Cairns) that this was the only time in recorded history where the rats swam *towards* the sinking ship.

By this action, Bjelke-Petersen had effectively signed his political death warrant. On Wednesday 25 November Sir Walter wrote to

Bjelke-Petersen summarising the events over the previous two days. In the meantime (though it is not clear exactly when) the Governor had been contacted by Gunn, Austin and Ahern, who had given him their views on the matter. Perhaps as a result of their representations, the Governor decided to treat the issue as a *political* rather than *constitutional* crisis, a point he made explicit in his letter to the Premier (Coaldrake 1989, pp. 20–21). Also that day the National Party's Management Committee met in Brisbane. Its purpose was to convene a meeting of the Parliamentary National Party for 10 o'clock the following morning (Thursday 26 November). It was invariably the party leader's prerogative to summon such meetings but, as Bjelke-Petersen now steadfastly refused to do this, Sparkes and his committee went over his head and called it anyway. At this point Ahern and Gunn announced the motion for a leadership spill and that each would be a candidate for the position.

On Thursday the meeting opened with Bjelke-Petersen the only absentee; having failed to persuade his Cabinet to boycott the meeting he now stood alone. Some residual support adhered to him when the spill motion was passed by thirty-nine votes to eight (one abstention). However, on these figures his support had shrunk to less than one-fifth (18 per cent) of the Parliamentary National Party. On the substantive motion as to who would succeed, Mike Ahern won with thirty votes (63 per cent); Gunn collected sixteen votes (33 per cent) and Hinze was humiliated with just two votes (4 per cent). To put all doubts as to propriety aside, after telephoning Sir Walter with the results Ahern caused two documents to be sent to Government House. The first contained two legal opinions from the Attorney-General/Minister for Justice and the Solicitor-General as to the legality, according to National Party constitution and rules, of the National Party Management Committee's convening the meeting of the Parliamentary National Party. The second was from Ahern himself, formally informing the Governor that, as he was now duly elected parliamentary leader, he thereby requested the Governor's commission to form a government. For good measure he appended a schedule, signed by all of the Parliamentary National Party members (except Bjelke-Petersen) both confirming and supporting this request.

Before swearing in Ahern and his Cabinet, and as a condition for so doing, the Governor required his new Premier to reconvene Parliament immediately and move a vote of confidence in his Government. Ahern readily gave that undertaking and was duly sworn in. On 2 December 1987, a day later, Parliament was recalled.

Ahern introduced the Motion of Confidence with a ritual denunciation of the Labor Opposition. He then devoted a mere three paragraphs to Bjelke-Petersen, before laying out four themes which he claimed would demarcate his administration from the previous regime. His primary concern was economic policy, where he pledged consultation with all stakeholders to ensure that "the centre-piece will be a State economic development strategy" (*QPD* vol. 307, p. 4805; see also chapter 7). Second, he articulated what he called his "vision of excellence", to be realised through:

> Quality decision-making ... efficient, cost effective Government ... consultation and co-operation between Government and all major sectors of the community and through rewards for performance. (*QPD* vol. 307, pp. 4805–6)

As if to underline his first two points and to demonstrate that he would remain his own man, he served notice on the National Party organisation, allowing only: "The wishes of my party ... will be given due consideration". He wanted to exercise control in the Cabinet room, not to be manipulated by party forces outside it. He sought this by emphasising that he did not owe primary allegiance to the party organisation. Sceptical observers, however, suspended judgment as to whether Sparkes would reassert his customary influence following the marginalisation he had lately received at Bjelke-Petersen's hands. Ahern, however, was conscious that his Government had to be seen to be free-standing, and not perceived to be under Sparkes's and the organisation's control.

Finally Ahern returned to an old theme, and one he had made his own during his extended spell on the backbench, namely a determination to restore dignity and standing to the Parliament. It was an elevated aim, and one not lightly set aside. While it did not necessarily strike a popular chord with the electorate, both contemporaries and colleagues were well aware that he had long championed this cause, despite few allies inside either his party or the Parliament. He continued to promote this ideal but, despite making worthwhile advances, his Government was denied the opportunity to accomplish wholesale parliamentary reform.

In his first parliamentary speech as Premier, Ahern had drawn together a number of important strands that characterised both his previous parliamentary and ministerial careers. His new order would be marked by technocratic managerialism, with efficiency and best practice guiding his Government's collective decision-making. He thereby gave notice that he would sweep aside the forces of cronyism, ad hocery, informal networking and populist localism. Parliamentary reform, a longstanding preoccupation, now received his imprimatur; and the partisan interference in Government decision-making that gave rise to ceaseless and ever-increasing allegations before the Fitzgerald Inquiry would be tolerated no longer. In short, the message was that his Government would not be run from National Party headquarters (Bjelke-Petersen House) in inner Brisbane's St Paul's Terrace, now sarcastically dubbed "The Bunker" by the media.

It was a short debate, involving only three other Nationals, two Liberals and two Labor Members. Gunn, now Ahern's deputy, in supporting the Premier devoted merely a few moments to Bjelke-Petersen, explaining, "The events of the past week were based as much on poor advice to the former Premier as anything else" (*QPD* vol. 307, p. 4807). The source of such "poor advice" was apparently left to posterity's imagination as Gunn proceeded to distance himself from his immediate past loyalty. Perhaps he was, as yet, under-confident as to how history would judge him.

Ian Henderson (Mt Gravatt), one of the so-called "Joh dog squad" of urban backbench Nationals, contributed his usual spiteful diatribe against the Liberals, as doubtless befitted one who had recanted from previous membership of that party. In his view the Liberals were "the Pontius Pilates of this Parliament ... nothing but unmitigated unrepentant political opportunists of the most despicable kind" (*QPD* vol. 307, p. 4822).

Of greater importance, however, given Henderson's hitherto uncritical and unswerving devotion to Bjelke-Petersen's stance on moral issues, was his defence of Ahern against the National's right wing. He affirmed that Ahern's would be a "mainstream National Government", which would support the (nuclear) family unit, sex education (especially related to HIV-AIDS) and law and order. Doubtless it suited Ahern to be endorsed by such a rabid fundamentalist, if only to forestall internal opposition from that quarter. However, Henderson's ministerial ambitions were not realised until Ahern's premiership was over. The Member for Mt Gravatt's parliamentary career was terminated by his electors in 1989, but not before he had advocated reinstating the death penalty, when Russell Cooper's Minister for Justice.

The final National Party contribution came from Tony Fitzgerald (Lockyer) who, in a curiously eclectic speech, paid the briefest obeisance to Bjelke-Petersen before mounting a defence of the zonal system. In this he reflected Ahern's views, but he chose to quote Malcolm Mackerras, who held the eccentric opinion (repudiated by all other commentators) that Queensland electoral results were a product of single-member constituencies rather than of the zonal system of vote weightage. Such a false interpretation was given much contemporary publicity by Sparkes. Fitzgerald was a dedicated parliamentary reformer, and his speech could only be construed as his toeing the party line. His namesake's report would render his position, and that of his party, untenable. He closed his speech by managing to keep a straight face when declaring that the National Party organisation had exercised no intervention in the Bjelke-Petersen leadership spill.

The Opposition parties did not seriously contest the debate, thus contributing to its set-piece character. Nonetheless they moved expected amendments to the Motion of Confidence, thereby flagging their respective priorities and concerns. The ALP, in the person of its leader, Neville Warburton (Sandgate), moved six amendments, emphasising the perceived deficiencies in the previous Government's record and highlighting Ahern's apparent complicity, given his seven years in Cabinet. Labor's amendments included: the abolition of the zonal system in favour of "one vote, one value", together with a 10 per cent tolerance; an immediate declaration of intent for a Public Accounts Committee and a Public Works Committee; a review of the education budget; plans to reduce unemployment (then standing at 9.3 per cent) and a Pecuniary Interests Register for MPs, spouses and their dependent children.

Labor's amendments appeared to be twofold in design. They were intended to exert maximum pressure on Ahern's reformist agenda as well as test the completeness of his break with the Bjelke-Petersen era. As many of these propositions had been dismissed out of hand by Ahern's predecessor, Labor advanced them to test Ahern's resolve. This none-too-subtle tactic was underscored by Warburton who, addressing themes that would recur during Ahern's premiership, alleged that Ahern was an inevitable part of the discredited Bjelke-Petersen period because of his years spent as a Minister. Labor's leader charged that the real National powerbrokers were Hinze, Austin, Gunn and Sparkes. Ahern, averred Warburton, "shows himself as an amateur and a novice" (*QPD* vol. 307, p. 4811). It fell to Opposition deputy leader Tom Burns (Lytton), while seconding Labor's amendments, to warm to these themes in his own inimitable style.

As was characteristic during this period in Queensland politics, the Liberals demonstrated their penchant for political ambivalence. Before moving their own set of amendments, their leader, Sir William Knox (Nundah), vouchsafed that they would support the Government's Motion of Confidence. Instead of a broad attack on the Ahern Government and its proposed policies, the Liberals contented themselves with a series of specific demands. They moved for action on the lack of police manpower; legislation against sexual exploitation of children; introduction of a statutory bodies review commission; implementation of the Savage Report recommendations on the Queensland Public Service; a foreign land ownership register; repeal of recent Education Act amendments; and the cessation of indiscriminate ministerial (land) rezonings. How they imagined, given their support for the Motion of Confidence, that such proposals would receive any consideration is open to speculation. Perhaps they hoped that by allying themselves to the new Government they could exert some influence over it. As the Government did not need their support to sustain its majority, this move could only be construed as an exercise in wishful thinking.

The seconding of these amendments was left to Angus Innes (Sherwood), soon to replace Knox as Liberal leader. He spoke after Henderson, and the following exchange took place. When Innes rose, White interjected:

> Are you aware that the Member for Mt Gravatt went to see Stefan [a well-known Brisbane hairdresser] today and had a blow wave as well?
> Innes: I had better not say what instantly occurred to me. (*QPD* vol. 307, p. 4828)

Since, according to the Queensland Legislative Assembly's Standing Orders, Hansard records interjections only if the speaker on his/her feet chooses to take them, this rather vulgar exchange suggests that the Liberals were prepared to repay Henderson in his own debased political coinage.

Such asides notwithstanding, it was an indication of the Parliament's ritualistic procedures that none of the amendments was debated. They could therefore be seen as constituting their sponsoring parties' ambit claims or, more correctly, prefiguring their forthcoming election manifestos (in 1989). As it transpired, both opposition parties managed to support each other's amendments, first expressed when both voted against the debate being gagged (47:36). Both sets of amendments went down by the same margin, but the Motion of Confidence was duly passed (57:27) as the Liberals rallied to the Nationals' cause. Ahern's Government had now won the requisite parliamentary approval, in part because the Liberals chose to cloak their continuing desire for a return to Coalition with high-minded rhetoric emphasising the need for (any) stable government. Gone was the White–Murphy ploy of negotiating for a minority Liberal Government supported by Labor from the crossbenches. Indeed, given the paucity of Liberal representation and the parliamentary ascendancy of the Nationals, such considerations were firmly relegated to the past.

Ahern's last action during this transitional period was to dissolve Parliament for the Christmas–New Year recess. During this political hiatus, the new National Party Government would attempt to put its administrative stamp upon Queensland. While parliamentary politics were now in abeyance, the coming of the 1988 parliamentary session would surely demonstrate the character of the new order.

Notes

1. In 1983 the slogan was "Now more than ever Queensland needs Joh and the Nationals". In 1986 it was "Joh Queensland". Thus had the person and the polity merged in true populist style.
2. While Liberal leader John Howard bitterly blamed Bjelke-Petersen for the loss, his own ineptitude during the campaign and the failure of the financial statistics for his health policy to add up were probably more important reasons for Hawke's third successive electoral victory.
3. Coaldrake, 1989, p. 15.

CHAPTER 6

The reform agenda

Ahern's premiership was to be a crowded one. Immediately upon taking office he declared, "My vision for Queensland is a vision of excellence. I realise there is an enormous expectation about my leadership" (*Courier-Mail*, 27 November 1987). And so it proved to be. The Nationals had experienced only three leaders in forty years although the second, Jack Pizzey had been leader for only a few months before his sudden death. Ahern was the youngest person ever to have led the Queensland Nationals and was widely expected to make a decisive break with his predecessor's policies and style. To follow such a dominant leader, and one long entrenched in office, could scarcely have been an easy task. Nevertheless, if his first press conference was any measure, Ahern seemed both enthused and energised by the prospect.

His administration was proactive on any number of fronts. It was concerned with machinery-of-government matters; it undertook several major policy initiatives, some left over from the Bjelke-Petersen era; it planned major economic projects; it began to grapple with the revelations before the Fitzgerald Inquiry and their consequences as defined by the Report; it brokered relations with both the Opposition and the National Party organisation; it addressed parliamentary reform and, perforce, conducted relations with the federal (ALP) Government.

From the outset Ahern was determined that his Government would be remembered as one of reform. He had spent his political life thus far planning to recast a National (or Coalition) Government, and assuming the leadership finally allowed him to implement his ideas. An opinion poll published ten days after he became leader showed that he enjoyed a high level of public support as Premier although, as an early warning, his popularity among National voters was soft. Many National Party rank-and-file supporters found it very difficult to adjust to Bjelke-Petersen's departure, let alone its attendant circumstances.

Public service reform

Before his first Cabinet meeting Ahern held discussions with Sir Ernest Savage who, five months earlier, had authored a report urging sweeping changes to the public service. Savage had recommended that the Premier's Department and the Coordinator-General's Office, which Bjelke-Petersen had merged, be re-established as separate departments further, he recommended that Cabinet establish a budget review committee, that an in-depth review of public service superannuation be conducted, and that the Government establish an economic strategy unit.

After this first Cabinet meeting the Premier gave the Government's response to these issues. It would set up an Economic Planning Committee; this would be chaired by his friend, Brisbane steel manufacturer Ross Palmer, with whom he had interacted as Minister for Industry, Small Business and Technology. In modification of Savage's recommendations, however, the title of Coordinator-General would be abolished and the last incumbent, Sir Sydney Schubert, designated Director-General of the Premier's Department. This department which would be divided into four: State Affairs, Economic Development Strategy, Special Projects and Arts. (This last division reflected Ahern's additional portfolio as Minister for the Arts.)

In other, though related, decisions Sir Leo Hielscher was retained as Under-Treasurer, reporting directly to Ahern in the latter's capacity as Treasurer, rather than to Austin as Finance Minister. Cabinet established a budget committee comprising Ahern (chair), Austin, Gunn and Vince Lester. As an earnest of Ahern's immediate priorities, this committee's first brief was to plan an economic development strategy, while also addressing social welfare and government infrastructure.

The adoption of major Savage Report recommendations, as well as Ahern's commitment to public service reform and modernisation, was soon demonstrated. In April 1988 the Public Service Management and Employment Bill was brought before the House. Austin, who had carriage of it, claimed that it gave public servants, particularly chief executive officers (CEOs), greater autonomy and responsibility for the administration of their departments. Additionally, he claimed that it would enhance the accountability of the public service, thereby creating a more flexible and responsive public sector with greater emphasis on performance management.

In summary, the legislation spelt out several initiatives. Merit would be the sole criterion for appointment to the service and promotion within it. All CEO and senior management positions would be by contractual appointment. Regular performance appraisals would be conducted, stressing achievement-oriented criteria. CEOs would determine staff salary levels within budget guidelines. The interchange of personnel between the state and federal public services, as well as between the state's public and private sectors would be encouraged. CEOs would have greater disciplinary powers, but a new appeals system would also be introduced. Redundancy packages were to be deployed only as a last resort.

The Government then proposed a devolutionary model: CEOs, with stronger and more direct hiring and promotional powers, would themselves be subject to five-year contracts. This last innovation opened up CEO and Senior Executive Service (SES) positions to outside appointment; in practice, however, and at least initially, most of these positions were filled internally. The Ahern Government thus began the process of repositioning the public service. This both brought Queensland into line with other jurisdictions and laid the foundations for the Goss Labor Government's more thorough, and not altogether popular, public service restructuring through its Public Service Management Commission (PSMC).

Labor, during the second-reading debate, declared its opposition to the contractual provisions. They were philosophically opposed to this development, and both they and the Liberals charged that such alterations at senior levels would encourage cronyism and nepotism. Given the widespread politicisation of the public service under Bjelke-Petersen (Coaldrake 1989, pp. 71–81), these objections were neither frivolous nor idle. Austin, in reply (*QPD* vol. 308, pp. 6299–301), chose not to refute these objections, stressing instead the popularity of the contract system with those so involved. He also highlighted the Government's commitment to extensive and ongoing consultation with the public sector unions during the implementation of these changes. Although Labor and the Liberals combined to divide the House on the second reading, the Bill was duly passed by forty-two votes to thirty-seven.

Another initiative in the area of public-sector administrative reform concerned Treasury. Austin introduced the Queensland Treasury Corporation Bill during the first Parliamentary Session of 1988. In part, this Bill represented Queensland's rather belated response to the federal deregulation of financial markets by replacing the Queensland Government Development Authority with the Queensland Treasury Corporation (QTC). The QTC's powers included extensive authority to borrow in Australia and overseas. It would also possess full lending powers, would act as the central borrowing authority for Queensland statutory authorities, and would have authority to invest on behalf of the Treasurer, state statutory authorities "and other persons". While the Government retained statutory power to limit QTC activities, in practice this Government envisaged a more distant approach to routine fiscal activity. The QTC's authority was underwritten because all its operations were guaranteed by the Treasurer, who in this case was the Premier.

Labor supported these financial arrangements and the resultant regulatory powers because it had proposed similar reforms at the 1983 and 1986 elections. The Liberals, however, were opposed. They charged that the QTC would impinge on, and usurp, the role of private enterprise. The Government and Labor then combined (68:9) to give the Bill its Second Reading. In committee, Keith De Lacy (Cairns), who later became the Goss Government's Treasurer, asked if QTC accounts would be open to scrutiny by the proposed Public Accounts Committee (PAC). Ahern replied, "absolutely". The Premier later explained that he would have preferred to establish the PAC before the QTC, but his Government had lacked time to bring on the PAC legislation. Paradoxically, timing considerations now necessitated establishing the QTC. At all events, he assured the house that PAC involvement with QTC operations would be covered by retrospectivity provisions in the proposed legislation to establish a PAC.

Penal reform

The final significant area of administrative reform concerned Corrective Services. The Ahern Government was determined to address the deplorable state of Queensland prisons, governed by a regime that had remained largely unchanged since the 1880s. In February 1988 it had appointed a review committee chaired by prominent businessperson Jim Kennedy. After a thorough examination, his report was handed to Russell Cooper (Roma), whom Ahern had appointed Minister for Corrective and Administrative Services.

Eight months later a trio of Bills was introduced to give effect to the Kennedy Report. The centrepiece was the Corrective Services (Administration) Bill, with consequential amending legislation contained in the Corrective Services Bill and the Corrective Services (Consequential Amendments) Bill. This last measure, a "tidying-up" Bill, revised relevant penal matters contained in the Criminal Code, Mental Health Services Act, Justices Act, Drugs Misuse Act and Public Trustee Act. The third Bill passed through all stages in four minutes on 16 November 1988.

Several important features arose when the two substantive Bills were debated. First, by his conduct in the House, the Minister appeared committed to the Kennedy reform agenda. This was Cooper's legislative debut, and he seemed determined to leave his imprint on this long-neglected policy area. It is relevant to recall that, before these Bills were introduced, there had been a number of highly publicised escapes from the Boggo Road gaol, as well as rioting and a high level of unrest among inmates in most of the state's gaols. These events had led to widespread community concern. Conscious of this background, Cooper spoke extensively in his second-reading speeches on both substantive Bills. Similarly his replies, both at the conclusion of the second-reading debates and in their respective-committee stages, were comprehensive, informative, explanatory and generous to all participants.

The second significant feature of the debates was the generous support that both opposition parties afforded to this legislative package. Kennedy's open hearings had ensured extensive input from directly affected stakeholders and other interested parties in the community and the welfare sector. Because consultation had also been a feature of the three Bills' drafting stages, there was broad acknowledgment that reform was long overdue. Such a sea change in attitudes was also evident in the fact that no Member who participated in these debates sought to exploit the law-and-order issue. For once, the "hang them, flog them" brigade was notable by its absence. To the credit of all participants, Parliament was able to grapple with sensitive legislative reform without being tempted into emotional grandstanding in a charged political atmosphere.

Both major Bills were comprehensive in scope and detailed in their drafting. Their major thrust dealt with the corporatisation of both the gaols and the corrective services procedures. Corporatisation was to be achieved by a Corrective Services Commission (CSC), comprising a nine-person board, which would oversee the administration of corrective procedures. The CSC board would include a lawyer, a member of the clergy or representative of a welfare agency, and an Aboriginal or Torres Strait Islander representative. All prisons would be under the control of a general manager, under whom would be specialist managers responsible for security, supervision, welfare, correctional programs, administration and finance. There would be two Visitors per prison to liaise with inmates, management and the CSC. The preferred emphasis for those incarcerated would be upon rehabilitation and community service.

The existing Parole Board would be replaced by a number of Community Corrections Boards (CCBs), located where prisons were situated. The CCBs would adjudicate upon the transfer of sentences from prison to Community Correction Centres. They would, in addition, decide parole applications from those serving sentences of more than five years and, in a welcome innovation, would be obliged to give specific reasons for rejecting such applications. Inmates could, if they chose, nominate a lay advocate to prepare their applications and, should these be rejected on three separate occasions, were empowered to lodge appeals. It was hoped that the establishment of Community Correction Centres would facilitate the participation of community and welfare groups in rehabilitation programs.

These reforms had several purposes. They addressed the overall corrective-services structure, via corporatisation, while being concerned both with the daily management of such institutions and the new regime to be introduced into the state's gaols — now to be designated Corrective Services Institutions.

The only contentious matter raised in this legislation concerned privatisation. This was not a hypothetical consideration as the Ahern Government planned to construct a new, privately administered prison at Borallon, between Ipswich and Esk. There was considerable local opposition however. Both Labor and the Liberals, perhaps to capitalise on these objections, declared themselves opposed to privatisation. Nevertheless, when Labor came to power it not only left Borallon in private hands, but also privatised the remand section of the new Wacol prison. The only division over the Bills was the move to delete the privatisation clause, defeated by forty-three votes to twenty-nine.

When the new structure was in place, Kennedy selected Keith Hamburger as its CEO. In effect Hamburger became the operational manager of the CSC. Kennedy warned Cooper to stay clear of managerial issues and let Hamburger do the publicity for CSC operations. Penal policy will always remain contentious, but Ahern and Cooper had successfully begun a long-term reformist process, albeit one that had to be fought anew at every subsequent step.

Social reform

Politically the Ahern Government's second year began on 19 January 1989 with a Cabinet reshuffle, when Leisha Harvey was sacked as Health Minister.[1] Craig Sherrin (Mansfield) was brought into the Ministry and given the Education, Youth and Sport portfolio. In this capacity, on 15 March, he introduced the Government's major domestic-welfare reform initiative, the Domestic Violence (Family Protection) Bill, Queensland's first legislative attempt to address the issue of domestic violence.

Sherrin, in his second-reading speech, discussed both the Bill's provenance and its major features. The origins lay in the report from the Domestic Violence Task Force (DVTF), *Beyond These Walls* (The DVTF had been established by Queensland's first female Minister, Yvonne Chapman, sacked by Ahern.) Submissions concerning the draft legislation had been received from the Law Society, the Bar Association and the Family Law Practitioners' Association. Its major feature was the Protection Order (PO), which could be issued against an abusive spouse, and the Bill itself was designed to give legislative effect to the Domestic Violence Awareness Program. Its implementation and enforcement would be overseen by the Domestic Violence Council (DVC), comprising representatives from relevant departments and community organisations.

Although applications for POs would be heard in Magistrates Courts they would not constitute criminal proceedings, hence no convictions would be recorded. The Bill envisaged that such applications would parallel civil proceedings, and would not be subject to the formal rules of evidence. POs would be granted to protect one spouse against violence, intimidation or indecent behaviour from the other. Violence would include wilful injury or damage to property, either actual or threatened.

The legislation defined domestic violence as that occurring between spouses, but provision was made to extend the definition to cover other family members. PO applications could be initiated by a spouse, by someone acting on that spouse's instructions, or by an investigating police officer. Penalties for breaching a PO were set at a maximum fine of $2400, or twelve months' gaol, or both. The PO would be enforceable for a maximum of 12 months but could be extended indefinitely on application. Provision was made for a spouse to be detained in the watchhouse for a four-hour "cooling-off" period. Interim POs could be ordered for up to thirty days, with the court being granted reviewing and monitoring powers. Finally POs could be reviewed, or varied, on appeal to the District Court.

The debate resumed on 11 April 1989 with seven speakers: two Labor, two Liberal and three National backbenchers. Although the House did not divide (as no one was opposed to the Bill), the speeches ranged across a number of concerns.

Labor speakers concentrated on the fact that domestic violence fell outside the criminal law, as a result of which the statistics kept were inadequate. They show a need for special police training in the area of domestic violence. The also advocated widening the provisions to cover family members other than just spouses, and to ensure enforcement in provincial and rural areas.

The Liberals raised economic issues as causal factors for domestic violence. They pressed for the monitoring of these laws to be brought under the supervision of a parliamentary committee, and expressed concern about giving the police extra discretionary powers, given current allegations against them at the Fitzgerald Inquiry. They also warned that these proposed reforms might conflict with the Commonwealth's Family Law Act.[2]

National backbenchers raised concerns about the negative impact of domestic violence on children. They questioned whether the legislation would keep families together, and expressed the hope that the Bill would prevent the cycle of domestic violence through appropriate intervention and appropriately empowering the police. Overall it was a wide-ranging debate free of partisan point-scoring.

In reply, Sherrin asserted that the Government had mounted a three-pronged attack on domestic violence. The Premier had, that day, launched a Domestic Violence Kit as part of a $200 000 domestic violence awareness program. Cooperation had been sought from the Commonwealth Government, and a Commonwealth Officer was attached to the DVTF. He undertook to refer this debate to the DVC (the third "prong") for comment. All police units, together with recruits at the Oxley Police Academy and all officers applying for promotion, would receive domestic violence training. Finally, the Government was confident that this legislation would act as a circuit breaker: police had reported that, in 85 per cent of cases, they returned to the same households, and this legislation would empower them to become proactive.

The Bill was given a second reading without division and reported out of committee without amendment. Given the complexities of domestic relationships, it is difficult to assess the Act's effectiveness. This reform measure was probably overdue, but the legislation could not have been initiated until the necessary research had been undertaken. There was some justification in the criticism that the police and the courts were to be used as the first line of attack, irrespective of the odium attaching to the police in the wake of the Fitzgerald Inquiry,[3] yet violence in relationships necessitated an interventionist strategy. This initiative represented the first attempt by any Queensland Government to address this problem, and it was deemed, by tripartisan consensus, to be a worthwhile start.

The drug issue

Legislation with the potential to effect important changes in the criminal law was introduced by the Attorney-General and Minister for Justice, Paul Clauson (Redlands), another of the Nationals' "young Turks". This was the Crime (Confiscation of Profits) Bill. Clauson delivered his second reading speech on 4 April 1989, and the debate resumed eight days later. All sides supported the Bill's general principles, but some of its specific provisions provoked enough disquiet to produce a stand-off in its committee stage involving Clauson, Innes and the ALP's Shadow Attorney-General and Justice Minister, Dean Wells (Murrumba).

In his 4 April speech Clauson referred to the precedent contained in the Drugs Misuse Act, which authorised forfeiture of property for those linked to drug trafficking and drug-related crime. To that date $1 million worth of property had been seized. However, a recent special premiers' conference on drugs had led the Standing Committee of Attorneys-General to produce model legislation: the Proceeds of Crime Bill, introduced in 1987. This federal initiative had been enacted in all states except Queensland which, while continuing to rely upon its Drugs Misuse Act, was evaluating the effectiveness of these new legislative initiatives in other jurisdictions. After this period of scrutiny, Queensland had now produced this Bill which in essence widened the provisions of the Drugs Misuse Act.

Clauson's Bill, by providing for a forfeiture order, covered the tracing, freezing and confiscation of proceeds from indictable offences. Such orders could also be made against convicted criminals on the initiative of their victims. Its provisions would apply upon conviction or, significantly, if an accused was acquitted on grounds of insanity or was deemed unfit to plead. The Supreme Court could order forfeiture to the Crown of an amount equal to any proceeds from publicity sold to media outlets concerning any crime. Such amounts could extend over a five-year period and be specifically directed toward victim restitution.

These provisions extended the orders to offences subject to joint Commonwealth–state law; for suspected "tainted" property, and for property that could be identified as deriving directly from criminal activity or that had been used to commit a crime. Clauson justified such extensive clauses by referring to the great profits flowing from the drug trade and the police's difficulty in identifying the source of money used to commit such crimes. He described this pecuniary penalty as a "super fine", and concluded by observing that such an order would prevent an accused from using such proceeds for living expenses, paying for his/her legal defence or repaying debts. The only limitation was that the order applied only to property deemed "tainted", and not to any other property owned by the accused.

Apart from a limited contribution from Fitzgerald, the only speakers were Wells, Innes and Clauson, who were among the most legally qualified persons then in the Chamber. In their second-reading speeches this trio largely prefigured the committee stage, where specific objections were canvassed.

Thus Wells emphasised the necessity for doing more to assist victims of crime. He noted that the Attorney-General, while empowered by the Criminal Code to make ex gratia payments to victims, was allowed to defer such payments indefinitely, and until the victim had exhausted all civil remedies. Wells wanted the Bill to address this anomaly. His major concern was the several instances where the Bill reversed the onus of proof. For instance, the court could assume that all property owned by the accused was "tainted", unless and until persuaded by contrary evidence. In certain circumstances, the police could search premises without warrant if they believed urgency was crucial. Finally, those acquitted by reason of mental defectiveness, or found unfit to plead, would be denied their civil liberties because they could still be covered by an order under the Bill.

Innes professed to share some of Labor's civil-libertarian concerns, but generally supported the Government. He was alarmed at the spread of organised crime, with its massive profits, and contented himself with the ludicrous claim that the Liberals would keep under surveillance both the use of the greatly enhanced search powers and the provisions reversing the onus of proof. He disagreed with Wells over the insanity provisions making the incredible claim that this amounted to a finding of guilty in all but name (*QPD* vol. 312, p. 4566). He concluded that, because of his hostility to "cheque-book journalism", he would support an order against making money by publicising crime in the media.

In a brief reply, anticipating that the debate would be joined in committee, Clauson agreed that more should be done for the victims of crime that, as property confiscation was a necessary prerequisite, it was appropriate that this Bill should precede any more general provisions for victim compensation. He further noted that a conflict arose among the interests of the victims, those of society in general and individual rights. By his account, this legislation did not aim to strike a further balance among such conflicts, but was deliberately restricted to confiscating the profits of (organised) crime.

The committee stage was taken six days later and, apart from White's occasional intervention, was once more confined to the three second-reading participants. The first dispute concerned clause 3, the issue of "tainted property". Innes thought this too wide, and urged that its scope be limited to serious offences carrying penalties of fourteen years or more; or to such other offences as the Minister would by regulation would have to bring before the Parliament for debate and approval.

Wells agreed, suggesting that, under clause 3, an accused could be deemed to have effective control over such property while not possessing legal, equitable or other interest. Clauson rejected Innes's argument, stating that, for example, theft by a servant, while carrying only a seven-year maximum penalty, was nevertheless deemed serious and often led to large "profits". The "tainted property" clause was deliberately drafted to cover conspiracy to commit an offence but, in repudiating Wells's claim, the Attorney-General was adamant that confiscation would follow only if there was a conviction. Although

Labor and the Liberals were in agreement, the house did not formally divide because Innes's amendment was lost on the voices.

Wells, following his second-reading objections, opposed the reversal of the onus of proof over "tainted property"; he parted company with Innes as the latter supported the clause, activated as it would be upon conviction. Clauson noted that this clause paralleled ones contained in the Commonwealth and West Australian Acts, whereby a property owner, duly convicted, was then required to prove that the property in question was not tainted. He also referred the House to more general safeguards for all property contained in the Commonwealth Cash Transaction Reports Act and the Australian Taxation Office tax file number system. Wells reiterated his position, identifying two issues at stake: whether the accused was guilty of a crime and whether such property as s/he possessed represented the proceeds of crime. In both cases the onus of proof should be on the Crown. Upon division the clause was passed by fifty-one votes to twenty-four, with the Liberals supporting the Government.

The third main area of contention was clause 30, covering search without warrant. Wells again opposed the clause, claiming the police possessed sufficient powers to cover this situation. White was disquieted by any increase in police powers, given their abuse in the recent past. Clauson again took refuge in similar federal and West Australian provisions, but promised to discuss these concerns with Police Minister Cooper. Apparently satisfied with this undertaking, the Liberals again joined the Government and the clause was approved by fifty-six votes to twenty-six.

The final dispute occurred over clause 59. Wells strongly objected to confiscation being ordered when findings were made as to insanity or unfitness to plead. He saw this as eroding the principle that prohibited punishment following acquittal. Innes again raised the matter of cheque-book journalism. He noted that the Supreme Court was to be given discretionary power; he considered this court had a good record when exercising such discretion, and so supported the Government. Clauson reiterated his intention to protect and recompense victims even if the accused was insane. He cited the case of New York serial killer "Son of Sam" who, though declared insane, had made a great deal of money selling his story. Clauson mentioned that support for this clause had been received from the Queensland Chapter of the Australian Journalists' Association. Debate on the clause then wound up with Innes and Wells attacking each other over the creation, in Wells's words, of "a subclass of not guilty people who will be treated as guilty" (*QPD* vol. 312, p. 4750). For the third time the Nationals and Liberals combined, and the clause was agreed to by fifty-five votes to twenty-six. The Bill was then reported out of committee with minor amendments (moved by Clauson) and given its third reading without division.

This Bill has been discussed in detail for two reasons. First, in any democratic society, the legislature must occasionally consider criminal matters that balance the exigencies of law enforcement against individual rights. When such rights are involved, it is necessary to address moral and philosophical concerns that affect the individual's standing before the law. Such boundaries are not immutable, and each occasion generates its own set of circumstances. The Crime (Confiscation of Property) Bill raised the extent to which the Government should sequester private property, both to impose a "super penalty" on convicted criminals and to provide victim compensation. The Government chose to widen the ambit, while the Labor Opposition sought to narrow it to the minimum extent consistent with the Bill's general principles — which the Opposition supported.

The Civil Liberties Council was correct to observe that this was a long Bill (50 pages) which involved some basic changes to the criminal justice system (*QPD* vol. 312, pp. 4732–33). As its passage took two weeks, one cannot charge that this was an example of rushed legislation; certainly no such claim was made in either the second-reading or committee stages. However, in any liberal democratic society, property confiscation will inevitably be a divisive issue. And further, while there were no political objections to such provisions applying to the drug trade, extending them to other criminal activities provoked active debate, which was no less spirited for its limitation to a small number of relevantly qualified Parliamentarians.

The second reason for giving detailed consideration to this Bill was that the dynamics of this debate were testimony to the balance of political forces at the time. The Nationals, under Bjelke-Petersen, had gloried in their reputation as proponents of law and order. This claim was seriously undermined, however, by the Fitzgerald Inquiry, which showed their law-and-order posture to be a sham, hopelessly compromised as it was by political and police corruption. By embarking on this legislation, the Ahern Government may have hoped, in part at least, to reclaim this ground. Its Bill relied on the twin precedents of the drug laws from other jurisdictions and the attorneys-general's model legislation. This was political terrain to be recontested, especially as the Bill was debated during the hiatus period between the conclusion of the Fitzgerald Inquiry and presentation of its Report.

Labor in Opposition could afford to be forthright in capitalising on the Government's embarrassment over the Fitzgerald Inquiry; Wells also possessed a strong civil-libertarian background. However, Labor was also playing the Opposition's traditional role, by assenting to the legislation's generalities while objecting to certain of its particularities. Here at work was the familiar Westminster system of adversarial politics. The Government proposed ambit legislation, while the Opposition chose the limits of its dissentient role and acted accordingly. Thus the ALP divided the House several times, choosing this tactic to reinforce its objections, reaffirm its credentials and delineate where, as the alternative Government, it diverged from the current administration.

While all this amounted to orthodox Westminster politics, it also illustrated the Liberals' dilemma. Third parties have no assigned role in a Westminster system and hence have difficulty defining their position. This debate demonstrated that there was in fact no viable third alternative. In the end the Liberals had to opt either for the stance of the Government or for that of the Opposition. As with all Ahern's legislation, this Bill would have passed irrespective of the position the Liberals chose to adopt, and Labor's points of objection would have been made with or without Liberal support. By playing both sides simultaneously, the Liberals lost to both. While they joined the Opposition in objecting to clause 7, they accepted defeat without forcing a division. By articulating their opposition to clauses 8, 30 and 59, yet voting with the Government, they risked the charge of hypocrisy. Such a judgment is too harsh, but it does illustrate the dilemma of crossbench occupation. The Liberals did not hold the balance of power, so their support amounted to no more than ballast for either side. Their essential irrelevancy on this legislative measure illustrated their wider political dilemma — one which was to persist beyond the change of Government in 1989.

The reform initiatives that comprised the Ahern Government's legislative agenda ran beyond social or economic policy. An important focus was parliamentary reform, but there were the other important issues to address first, the origins of which lay in the previous administration. These were the Electricity Authority Industrial Causes Act Amendment Bill and the South Bank Corporation Bill.

The electricity industry and the Electrical Trades Union

The first of these pieces of legislation was the Electricity Authority Industrial Causes Act Amendment Bill. This was, in effect, the final scene played out in relation to the 1985 SEQEB strike, itself one of the ugliest industrial confrontations of the Bjelke-Petersen era. His Government was determined to break the power in the electricity industry of the Electrical Trades Union (ETU), long a dominant player in the Labor Unity faction of the ALP. After escalating confrontation, the union ordered its members to strike, the Government declared a State of Emergency and sacked the workers. It then offered re-employment on its own contractual terms, which the ETU predictably rejected. Those workers who refused this offer were then denied their superannuation entitlements. The Government established its own alternative union, the Power Workers Union (PWU), to cover those who had accepted the Government's conditions and returned to work. The legislation that gave effect to the Government's actions had stayed on the Statute Books, a reminder of the extent to which that Government was prepared to go to create a pliant workforce in the electricity industry.

Although it is significant that an early action of the Ahern Government was to complete the passage of the amendment Bill, this initiative began before to Bjelke-Petersen's overthrow. On 12 November 1987 this Bill had been introduced Brian Austin. After his second-reading speech the legislation lay on the table until 8 March 1988 when Martin

Tenni (Barron River), Ahern's Minister for Mines and Energy, moved the debate's resumption.

In his speech Austin had noted that the original Act created a separate tribunal for electricity workers, and outlawed strikes or any similar industrial action designed to reduce electricity output. While the amendment Bill would repeal all emergency provisions, it would retain those measures that governed the dismissal of electricity workers, and the contractual provisions under which those who opted for re-engagement now operated. Superannuation entitlements owed to those dismissed would not be restored.

In this resumed debate only five Members, apart from the new Minister (who wound it up), spoke. Neither Opposition party opposed the amendment Bill, but all briefly took the opportunity to revisit the crisis, and their previous positions. For Labor, Bob Gibbs (Bundamba) attacked the continuation of the tribunal established to deal with the strike and its aftermath (especially as it was chaired by Labor's bête noir, Judge Eric Pratt). He denounced the PWU as a "scab" union, noted that the Government had "quietly" stopped its funding, and asked how much money the Government had spent on it. He condemned the prohibition on superannuation payouts and attacked contract labour provisions which, he claimed, disadvantaged workers.

According to Gibbs's colleague Anne Warner, the Ahern Government was embarrassed by this Bjelke-Petersen legacy. She claimed that this legislation would not restore democracy to the electricity industry. She further asserted that the original legislation was unenforceable and said that, as the High Court "had deemed that the legislation was incapable of implementation", it should be fully repealed (*QPD* vol. 307, p. 4944).

The Liberals fielded two contributors, their former leader Knox and current deputy Peter Beard (Mt Isa). The first reiterated his support for both the original Act and this amendment, stating that the Government had compounded its problem by not changing the award conditions when it established the tribunal. Those who turned the power down, or off, were not dismissed, no strike organisers were prosecuted and the sole "victims" were ancillary and/or outdoor workers, only 250 of whom had been sacked.[4] Beard supported Knox in general, but moved further by attacking the former Premier for his lack of understanding of Australia's working culture. He called for a sense of compassion and humanity (but not justice) to be shown to the strikers who had been defeated in the dispute. He was, after all in an invidious position, having won this quintessentially mining seat as a Liberal in 1986, and having to appear sympathetic to the MIM Holdings workforce to have any chance of retaining it.[5]

Fitzgerald was the sole Government backbencher to speak, asserting that the legislation now to be repealed had never been used. He euphemistically claimed that the dispute resulted from a new approach to the power industry. According to him, the imbroglio was traceable to two (unnamed) ETU officials who fomented the confrontation to arrest their declining power in their union. He supported the contract labour provisions because they gave the workers freedom of choice.

Tenni, in reply, justified the previous Government's actions of 1985, claiming that no one was sacked because the dismissed workers were twice offered their jobs back (on terms unacceptable to them or to the ETU). In a rhetorical ploy, he offered those dismissed the return of their superannuation entitlements if the ETU would compensate the community for lost money and damages incurred during the strike. In reply to Gibbs, he noted that the Government had paid its PWU $200 000.

This amending legislation laid an industrial ghost to rest, but the political landscape had altered. Passions had been aroused, at the time,[6] and while future labour historians will no doubt regard this as one of the more significant industrial crises in Queensland's recent past, no high drama attended the denouement. Rather, a sense of necessity pervaded the parliamentary proceedings, with neither side seriously attempting to reignite past hostilities. As if by tacit consent, Parliament took the necessary action to conclude the matter and put this aspect of the past behind it.

The establishment of South Bank

The South Bank Corporation Bill had profound and ongoing consequences for Brisbane and the provision of public recreational facilities. The Bill addressed a question of considerable contemporary interest, not to say public importance, as it provided for the redevelopment of the Expo 88 site on the south bank of the Brisbane River. The six-month Expo had been an enormous success, with fourteen million visitors attending (compared to the seven million originally predicted) attending. Expo was an exciting carnival-style event which had, by common consent, transformed Brisbane's self-image. However, to some general despondency, the Expo Authority had decreed that the site be dismantled immediately the exposition ended. Thus the area stood empty (except for the three Heritage-listed buildings it incorporated) while controversy swirled as to what redevelopment should occur. This Bill represented the Government's solution, although the comparative brevity of the parliamentary debate belied the importance attached to it by public opinion in Queensland (and especially Brisbane).

Neither the ALP nor the Liberals opposed the Bill or its provisions, designed as they were to facilitate the envisaged redevelopment. Instead, the debate concentrated upon the project's financial aspects and the need for a comprehensive and authoritative statement from the Government in the face of widespread rumour, claim and counterclaim as to what had been decided. The Premier was the sole Government speaker, with the ALP's contribution coming from Ken McElligott (Thuringowa), a former Deputy Mayor of Townsville. The Liberals put up Denver Beanland (Toowong), Brisbane's former Deputy Lord Mayor.

In his second-reading speech (incorporated in Hansard by leave) Ahern spelt out the details. The Bill would establish a statutory authority for the purposes of the State Bodies Financial Arrangements Act and the Financial Administration and Audit Act. As the body charged with the redevelopment of the Expo Park and South Bank–West End precinct, it would be overseen by a committee of five, two of whom would represent the Government and two the Brisbane City Council (BCC). It would have a minimum number of employees and would be empowered to use both private contractors and public-sector expertise. Its goal would be to cater for the widest possible public interest and not generate private profit. It would be wound up when the redevelopment was complete. Initially its operations would be exempt from the BCC Town Plan but, as redevelopment of each section of the site was completed, such areas would revert to coverage under the plan. Ahern further noted that the 4.6 hectares occupied by the original site would be augmented to a total of 9 hectares. The extra land would have to be acquired by agreement and ministerial approval; the South Bank Corporation (SBC) would not be given compulsory acquisition powers.

McElligott began by strongly criticising the lack of action during the previous six months. He alleged that unknown lenders had produced $182 million of debt during this period; at a 14 per cent interest rate this increased total indebtedness by $500 000 per week. The *Courier-Mail* (30 March 1989) had reported Expo's profit at $653 000 from outlays worth $480 million, but any such "profit" depended on the recovery of $18 million worth of debt.

McElligott went on to ask a series of questions. How much was needed to secure the land and infrastructure? How much was owed, and to whom? What were the conditions of repayment? Who would pay for what was unrecovered by the land sales from the development rights? Additionally he sought details as to which companies were awarded contracts for public relations and other similar concessions. After making a couple of fairly restrained attacks on the Government, he concluded that the Opposition wanted:

> ... a complete, unedited financial account of Expo from go to whoa — a statement that itemises debts as well as receipts and explains the smaller type of terms of interest payments. (*QPD* vol. 312, p. 5051)

The BCC was then controlled by the Liberals under their high-profile Lord Mayor Sallyanne Atkinson, and Beanland could not resist claiming credit for the Liberals in leading public opposition to initial redevelopment plans as proposed by the River City 2000 consortium led by National Party identity Frank Moore. Like McElligott, he approved the Bill's provisions, but echoed the financial concerns.

Beanland also asked that Expo's financial affairs be tabled, claiming that the Expo Authority had two major debts: $11 million as a result of royalties and merchandising and $17 million to the World Expo Park. As these debts had provoked disputes, Parliament should have the facts. As at 30 June 1987 the Auditor-General's report had shown the debt to be $182 million, increasing to $227 million twelve months later.[7]

Money had been borrowed, initially through the Queensland Government Development Authority and then through the Queensland Treasury Corporation. He claimed that no indication had been given as to what the transfer amount would be, or how much the Corporation would pay the Authority for land transfer.

In reply, Ahern described Beanland's speech as "cretinous". In response to Beanland's claim (in committee) that the Government had wanted to sell Expo's river frontage but had been prevented from so doing, Ahern accused him of talking, "absolute nonsense" and of demonstrating "crass stupidity" (*QPD* vol. 312, pp. 502–8).

More importantly, the Premier directly addressed the fiscal issues. Expo's (unaudited) debt was at that stage $224 million, while the overall financial position would be tabled when the Authority's term expired. The SBC would then take over valuable assets which would generate money to cover debts, especially as Government had received estimates that land values in the area would rise. SBC borrowing conditions were identical to those of other semi-government authorities, while its debts would accrue to the Crown, and hence would be pursued by the Crown. The Government's current advice was that debt-recovery prospects were satisfactory. Ahern then drew his speech to a close by observing that the Government would not permit South Bank to become a commercial site, because this would not be a fitting memorial to Expo. Thus his Government was prepared to carry any overall cost. He asserted that the six-month delay had not been wasted because the time had been used for extensive planning and consultation as to the future of South Bank. The SBC would now institute a further review before the legislation was implemented. In fact, the Government had to write off $150 million of Expo Authority debt to reduce its total indebtedness to a manageable level.

The popularity and continuing success of the South Bank Parklands, with its mixture of leisure, commercial and cultural precincts, suggests that those concerns were more than satisfactorily addressed by this Bill. In hindsight, six months of public discussion and disputation seem a small price to pay for the development of such a superb, and progressively enhanced, public facility.

Parliamentary reform

As Premier, Ahern had promised parliamentary reform at his first press conference. True to his intention, four major initiatives were now undertaken: the Parliamentary Services Bill, Public Accounts Committee Bill and Public Works Committee Bill, and the Register of Members' Interests.

The Queensland Parliament had long been criticised by commentators and observers, as well as some Members, for an inability to respond to its marginalisation at the hands of successive Governments. The establishment of a strong party system pre-dated the 1915 election of the Ryan Labor Government, and from then on had imposed a rigid template on the Parliament. This was exacerbated by successive long periods in power of ALP, Coalition and National Governments. These Governments had, over time, provided a series of autocratic premiers who dominated both their Governments and the Parliament. No Speaker had been genuinely independent because all were appointed by, and from, the ranks of the Government. It was little wonder that, lacking any semblance of a committee system, Parliament's status was reduced to that of a cipher. It met infrequently and then at the Government's behest; backbenchers had few opportunities, outside the set-piece Address in Reply, Budget and (limited) Estimates debates, to raise issues of importance. Question Time stood unreformed, dominated by Dorothy Dix questions from Government backbenchers and often long-winded, time-wasting ministerial replies. The Opposition parties were deliberately starved of resources, which achieved its purpose of limiting their ability to respond to Government initiatives.

One widely acknowledged source of many problems was that Parliament's budget was determined by the Premier's Department (including funding for the Opposition Office). This meant that Parliament's resources were directly controlled by the Executive, and Parliament was denied any effective input into its own financial or institutional arrangements. Members would, on occasion, complain about this situation, but no sustained reform campaign was ever mounted. Government Members were unwilling to advocate any measure of parliamentary autonomy, as this would put them at odds with the Executive; during Bjelke-Petersen's long tenure as Premier (as Ahern's case demonstrated), this would immediately frustrate any ministerial ambitions that such a person might have. Alternatively, any publicising of these matters by the ALP invited the riposte that they had initiated this situation when in government, and therefore deserved the conditions to which they now objected. A cynic might have noted that the Liberals became converts to parliamentary reform once they lost office, although in 1983 a minority of them brought down the Coalition (in practice if not by intent) when attempting to provoke debate over the establishment of a Public Accounts Committee.

For proponents of parliamentary reform the unpalatable reality was that, while this was properly the business of the Parliament and could not be imposed upon it by external forces, reformist measures would occur only on the initiative of the Executive, or at least with its active support. There was not the faintest chance that this would be seriously contemplated by Ahern's predecessor. There is no greater measure of the decisive break between these two Governments than the question of parliamentary reform.

The first initiative was the Parliamentary Services Bill, which Austin introduced on 7 September 1988, ten months into the Government's term. Its object was to create the Parliamentary Service Commission (PSC), consisting of a seven-person committee representing all parties in the Legislative Assembly and chaired by the Speaker. The only Ministerial representative would be the Leader of the House, who would table the PSC's estimates. The Clerk of the Parliament would be its CEO. This would preserve the PSC's independence from the Executive, as the Clerk would be given responsibility for both managing the Parliament and framing its budget. Austin then outlined four tasks for the PSC:

- to determine policy and guide service delivery
- to prepare operating budgets
- to decide the size and organisation of the parliamentary staff
- to set their terms and conditions of employment (including salary levels).

PSC employees would be independent of both public service legislation and Government control, but anyone currently employed could choose to remain under public service conditions.

Austin concluded his second-reading speech by linking this Bill with the proposed Public Accounts Committee (PAC) Bill (introduced one month later), asserting that both would make Parliament substantially independent of Government (*QPD* vol. 309, p. 655).

Labor, in response, put up five speakers, the Liberals four, and the Government a further two. This was not controversial legislation in the sense that it excited opposition from non-Government quarters, but it went to the heart of the Parliament's operations and its future. Because the Parliament is the only constitutionally sanctioned forum for Opposition political activity, those on the Speaker's left took a close interest in this legislation, using the debate to air a variety of past grievances while expressing their hopes as to future improvements.

Keith De Lacy (Shadow Treasurer) noted that Federal Parliament had introduced similar legislation, on the initiative of the Speaker and Senate President. He observed that in the United Kingdom the Speaker determined the House of Commons Estimates and brought them before the Parliament. While this would be done in Queensland by the Leader of the House, he considered that it nonetheless bestowed financial independence on the Legislative Assembly, and such financial autonomy was a necessary condition for Parliament's independence. He drew attention to similar legislation in Victoria (1975), South Australia (1985) and New Zealand (1985), considering that the final example would best serve as the appropriate model for Queensland.

Terry Mackenroth (Chatsworth), who subsequently became Leader of the House in both the Goss Government and the first Beattie Government, charged that previous Speakers were "too gutless" to stand up to Bjelke-Petersen (*QPD* vol. 309, p. 1255). He complained about the so-called over-staffing of Parliament, especially security staff. He wanted parliamentary staff to be unionised so that their union could then negotiate with the PSC. He concluded by requesting increased research facilities for Members, including enhanced electronic equipment.

Ed Casey (Mackay), a former Opposition Leader, felt that the Parliamentary Draftsman's office was understaffed. He suggested greater interchange with Members from other jurisdictions and blamed Bjelke-Petersen for "poisoning" relations among Members.[8]

The final Labor contributor was Les Scott (Cook) who, evenhandedly, praised both Speaker Powell and Premier Ahern for the Bill but then criticised the lack of adequate planning for the Parliamentary Annexe. As a backbencher serving a large and remote rural electorate, he wanted better facilities and increased travel entitlements. Thus were parliamentary concerns conjoined with the needs of particular electorates.

Supportive speeches also came from the two Government backbenchers, Sherrin and Fitzgerald. Sherrin (not yet elevated to Cabinet) believed that the power of Parliament had declined owing to strong party discipline, administrative complexity and ineffective parliamentary practices. Fitzgerald limited his speech to a reiteration of some of Austin's points, while claiming that Parliament was its own master because it decided its standing orders through the Standing Orders Committee. This claim was specious, as this committee did not meet between 1950 and 1980 (Coaldrake 1989, p. 59). Further, if Parliament was indeed the master of its own destiny, there should have been no need to enact this legislation — which he supported.

The Liberals, with their nine Members (four of whom spoke), had the greatest investment in parliamentary reform. They were the most marginalised of the parliamentary parties, possessing few non-parliamentary forums, or resources, to make any political impact. Innes was therefore anxious to have Liberal representation on the PSC confirmed. He also observed that, as half the Government Members were either Ministers or had specific political duties, they could control the Parliament by constant caucusing. He praised the standard of parliamentary renovations (undertaken between 1979 and 1982) and suggested that the PSC would need to be sensitive to its employees' needs.

Lickiss commented on the role of the Clerk, and Knox expressed the hope that the PSC would provide the best of resources to assist Members to serve their electors. While attacking both Government and Opposition for "collusion" in the allocation of questions at Question Time, he praised the quality of staff in the Table Office and urged that television film clips of parliamentary proceedings be made available to the media.

The most comprehensive contribution to the debate came from White who, together with Ahern and Hewitt, had long been active in the cause of parliamentary reform. He considered that Parliament was now more effectively managed, and attributed this to the efforts of the two most recent Speakers, Kevin Lingard (Fassifern) and Lin Powell. He urged Members to put aside their ideological and partisan differences in adopting a new unity of purpose towards Parliament. He then listed the important roles played by Parliament: enforcing accountability on Government by legislative debate and the questioning of Ministers', scrutinising administration, granting Supply, and forming Government by supplying Ministers. He considered, with some justification, that the Parliamentary tasks worst performed in Queensland were holding rational debates and scrutinising public administration. He thought that the only way to rectify this situation was through Select and Standing Committees of the Parliament which could call public servants to account. Governments would have to learn to accept a certain level of criticism from these committees, but this would lead to better decision-making. He concluded with the apparently obligatory denunciation of Question Time, the effectiveness of which was all too often limited by poor ministerial performance. As a former Minister he observed that, if Ministers could not cope with questions "off the cuff", they were either not performing or were unfit for their positions.

In reply, Austin overrode most of these speeches by observing that the Bill was not about what occurred in the Parliament but what happened outside the Chamber. He likened the PSC to a Board of Directors that determined policy, and, as an employing body, was empowered to manage and control parliamentary staff. He reassured the Liberals that they would have representation on the PSC, and told the House that Treasury would not determine the PSC budget. He also praised the performance of Speaker Powell.

Although high hopes had been expressed for the PSC, in reality the corporatisation of parliamentary operations was, at best, a qualified success. Treasury strongly resisted any attempt to yield control over the parliamentary budget and, despite Austin's best efforts, Cabinet supported Treasury (Austin, interview 7 July 1993). Thus parliamentary financial independence remained more apparent than real.

Additionally, the PSC was constantly plagued by dissension. Jim

Fouras (Speaker 1990–96) repeatedly complained to me that the party representatives used PSC committee meetings to indulge in backbiting and political point-scoring. Fouras's critics responded that he lacked the capacity to handle these meetings with the requisite firmness. Importantly, the Speaker's office remained chronically under-resourced, a matter never seriously addressed by either the Goss or Borbidge Governments, but partially addressed under the Beattie Government by Speaker Hollis.

To some extent the budgetary independence of the PSC was superseded, under Goss, by the establishment of Estimates Committees. PSC Estimates were scrutinised by Estimates Committee A and debated in the House, the Speaker in reply. In 1996, shortly before the change of Government, the PSC was wound up by apparent agreement on all sides (Moroney, 1997). Not one of the original protagonists then remained in the Parliament; the current Members apparently regarded it as an experiment that had outlived its usefulness. White's passionate exhortation for a unity of purpose regarding the Parliament and its operations remained simply unachievable. Ahern's legislation had to some degree moved Parliament towards genuine independence, but in the end (thanks to Treasury's intransigence) the Speaker's limited role over the scope of the Parliament's budget had curtailed the Legislature's ability to differentiate its operations from those of the Executive.

Parliamentary committees

In the 1980s, there was no issue, more symbolic of parliamentary reform than the establishment of a Public Accounts Committee (PAC). Queensland, alone among Westminster-style parliaments, did not possess one. Although taken for granted today in Queensland, the establishment of a PAC had, by the end of the Bjelke-Petersen era, assumed totemic and symbolic significance among those advocating parliamentary reform. Aspects of this controversy have been discussed above, but in essence it was Bjelke-Petersen's obdurate hostility, together with the events of 1983, that precluded the establishment of a PAC under his Government. His line of reasoning was as brutal as it was unambiguous. If the public had subscribed to a PAC and all it symbolised, they would not have returned the Nationals to power in 1983 or 1986. According to Bjelke-Petersen, governments were elected to lead, to govern and to take necessary initiatives. Parliament could not interfere with the Executive, and any attempt to increase surveillance over the Government could not be countenanced, as this would diminish Cabinet's decision-making role and its executive duties.

Although this view prevailed within Government until the fall of Bjelke-Petersen, it was strongly contested outside Government ranks. Ahern, whose support for a PAC was both public and longstanding, had no qualms about reversing Bjelke-Petersen's position. Within two weeks of becoming Premier, Cabinet had decided in principle to legislate for a PAC and had detailed two National Party backbenchers, Gilbert Alison (Maryborough) and Des Booth (Warwick), to investigate the matter. They had collected evidence from all Australian jurisdictions (except Tasmania) concerning the operations of their PACs, and reported to Cabinet. The legislation was introduced on 11 October 1988, with the debate resuming on 10 November. However, in the cruellest irony of all, the day before the debate's resumption (9 November) Lane admitted before the Fitzgerald Inquiry that he had abused his ministerial expenses for private gain, and claimed that all other Ministers had done likewise. Such revelations created uproar in Parliament (dominating Question Time before the legislation was debated) and inevitably poisoned the atmosphere surrounding this long-awaited debate.

Ahern, in his second-reading speech, claimed that the Public Accounts Committee Bill constituted proof that his Government was committed to accountable Westminster-style government. He placed the Bill in the tradition of the Financial Administration and Audit Act, the Public Service Management and Employment Act and the Parliamentary Service Commission Act.

The Bill provided for a seven-person Public Accounts Committee (PAC), four of whom would be Government Members. It would have four chief functions: to review financial statements and other pertinent reports or documents; to inquire into any matters relevant to such statements, reports or documents; to report to Parliament on its reviews or inquiries; and to refer any matters arising from its reviews or inquiries to the Auditor-General for further detailed investigation. The

PAC could also review the financial operations of all line departments, statutory bodies or other Government agencies. It would be given wide powers to obtain information, summon witnesses and use contempt procedures. Its hearings would be in public unless it otherwise decided, and it would be resourced by the Parliamentary Service Commission (PSC), although for the 1988–89 financial year (in the absence of the PSC) the Government would provide an establishment grant of $200 000. The most controversial aspect of the legislation was the time limitation the Government placed on the PAC, specifying that it could not investigate any matter that occurred before to 1 December 1987 (the day Ahern took over from Bjelke-Petersen).

The PAC debate was an interesting example of how the Parliament chose to scrutinise and comment upon its own operations. A dozen Members participated (five ALP, four Nationals and three Liberals) and, while none opposed the Bill, there was repeated criticism of certain of its provisions which were subject to divisions in the committee stage. Inevitably, background matters such as Lane's admission of corruption, aspects of the Bjelke-Petersen era and the fall of the Coalition Government were revisited. The debate, while at times heated, nevertheless showed all sides to be committed to parliamentary reform insofar as this entailed a greater measure of executive accountability. Predictably the major difference amounted to Labor (and the Liberals) attempting to widen further scrutiny of Government, against the limits imposed upon the PAC by Cabinet.

Wayne Goss (Logan), as Leader of the Opposition, opened the resumed debate and immediately raised the issue of ministerial expenses by claiming that Lane's allegations were not new, quoting questions from his predecessor, Nev Warburton, to Bjelke-Petersen on 29 July 1987. He attacked Health Minister Leisha Harvey for paying Health Department moneys to National Party branches and using departmental funds for her personal expenses. As ministerial expenses were only summarily reported to Parliament, this Bill would give Ministers the power to veto any such PAC investigations. Similarly, he charged that the Treasurer's Instruction #330 weakened the ability of the Auditor-General to investigate. He sought to sow division between Booth and Alison, by noting that the former had said that investigation of ministerial expenses was a proper function for the PAC, while the latter had repudiated this. According to Goss, Booth's views had cost him the chair of the PAC, Cabinet having nominated Alison.

Clem Campbell (Bundaberg) surveyed the workings of PACs in other Australian jurisdictions and elsewhere in the world. He discussed the PAC's relationship with the Auditor-General, noting that the Canadian Auditor-General regarded the PAC as a useful tool to force reluctant bureaucrats and their departments to disclose relevant information, and further predicting that a close working relationship would develop between the Queensland Auditor-General and the PAC. He emphasised that the PAC must retain its independence. He foresaw a problem because the PAC was being established in a climate of mistrust and conflict, but welcomed the provision that Ministers must respond to the PAC's investigations within six months. He noted that there was no provision for a Deputy Chair and saw the PAC as limited by three constraints: time limitations (1 December 1987), ministerial veto and departmental cooperation.

Mackenroth (Chatsworth) linked the ministerial veto to the time limitation because Ministers could now veto any investigation of past and present expenses. In reference to White's earlier contribution, he attacked his credibility by charging him with hypocrisy. According to Mackenroth's interpretation of events, White had been offered the Liberal leadership in the Members' Bar in 1983, the night before he crossed the floor, and had used the PAC as a convenient ploy. Originally White wanted no time limitations on PAC investigations but, after Lane's allegation that all Ministers from 1980 had abused their expenses, White now supported the time limit. In Mackenroth's view this was because he and other former Liberal Ministers were now implicated and would be investigated by Fitzgerald's prosecution team (*QPD* vol. 309, pp. 2421–22).

The next Labor speaker was De Lacy, who observed that contemporary problems had arisen because the Government had been in power too long and had allowed lax financial practices to develop into dishonesty. In a swipe at Ahern, he noted that Treasurer's Instructions had been replaced by "new public financial standards" but, because the Premier would not table these, the House could not be sure of their existence (*QPD* vol. 309, p. 2452). He claimed that there were three flaws in the legislation: the time limit of 1 December 1987, the ministerial veto, and its failure to oblige the Auditor-General to co-operate with the PAC. He closed by foreshadowing divisions in committee on these questions.

The final round of Labor objections came from David Hamill (Ipswich), who stated that the ministerial veto was unnecessary because there was a body of Australian and British law covering cases of Crown privilege. Further, in Sankey's case (concerning the 1975 dismissal of Prime Minister Gough Whitlam), the High Court had determined which documents had Crown privilege attaching to them. Hamill considered that the Auditor-General's brief was too specific for the PAC Bill to provide the widest possible range of financial accountability, and concluded that the Auditor-General would become the "protector" of the Government. In a reference to past and present practices, he noted that Ministers consistently failed to give information requested both in Questions Without Notice and Questions Upon Notice, and wondered if they would be frank with the PAC. He closed with a reference to clause 23, which prohibited anyone from breaching the secrecy provisions of the Financial Administration and Audit Act. He believed this provision would prevent a complementary approach between the PAC and the Auditor-General's staff — a necessary prerequisite, according to Hamill, for the PAC to perform adequately.

The Liberals' contributions were more general than those of Labor, with White reprising the events and personalities of 1983, while observing that the Government's arrogance had led to the corruption uncovered by Fitzgerald. A PAC would have prevented most of this, particularly the cronyism involved in public tendering. White then charged that the ministerial veto provision demonstrated that the Nationals had not fully embraced the concept of public interest, since in no other jurisdiction was this provided for in PAC legislation. He was critical of Alison's nomination to the PAC chair by the Government, partly because the PAC should elect its own chair and partly because, as a known Ahern supporter, Alison was now receiving a career lift. He finished by emphasising the need for a Ministerial Code of Conduct.

Innes's opinion was that, since the PAC was only one part of the complex process of accountability, it should not have been delayed for eleven months. He considered that Ahern should have enacted the necessary legislation immediately he became Premier. Innes deplored the lack of guidelines for financial accountability and charged that too many Ministers were lazy and incompetent, using their public servants to rescue them. In a short speech, Knox bemoaned the abolition of the Internal Operational Audit Unit, but claimed that the Financial Administration and Audit Act had originally been drafted to complement a PAC, should one ever be established.

The Government put up four speakers in addition to Ahern, of whom the most important were the PAC investigators, Alison and Booth. Alison began by defending the taking of privilege on certain documents, suggesting that if clause 22 (on the inadmissibility of documents) proved to be against the public interest and hindered the PAC's work, it would be reviewed. The secrecy provisions for the Auditor-General's staff were consistent with professional requirements, he contended.

Alison informed Parliament that he and Booth were satisfied that all PACs they investigated operated in a bipartisan manner. Most had five members, reflecting the political composition of their Chambers, and all were chaired by a Government backbencher. He defended the nominated time limit, noting that the PAC could conduct investigations into events before 1 December 1987 to gather material "which has, or may have, a continuing effect on the financial administration of public monies" (*QPD* vol. 309, p. 2413). Although the PAC had the power to look at all Members' expenses (including those of Ministers), in all state and federal jurisdictions it was the prerogative of the Premier or Prime Minister to ensure that Ministers were properly accountable for their expenses. Finally, he denied that the PAC Bill had been the subject of delays, as they had been given their brief by Ahern within a fortnight of his becoming Premier. A detailed, nine-month process had been set in train to bring the legislation on for debate.

Booth was somewhat equivocal in his support of the Government's position, perhaps reflecting the accuracy of Goss's charge. For example he agreed with the need for a Deputy Chair. He was unsure whether or not it would be better to have the PAC chaired by an Opposition Member, and was equally uncertain whether 1 December 1987 was the appropriate date for limitation. More positively, he considered that the PAC had adequate power to act on its own initiative, and that it would improve the flow of information to Parliament and increase its surveillance of statutory authorities. He also stated that he and Alison had deliberately refrained from giving Ministers the right to refer matters to the PAC, to prevent both PAC work overload and "buck passing" by Cabinet.

Len Stephan (Gympie) and Fraser (Springwood) made short contributions. Stephan claimed that Ministerial veto powers were the same as those for the Subordinate Legislation Committee and, because they had caused that committee no problem, were unlikely to be problematic for the PAC. Ministers carried a heavy responsibility to decide whether disclosure was in the public interest, while the Ministry as a whole would now be subject to greater scrutiny.

Fraser defended the time limit and was of the opinion that being an investigative body was the PAC's chief role. It could investigate ministerial expenses, and those of all Members and departments, the PSC and local government. He foresaw that the PAC would be independent and bipartisan, and claimed that it would publicise any disagreements it had with the exercise of any ministerial veto.

In reply, Ahern covered most of the points that had been repeated and contested in debate. He defended the time limit because the PAC was to be concerned with the present and the future, not the past. However, clause 13(3) did exempt anything that had, or might have, a continuing effect on the administration of the state's finances. He rejected the charge that the legislation conferred a ministerial veto because, if a restriction was imposed on certain information, this could be brought before the Parliament, and the Government would have to endure the consequences. Clause 22(b) (inadmissibility of documents) was similar to procedures in all states for all parliamentary committees, and the Auditor-General was not muzzled by the Financial Administration and Audit Act. The Auditor-General could report to the Parliament at any time and on any matter, and so was not the Government's protector. Self-incrimination procedures were included to protect basic individual rights and, because Ahern's was a private-enterprise government, the work of the Internal Operational Audit Service had been privatised.

Because neither the Opposition nor the Liberals opposed the Bill as a whole, it was given its a second reading without division. However, these parties did object to several specific clauses, as a result of which the committee divided five times, with the Liberals joining the ALP on three occasions.

Committee proceedings began with the Government accepting a Labor amendment to provide for a Deputy Chair. This was important to the Opposition because, in the interests of PAC bipartisanship, an Opposition Member could expect to fill the Deputy's position if a Government backbencher took the chair. This subsequently became standard practice for all parliamentary committees. Innes attempted to take this principle a stage further by moving that the chairperson not be a Government Member. This was defeated by forty-two votes to thirty-four, with Labor combining with the Liberals. Innes then moved for the Auditor-General or his/her representative to be present at all PAC meetings, but this motion was defeated by sixty-eight votes to eight as the ALP joined the Government. Goss moved to delete the time-limitation clause (defeated 42:34), and then to delete reference to failure to provide material to the PAC which was "against the public interest" (defeated 41:34). His final move was to have the secrecy provisions deleted (defeated 49:26), with the Liberals combining with the Government. The Bill was then reported with amendments and read a third time without further division.

There is no doubt that, with its companion the Public Works Committee Bill, the PAC Bill was a significant reform measure. Their gestation had been long and controversial, but in retrospect such controversy is hard to understand. As a standard feature of the parliamentary landscape, PACs in other jurisdictions seldom engage in controversial work or cause undue problems for governments whose financial procedures meet reasonable expectations of accountability. This has now proved to be the case in Queensland. Under Labor and Coalition Governments the PAC has worked efficiently and non-controversially. Its work has been enhanced and complemented by the

In 1969 Mike Ahern represented Hon. A. M. Hodges, Minister for Works and Housing, to open the new premises of the Queensland Government Tourist Bureau in Newcastle (NSW). This was the first occasion he had opened anything. With Ahern is the local manager of the office on the left and the then Director-General of QGTB on right. (Photo courtesy *Newcastle Herald*)

In 1969 Mike Ahern represented Hon. V. B. Sullivan, Minister for Lands, at the opening of the annual Field Day in Kingaroy. Representing ministers, or the Premier, at public events is stock-in-trade work for younger government backbenchers.

Mike Ahern's How to Vote card for the 1972 General Election. Note that the National Party is still called by its original name of Country Party. The re-naming occurred in 1974.

Mike Ahern's How to Vote card for the 1977 General Election. His party now bears its new name, and his only opponent is the Labor nominee.

The last Coalition Cabinet. The Liberal leader and Deputy Premier Sir Llew Edwards sits on the Premier's right, while Mike Ahern sits five seats down from the Premier against the wall, 1983.

Alan Moir, then the *Courier-Mail*'s cartoonist, mercilessly and skillfully lampooned the old-style National Party. Standing behind the Premier are (left to right) Russ Hinze, Ivan Gibbs, Vic Sullivan and Bill Gunn. Sullivan was forced to resign the deputy leadership, and the other three, plus Ahern, were contenders. Gunn beat Ahern on the fourth ballot by one vote. *(Courtesy of Alan Moir)*

The Cabinet prior to the Nationals' greatest election victory, 1986. Mike Ahern is fourth on the Premier's right.

In his capacity as Member for Landsborough, Mike Ahern cuts the ribbon to open the new Bruce Highway Beerburrum deviation, 1987. Russell Hinze was there as the Minister for Main Roads.

Mike Ahern and his first Cabinet after the swearing-in ceremony. The Governor, Sir Walter Campbell, congratulates the Premier. (Photo courtesy of Queensland Newspapers/George Fetting)

Mike and Andrea outside the Parliamentary Annex when he became Premier. Their lifetime of devotion to each other is amply demonstrated in this photo.

All the world came to Brisbane for Expo 88. This photo at Government House shows Mike Ahern and Sir Walter Campbell with HRH the Duke and Duchess of Kent.

The first Cabinet in session. This Ministry lasted from 9 December 1987 to 19 January 1989.

The second Ahern Cabinet is sworn in by the Governor. This ministry ran from 19 January 1989 until 25 September 1989 when Mike Ahern was replaced by Russell Cooper as Premier.

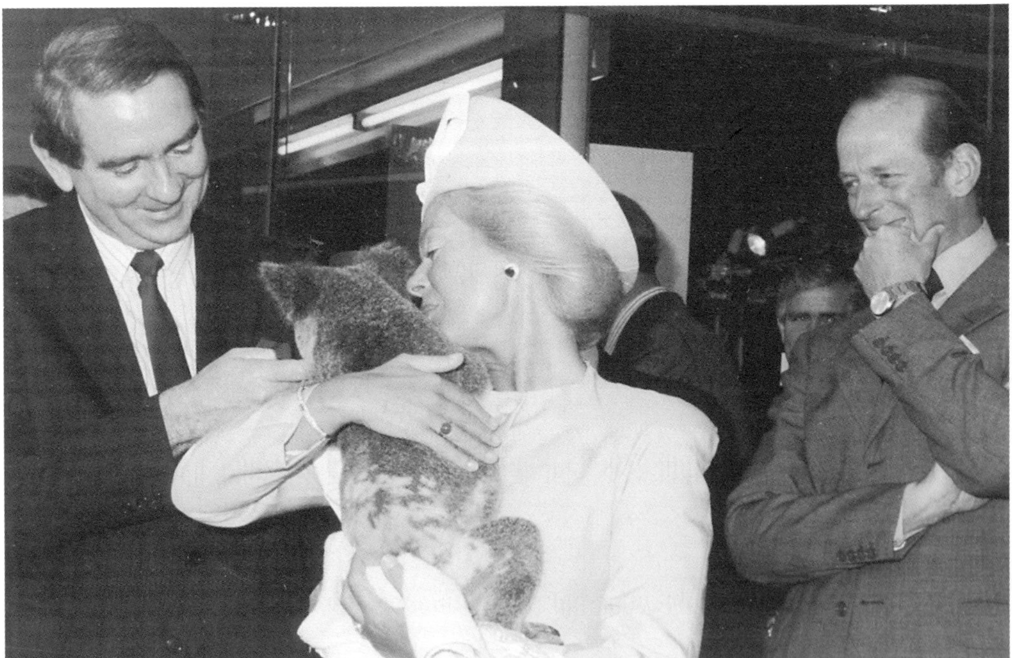

The Duchess of Kent has a close encounter of a koala kind, to the evident amusement of the Duke. From the Premier's viewpoint, an ideal photo opportunity.

The Ahern family at Expo 88. Left to right: Christine (10), Claire (14), Louise (16), Sharon (7), John (12), Andrea and Mike. His government's enthusiasm for the post-Expo site development bequeathed a magnificent public asset to Brisbane.

In his capacity as Premier and Minister for the Arts, Mike Ahern opens Movie World, the third major theme park in South-East Queensland.

Mike Ahern visits Warwick with local member Des Booth in April 1989 to attend the 25th Anniversary Dinner of the Warwick Branch of the National Party.

In 1989 Mike Ahern opened the Burdekin Dam, along with the prime minister, Bob Hawke, and Don Neal, Queensland Minister for Water Resources.

Mike Ahern opens the South Pacific regional office of the Sheraton Hotel Group. Sailyanne Atkinson was then Lord Mayor of Brisbane.

establishment of Estimates Committees, and those hopes originally held for it, and expressed at the time of the debate, have been fulfilled. Its features to which the non-government parties then took exception have not hindered its work, and no subsequent Government has found its existence, or its remit, as constituting frivolous or vexatious behaviour.

By contrast, the Public Works Committee Bill excited little controversy. This was somewhat surprising, given the heavy criticism by Fitzgerald of the Bjelke-Petersen Government's tendering processes (or lack thereof). However, the Bill was debated two months before the Fitzgerald Report was published and six months after the PAC debate. Thus many substantive matters covering Government's financial accountability had already been rehearsed, while the full indictment had yet to be handed down.

The Bill was introduced by Austin on 5 April 1989. He placed it in the context of other reforms and said that it would give the Public Works Committee (PWC) greater scope than in South Australia, Tasmania or the Commonwealth. The PAC and PWC would be complementary, adequately informing Parliament as to financial appropriations for government purposes, together with the results achieved. He observed that public works constituted a significant percentage of the money spent by both government departments and statutory bodies. The PWC could:

- enquire into any public work
- assess its suitability for the purposes stated
- enquire into the necessity for the work and the advisability of carrying it out
- the value for money achieved by the work
- the present and prospective public value of the work
- its impact on the economy, the environment and the community
- and how well the various participants performed.

In scope the PWC would cover public works by all departments, statutory bodies and other government instrumentalities where the work was financed from appropriations voted by the Parliament, and where the capital value of the public work exceeded $2 million (at 1989 indexed prices). Works of any value could also be referred to the

PWC by parliamentary resolution or Orders in Council. PWC inquiries could occur at any stage of construction, even after completion. However, only in exceptional cases would work be halted until the PWC completed its investigations — thus the PWC's emphasis would be on auditing works, rather than approving them.

PWC powers would be similar to those for the PAC, with permanent staff supplied by the PSC, and with empowerment to employ specialist staff. Unless the PWC decided otherwise, it would hold public hearings as part of its investigative charter. Austin then concluded by observing that the Government had consulted widely on the Bill's principles which had received near-unanimous approval from all quarters.

The second-reading debate resumed five weeks later, on 12 May, with five speakers — three Labor and one each for the Liberals and the Government.

De Lacy led for the Opposition, noting that the basic value of the PWC lay in its existence rather than its operations. Labor welcomed the Bill because a PWC would promote better procedures. Companies would now be aware that their tenders would be open to scrutiny, while Government would ensure that its own procedures were honest. He likened the PWC to a company auditor who established guidelines and ensured compliance. Additionally a PWC could protect governments, because Ministers could use it to refer matters and publicise procedures. Any temporary embarrassment suffered by Government was far preferable to the general disrepute into which previous tendering procedures had fallen. The existence of a PWC would lead to expressions of interest before tendering took place. Paradoxically, introducing flexibility to such procedures could also lead to abuses such as nepotism and cronyism; however, a PWC could maximise the positive aspects and minimise the negative ones. He claimed also that its activities would increase investors' confidence as most public works are financed by loans. The PWC would stop practices such as those revealed to Fitzgerald, whereby Citra Constructions won a $50 million contract after donating $250 000 to the National Party, and Hinze was "lent" $200 000 by Eddie Kornhauser after the latter had won the Surfers Paradise "Paradise Centre" contract.

De Lacy drew his speech to a close by noting that the PWC could not investigate any work done before 1 December 1987. Labor was against this limitation; but it had vented its opposition during the PAC debate and would not again divide the House. While the legislation did not specifically allow the PWC to investigate tendering, the ALP presumed that this was not excluded from its investigatory charter. He observed that the PWC was prevented from investigating "any matter of general public works policy" (*QPD* vol. 312, p. 4512). While the Opposition generally supported this, it was something of a grey area because of the inevitable overlap between policy formulation and implementation.

Labor's Glen Milliner (Everton) used the opportunity to affirm support for the select committee process, and praised the Minister for resisting objections from the construction industry. He was concerned at the $2 million threshold, claiming that public works often came in below that figure, and that there were as many rorts in small contracts as in large ones. To illustrate his disquiet over the time limitation, he cited several unresolved allegations from the past, including some that arose in 1984 when Austin was Health Minister.

Campbell (Bundaberg) went back to Ahern's 1975 report to Government urging the establishment of a parliamentary committee system (see chapter 2). He too attacked the time limitation, on the basis that it would prevent investigations into the upgrading of the Kingaroy airport and the construction of the Bjelke-Petersen Dam, which was initially costed at $17 million despite DPI advice that this figure was unrealistic. The dam in fact cost $42 million.

He noted that, while the PWC had no role in policy-making, it could question whether money spent on a project in one area would be better spent elsewhere. He finished by asking whether major projects would be leased by developers to circumvent the legislation, whether provision would be made for site selection, and whether proper cost/benefit and discounted cash-flow analyses would be carried out for all capital works projects.

White proffered the support of the Liberals, predicting increased Government accountability, a rise in information available to Parliament, better value for taxpayers' money and better-informed debate.

He observed that such committees are "watchdogs, not witch-hunts". However, with the abolition of the Internal Operations Audit Section, the PWC and PAC would be both heavily reliant on the Auditor-General.

National backbencher Sandy McPhie (Toowoomba North) praised the legislation, supporting the time limitation as appropriate because "that is the date from when we in this state stand proud over our achievements and from when we had completely open and accountable Government". (*QPD* vol. 312, p. 4513). He felt the $2 million base was appropriate given the provisions in the Bill for indexation, and that the *Courier-Mail* was wrong to see the confidentiality provisions as an abuse of parliamentary powers; he considered these necessary for commercial reasons. Penalties for contempt were also necessary to prevent "shoddy operators" from getting away with substandard work.

By McPhie's account, Queensland's PWC would be superior to those in other jurisdictions because, while other PWCs could investigate public works before they commenced, this was not appropriate for Queensland given the rate of development and the need to avoid both delays and cost increases. However, in exceptional circumstances the PWC could do this. He finished by noting that only one of the eight organisations consulted had any objections to the Bill's provisions.

In a short reply to Milliner, Austin answered that when he was Health Minister the Government had implemented a construction-management program to redevelop a large number of public hospitals. After the project's conclusion, he engaged a private consultant for a construction audit to ensure value for money. If the PWC had existed, it would have performed this task.

The secrecy provisions in the Bill had nothing to do with the Government and would be invoked by the PWC only if that was its decision. Austin's judgment was that investigation as to where public works would best be located was outside the PWC brief, while the term "tender" had been avoided to incorporate day-labour projects. The Government had not nominated the chairperson in advance (as it had before the PAC debate); nevertheless, he praised McPhie's contribution and hoped that, in line with Government wishes, McPhie, would be elected to the PWC chair.

The Bill was then given an unopposed second reading. In committee, Campbell asked, with reference to clause 4, why a veto power was included and what bodies were proposed for exclusion. Austin replied that this was taken from the federal legislation to exempt both Qantas and Australian Airlines, which operated competitively. He would exclude SGIO (later Suncorp) which used policy-holders' money rather than public funds.

In a further response on clause 18, Austin told Campbell he was unsure whether leaseback arrangements were covered by this legislation but, if not, they would be covered under the PAC Act. Thus the Bill was reported out without amendment, and given an unopposed third reading.

As the companion to the PAC Act, the PWC legislation completed the Ahern Government's plans for institutional parliamentary reform. The legislature had now established two key committees, both of which commenced work in the manner prescribed. Although changes to the overall committee structure occurred under future Labor and Coalition Governments, the foundations for a permanent investigatory parliamentary committee system had been laid. Queensland had, in this respect, lagged far behind the other states and the Commonwealth, but it now had a Government committed to the Parliamentary reform agenda and prepared to do the necessary work to facilitate its implementation.

The final parliamentary reform issue was the Register of Members' Interests, which was a Resolution of the House introduced by the Premier on 18 April 1989 and debated the following day. Because it was a Resolution, rather than a Bill, the debate upon it proceeded as if the House was in committee — that is, with no long speeches and Members permitted to speak more than once. This was a very sensitive issue: Lane's allegations concerning ministerial abuse of expense accounts hung over the Parliament and once again, the debate occurred after the Fitzgerald Inquiry had concluded, but before he had reported. Moreover, the Queensland Parliament had never before debated this question.

Immediately Ahern had assumed the premiership, he required his Ministers to provide him with a summary of their business, financial and other interests, which he kept within his office as a confidential register. One year later, in December 1988, a further accountability package was introduced. This strengthened the Ministerial Code of Conduct, and provided for publication of Ministers' personal business interests. It also extended the confidential register to cover the business interests of the Ministers' immediate families, and adopted strict guidelines for Ministerial expenses, including any gifts received.

The Premier proceeded to a full explanation. From 1 July 1989 ministerial offices would become cost centres, with ministers fully accountable for their office expenses. Standard guidelines would be issued and cash advances (except foreign currency for overseas travel) would be abolished. The Premier would annually table details of ministerial travel expenses. All Ministerial gifts would be deemed public property, with the Minister having to declare the gift(s) within fourteen days of receiving same. All gifts would then be recorded on the public register. Should a Minister wish to purchase a gift, s/he would have to pay to Consolidated Revenue the difference between $100 (for a privately donated gift) or $250 (for one from official sources) and the wholesale value of the gift as calculated at its place of origin.

Ahern then observed that the same standard of probity should be required of all other Members. Thus he proposed a Register of Interests, based upon that adopted by the Commonwealth Parliament, comprising four major features:

- There was to be registration and declaration of Members' interests.
- Each Member would furnish a statement of registrable interests.
- Explanatory notes would be provided as guide-lines to Members, to help them complete their entries.
- There was to be notification within twenty-eight days of any alteration to a Members' interests.

The Clerk of the Parliament would be the Registrar of Interests. The Register, maintained by the Clerk, would be open for public inspection under the following conditions.

- Inspection would occur in normal business hours.

- Anyone wishing to carry out an inspection had to provide their name and address.
- A record of all who had inspected the Register would be available to all others who wanted to do so.
- No photocopying would be allowed (note-taking only).
- Publication of information so acquired by those inspecting the Register would be limited to a fair and accurate summary.

Members failing to supply the required information would be deemed to be in contempt of Parliament and would be dealt with as the Parliament saw fit. These procedures would apply only to the current Parliament and would have to be reintroduced to the next one. The extent and range of Members' interests were not covered by the proposed resolution, and neither were those of their spouse, but they had to declare any interests vested in children. A spousal exception applied where property was jointly owned.

The following day Ahern formally moved the Resolution of Members' Interests. It was extremely comprehensive and included:

- shareholdings in public and private companies, including the names in which the shares were held;
- family and business trusts and nominee companies in which the beneficial interest was held, the name of the trust, the nature of its operations and beneficial interest, together with such details for dependent children;
- real estate owned, its location and purpose;
- company directorships;
- partnerships, including the nature of their interests and activities;
- liabilities — their nature and the creditors;
- bonds, debentures and similar investments;
- savings and investment accounts, name of the bank(s) or other institutions;
- the nature of other assets valued at over $5000, excepting household and personal effects;
- the nature of any other substantial income source;
- gifts over $250 from official sources, or over $100 from non-official sources, where the Member is of the opinion that an appearance of conflict of interest may be seen to exist;
- sponsored travel or hospitality;
- any other interest that might lead to conflict of interest.

It is unknown whether Members were expecting such a comprehensive itemised list of registrable interests, together with some "catch-all" categories. Ahern was determined that institutional corruption, at both the ministerial and parliamentary levels, would not again grow from lax governmental and political processes and disfigure Queensland's public life. There was general assent to the Resolution (it would have been a brave Member or party to oppose it after the revelations at the Fitzgerald Inquiry), but some underlying resentment was discernible in the subsequent debate. Members rightly suspected that, although the register would, in theory, be open to all, in practice it would be the journalists who would use it most. Accordingly, Members feared that journalists would write negative stories about them based on such research.

Four amendments were moved in debate. The first, moved by Goss and seconded by De Lacy, was aimed at including spousal interests. Goss asserted that this was a question not of the invasion of privacy (as Ahern had maintained), but of openness and accountability in Government. The risk was that, to avoid disclosure, MPs would transfer all their assets to their spouses. De Lacy concurred, citing the case of Hinze who, he alleged, had placed everything in the name of his second wife (*QPD* vol. 312, p. 4956). They argued that their amendment was only fair and just, if spouses were then to be written into Members' entitlements.

Typically, Innes sought to take the moral high ground without supporting the Opposition. He backed the Government's privacy argument, but argued for "a code of conduct for all Members backed by a Register of Interests of limited access, with a far more comprehensive and compulsory code for the Ministry" (*QPD* vol. 312, p. 4960). No wonder, before the vote, Ahern asked Innes for clarification of the Liberals' position. They voted with the Government, and the spouse amendment was lost by fifty-six votes to twenty-four.

Innes moved the second amendment, to alter the register annually rather than within the twenty-eight-day period. Ahern refused to accept this, no Labor Member spoke, and the Opposition sided with the Government to defeat the amendment, by seventy votes to ten.

Innes had more success with his third amendment. Those wishing to access the register would have to provide identification and state in writing the reason for such an inspection. The Clerk would then be required immediately to tell the Member the applicant's name, address and reasons for wishing to inspect the entry. Innes maintained that this amendment would prevent "undesirables" and those with prurient motives from accessing the register. Beard seconded it, asserting, with some justification, that backbenchers possess little political influence compared to that of media owners. He considered that lobbyists and journalists should have to register their interests before Members were so required — surely another testimony to the impotence of the Liberals on the crossbenches.

Goss, on the Opposition's behalf, opposed the amendment. He believed it would achieve nothing because, even with limited inspection, the media would publish the information either in full or in part. His deputy, Burns, added that the whole point of the register was to enable members of the public to check the veracity of Members' declarations. If this access was restricted, it would seem that MPs had something to hide.

Ahern accepted the amendment, with Austin observing that anyone, MP or otherwise, who abused information from the register, could be held to be in contempt of Parliament. The amendment was then passed by fifty-six votes to twenty-four. Parliament had its fig leaf.

In a final attempt to gut the register, Lyle Schuntner (Mt Coot-tha), a Liberal "oncer", moved an amendment to prohibit publication of matters contained in the register, "unless there is some reasonable ground for believing that a Member is, has been, or is likely to be guilty of conflict of interest" (*QPD* vol. 312, p. 4974). While this move would not have impeded access, it would have effectively prevented dissemination of material in all except conflict-of-interest cases. Knox seconded it, while Labor Members showed their disdain by not bothering to speak to it. Ahern refused it, using the words "nonsensical and unworkable". Labor and the Government combined to defeat it (69:10). At 1.44 am on 20 April 1989, the Queensland Parliament gained a Register of Members' Interests.

By its legislative record, the Ahern Government now had the reputation of being a reformist one. Ahern had come to office with his own agenda, and directed his Government as it set about fulfilling its self-imposed tasks. Ahern was very much in charge, but he had an able lieutenant in Austin, his deputy in all but name. His promotion of younger backbenchers to the Ministry on the basis of performance expectations broke the grip of seniority on Cabinet preferment. When the Ahern Government fell, it did so because of internal pressures and not through legislative incompetence.

Notes

1. See chapter 8.
2. In this case Commonwealth law would prevail to the extent that both Acts were in conflict.
3. At the time of this debate Fitzgerald's hearings had ended, but his Report was yet to be handed down.
4. Warner disputed this in her speech, claiming a figure of 1100.
5. For the circumstances in which Beard won Mt Isa, see Reynolds (1987). Beard was decisively beaten in 1989 by the ALP's Tony McGrady, later Mines and Energy Minister in the Goss Government and first Beattie Government, and Minister for Police and Corrective Services in the second Beattie Government.
6. See *Mood of '85. The People's Response. Essays, Poems, Letters and a Short Story About the SEQEB Strike of 1985*, Australian Studies Centre, The University of Queensland, 1988.
7. It should be noted that 30 June 1987 was ten months before Expo began; thus the Authority did not possess any appreciable revenue base to offset its debt. By 30 June 1988, Expo had been running for only two of its six scheduled months.
8. Bjelke-Petersen had forbidden Government Members to dine, drink or otherwise associate with their Labor counterparts.

CHAPTER 7

State economic development strategy: "Quality Queensland"

Mike Ahern had brought to his premiership some definite views as to Queensland's appropriate economic direction, and wasted no time in signalling these when he took office. He had been honing his ideas since 1980, when he entered the Ministry, but they had begun to take coherent shape when he was called upon to establish Technology as one of the subset of three ministries he assumed upon leaving Primary Industries. This new portfolio had jolted him out of traditional Country Party thinking, had built upon his Bachelor of Agricultural Science foundations, and dovetailed well with his evolving views on the necessity to adopt a more modern approach to public administration. Increasingly he perceived the technocratic imperatives that the private sector needed to bring to its decision-making processes.

Ahern had become increasingly dismayed by previous economic practices. The lax, ad hoc approach to Government tendering processes had, for example, become a matter of notoriety, and was in due course roundly condemned in the Fitzgerald Report. Ahern, however, was not merely responding to the flow of events. His experience in establishing an innovative department had brought him into contact with Brisbane's business community, and familiarised him with current thinking that emphasised the necessity for strategic economic planning, including medium- to long-term goal setting, indicative planning and rational resource allocation. To this he added a commitment to technological innovation and a deep seated adherence to the view that, for balanced economic development, Queensland had to move in this direction, while continuing to exploit its advantages in developing natural resources. He saw his task as essentially twofold. Primarily his Government had now to articulate appropriate goals for the new economic direction he perceived for the state; second, it needed to argue the case for the development of appropriate economic, social and technological infrastructure to ensure the realisation of these initiatives.

Ironically his model, and its impact upon the upper reaches of the state's public administration, has been accurately described in an account of the first Goss Government:

> If Cabinet acted in a corporate fashion, agreeing on policy and direction for all public agencies, it could achieve its central vision more effectively. These agencies, in turn, would employ program budget and strategic planning mechanisms, so ensuring the alignment of goals and activities. Ahern talked the language of transformational leadership, of developing an "ethos of strategic thinking and constructive change" throughout the public sector. Here was a managerial model of coordination, with the Premier as the chair of the corporation and government held consistent through shared objectives rather than personal fiat. (Davis 1995, p. 10)

This in summary was the model to which Ahern aspired and which, despite the brevity of his term in office, he consistently pursued. The fact that he was largely unsuccessful owed much to the circumstances of his tenure, and to the pressures to which he and his Government were subjected. Furthermore, these aspirations were a novelty for Queensland and, in Davis's terms, "his colleagues did not share the vision and panicked over more pressing problems".

Ahern had flagged his intentions at the outset in an interview he gave to the *Sunday Mail* (29 November 1987). In a wide-ranging discussion he affirmed his economic, political and strategic intentions by stating, "The Government's centrepiece will be its economic policy". He proposed a state economic development strategy comprising a "sensible working partnership" between Government and industry. He stated, "We've got to do better than depend on coal, cane and copper and now tourism."

He was not about to mindlessly repudiate the past, as was seen in his wish to retain the services of both Under-Treasurer Sir Leo Hielscher and former Coordinator General Sir Sydney Schubert. He also announced the establishment of "specific advisory groups comprising business people which would give separate economic advice from Treasury". As he noted, "These groups [were] coming together already. A number of people could see the inevitability of what was happening and came to see me". (Ibid.)[1]

While these views were clearly those of a man eager to seize the reins of power, it became obvious that he had done a considerable amount of work over the Christmas–New Year period (1987–88), as seen by his press release of 9 February 1988. In this he spelt out his earlier thoughts, under the typically grandiose heading "First Step in the Ten Year Economic Strategy". This statement announced that a select group of five local management consultant companies would be invited to put forward proposals to help the Government develop its State Economic Development Strategy (SEDS), the aims of which would be to:

- place Queensland in a global content and identify its economic strengths and weaknesses
- boost value adding in manufacturing
- seek greater cooperation between industry and the state's tertiary institutions
- seek wider technological development, new managerial practices and commercialise innovations
- develop South-East Queensland (SEQ) as a major centre for advanced technology
- establish Queensland as a centre for international business education, research and commerce
- develop further tourism, agriculture and mineral production.

As a policy initiative, this announcement traced Ahern's lineal descent from his earliest days in Cabinet. It was his firm belief that only by harnessing technological innovation, together with modern administrative and managerial strategies, could Queensland secure a viable future direction. In part this was his reaction to the cronyism and political jobbery of the Bjelke-Petersen era, but it also reflected Ahern's desire to initiate rational planning, a priority he had taken with him from his experience in previous ministerial appointments.[2]

However, because this represented an innovative departure from the low priority that Queensland's previous political leaders had given to economic policy, it inevitably attracted critics, doubters and scoffers. To Ahern's political opponents his aims represented yet another example of his inability to "get on with the job".

Ahern's denigrators perceived Government to be about quick, decisive decision-making, not waylaid by the lengthy processes of gathering data, carrying out research, setting goals and consulting stakeholders. A mind that is academically trained and expends time in focusing on problems before finding solutions is unfathomable to those who cannot appreciate, or come to terms with, such an approach. In Queensland, the so-called men of action, socialised by the so-called university of hardknocks, are very suspicious of the academically trained and hence gave free rein to crudely voiced anti-intellectualism.[3]

Ahern was not to be swayed by such opposition. He had long identified as one of the basic weaknesses in Queensland's public administration the failure to be goal-oriented in measuring achievement. Treasury, even by its supporters, had often been dismissed as a "bean-counting" department, and it seems that no other department had been actively encouraged to develop strategic planning. Indeed line departments had little incentive so to do when their considered advice could be so easily overturned by the whim of a Minister or his Cabinet colleagues, depending upon who had last spoken to them, or who offered them the more significant inducement.

A month later (14 March 1988) Ahern announced that the Stanford Research Institute and Brisbane Strategies Pty Ltd had won the contract to develop SEDS. Ahern hoped that the international reputation of Stanford University, together with the local input from a Brisbane consultancy firm, would provide the best balance for this innovative exercise. However, it was another nine months before these preparations came to fruition, when SEDS (by now renamed Quality Queensland) was launched before an audience of businesspeople, academics, entrepreneurs, politicians and selected others at Parliament House on 12 December.

In the meantime economic initiatives had proved to be something of a mixed bag for the Government. On 3 May the Government had proclaimed the Cape York/North Queensland Enterprise Zone (CYNQEZ). This, it was hoped, would become the first of several regional areas targeted for special departmental attention, in an effort to decentralise significant economic decision-making and ensure a more balanced approach to economic development.

Partly to reassure the agricultural lobby that it was not being overlooked in this rush to embrace high technology, a $50-million primary industry productivity enhancement scheme was announced and given to the QIDC to administer. A month later, in September 1988, the Government set aside $1.7 million to encourage and support the study of ethanol production.

While the Government, in the person of the Premier, appeared sensitive to this economic balancing act, it was hard to keep all the balls in the air. The president of the Chamber of Mines, for example, criticised the Government's space-base policy, and its emphasis on high-technology-based manufacturing, because he feared core economic activity (mining, obviously) would be downgraded. *Courier-Mail* state roundsman Peter Morley, almost certainly reacting to economic briefings from industry, wrote an article criticising the Ahern Government for failing to implement what he termed "real economic change".

A more literate economic critique was provided by Murray Massey in the *Australian Financial Review* (22 November 1988). He opened his piece by reporting Queensland business people's discontent with the Government's purchasing policy, allegedly because business was uncertain as to the Government's economic direction. More ominously, Massey reported that Wayne Goss, who had become Leader of the Opposition the previous March, was increasingly receiving invitations to speak at business functions and to meet industry leaders — "more than most National Party Ministers". According to him:

> Goss maintains contact with the likes of BHP, MIM and Qintex and has no fear of praising the decisive style of the former Premier Sir Joh Bjelke-Petersen in a bid to exploit the growing frustration of the private sector with what it complains is the slow grind of the Ahern Government.

To complete this Greek chorus of criticism, three days after the launch of the Quality Queensland strategy, the influential (in National Party circles) journal *Queensland Country Life* argued that agriculture's role and place had now been downgraded as a result of the Government's new strategy.

Ahern's media release on 12 December 1988 hailed the Quality Queensland strategy as "the start of a major process of change in the future economic development of Queensland". In keeping with Ahern's predilection for setting long-term goals, the emphasis was on "a series of major initiatives for Queensland over the next two years". Highlighted for attention were the following:

- *Taxation*: Review of current tax structures to minimise state taxes/ charges, emphasising resource-based proposals
- *Banking*: Encouragement of a large Queensland-based private enterprise bank
- *Tourism*: Policies to encourage future initiatives.
- *Education*: An upgrading of the Queensland education system to emphasise life long education
- *Regionalism*: Establishment of Centres for the Development of Regional Opportunities and the decentralisation of key departmental activities
- *Agriculture*: Provision of technological, financial and marketing information for all producers, and especially for those producing high-value-added and perishable goods; identification of the fiscal needs of small to medium producers.
- *Transport*: Improved national and international transport to both Brisbane and Queensland, and an upgraded transport infrastructure within Queensland.
- *Small business*: Integrated policies to encourage greater investment.
- *A world trade centre*: To support world trade centre owned and managed by the private sector.

For Ahern, this announcement was the culmination of a longstanding process of policy formation. Indeed, in the time remaining to him as Premier, he began to move on a number of fronts to add specifics to these general aims. In January 1989 he created a Division for State Economic Development within the Premier's Department. In February he established an Office of International Business as a "one stop shop" for foreign businesses dealing with Queensland. In March a two-month marketing campaign was launched to attract business investment to the state, while Rockhampton was chosen as the next centre for regional development grants. In April Ahern urged industry to give more encouragement to science and education through research and development. In May advertisements were placed for expressions of interest in the CYNQEZ, and in July increased funding for tourism was announced.

However, to his critics (both within the National Party and elsewhere) "Quality Queensland" was brushed aside, either as a wish list or as an example of Ahern choosing "pie in the sky" over hard decision-making options. Austin spoke contemptuously (interview 7 July 1993) of the exercise, saying that he had kept the Stanford report "in his bottom drawer" until he had time to rewrite it in a way that was comprehensible for the major stakeholders. Dr Gary Chittick, who was then the Opposition's economic policy adviser, alleged that the Stanford Institute had merely attached a Queensland cover to a generic report which was bland and full of "economic-speak" because they had never seriously investigated the Queensland economy.

It is undeniable that for "Quality Queensland" to be judged a success the Government required the necessary lead time to implement these policy initiatives, as well as an administrative team dedicated to pursuing these objectives. Ahern, by implication, realised this when he optimistically announced that SEDS would guide the Government's economic policy over the following two years. An observer did not have to be overly sceptical, or particularly hostile to the Government, to predict that such a time frame was precisely what the Ahern Government lacked.

The "Quality Queensland" strategy had taken the best part of a year before it could be announced and placed on the policy agenda. But when this occurred, only twelve months remained to the Government before it had to go to an election. Thus a two year timetable was an excessively optimistic political forecast, given the realities that faced Ahern's Government. Also, both the media and, by extension, public opinion, were exclusively focused upon the Fitzgerald Inquiry (which closed its hearings in December 1988, the month "Quality Queensland" was announced). This made it impossible to distract media opinion with a visionary statement or economic blueprint designed to take Queensland into the 1990s and beyond. The opinion marketplace was simply incapable of paying this policy area any sustained attention. By now most industrial and economic opinion leaders had largely given up on a Government that preferred to discuss their needs in what today would be called "big-picture" terms. In the late 1980s this was an altogether unfamiliar perspective for Queensland industrialists and leaders in commerce who had, for years, been socialised into the culture of decisive (if erratic) decision-making at the micro-economic level, and who had been encouraged to present themselves to Government as a succession of special pleading stakeholders. Ahern was now attempting to inculculate a holistic economic perspective in Queensland's policy and public administration processes, and to present this to the domestic, national and international business forces with which the Government would do business. By any criteria this was a tall order, and one that would have been extremely difficult even in more propitious times.

In hindsight it can readily be appreciated that these times were distinctly unpropitious. The question remains, why did Ahern persist with a policy stance that, in the eyes of many, marked him out as a poor politician — one who pursued an economic (and therefore political) strategy that was simply inappropriate for that time and season?

There are several possible answers. First, Ahern was completely convinced that his way was the only way to proceed. Even leaving aside the corruption issue (if that were then even remotely possible), he was unshakable in his conviction that the previous lack of planning, the frequent overriding of technological and expert advice for personal, and/or political advantage and the excessive focus on micro-economic opportunities had simply no place in any modern society. Such an approach belonged to a bygone era where problems were so simple in their definition that they suggested their own immediate solutions, and could be simply addressed and treated. Moreover, such a populist approach, whereby short-term political advantage was always paramount, challenged all that Ahern had stood for in manoeuvring for the premiership. Despite coming from the land, Ahern was not a populist and led the revolt within his party against the preceding populist style of rhetoric and decision-making. He was determined to sweep away the past decision-making mind-set, and replace this with a technocratic, managerial, political model based upon rational analysis and dispassionate advice which would set the economic decision-making parameters. Within these could be accommodated the regional and local factors which must, inevitably, influence micro decision-making choices.

In addition, to this ideological conviction (if it could be so termed), there was Ahern's often underrated quality of tenacity. At any point during his long and often frustrating parliamentary career, Ahern could have left to pursue more personally profitable goals in agriculture, industry or commerce. He chose to stay in the political arena, convinced that his time would come and that his reforms would be accepted as the inevitable way forward. Thus, when he came into his political inheritance, he refused to capitulate to contrary forces who urged caution and the retention of past ways to secure a political future. He had no intention of repudiating his *raison d'être* for such expediency. He was determined to make his mark, both on his own times and on Queensland's future direction. His economic vision was integral, central even, to this self-proclaimed intention. At times, he seemed to want to transform Queensland into a vast Silicon Valley, but more plausibly, and half a decade before Paul Keating, he saw the possibilities of expanding Australia's knowledge industry to service the growing Asian economies. He wanted Queensland to be positioned to take advantage of such an opportunity.

Finally there were the considerations of pragmatic politics. Ahern was well aware that his Government was being badly damaged by the Fitzgerald process. To counter this he advanced several strategies, none wholly successful. He attempted to draw a line under the Bjelke-Petersen era by proclaiming that both he and his Government were fundamentally different. His next ploy was to commit himself, sight unseen, to implement the Fitzgerald recommendations, "lock, stock and barrel". Lastly, he tried to shift his political focus to other areas of policy, to demonstrate that his was a Government that could and would address contemporary issues, especially those he considered salient for the future.

While such strategies were geared to important immediate political requirements, all involved high political risk-taking. For example, how could Ahern credibly sign off on the Bjelke-Petersen era when he had served in Bjelke-Petersen Cabinets from 1980 to 1987? How, also, could he repudiate this *ancien régime* when he led a Parliamentary National Party entirely composed of Members elected during the tenure of Bjelke-Petersen's premiership? Importantly, Ahern's various Ministries attested to the pervasiveness of the Bjelke-Petersen era. Although, on assuming office, he had dropped some of the National Party "ultras" (for example Lane, Hinze and Chapman), and promoted some backbenchers of varying and dubious talents (for example Borbidge, Cooper, Harvey and Sherrin), the core of his Cabinet was populated by older men whose positions and seniority resulted from their faithful service during the Bjelke-Petersen years. Instant transformation, on either their part or that of public perception, could not come readily or easily.

While the "lock, stock and barrel" pledge served to insulate Ahern personally from any collateral political damage deriving from the Fitzgerald findings and recommendations, it failed to ease the pressure on the Government as a whole — either during the hearings or in the seven-month hiatus between the ending of the inquiry and the presentation of the report. Ahern's political problem was always going to be intractable. How could he direct media and public attention from these revelations for anything other than the shortest time? Any attempt to provide other political foci (including economic ones) was doomed. It was essential to try, in order to prevent Fitzgerald-generated political paralysis from taking hold of his governmental processes, but the political foreground was simply too crowded to give space to other priorities. Moreover, when these entailed visionary perspectives which encouraged the public to engage in abstract speculation about defined but hitherto unrealised goals, few, if any, opinion leaders within the politically attentive public paid any heed.

In more settled political times this economic policy of Ahern's might, perhaps, have constituted a viable strategy. It should be said, however, that all state governments are well-nigh exclusively focused on the political advantages to be reaped from governmental outputs within the time before the next election. It should be acknowledged that Ahern tried to shift such attention to broader economic horizons. It is altogether unsurprising that he failed, although in part he did point the way forward for the incoming Goss Government.

As Davis's account makes clear, Labor while in Opposition was increasingly turning its attention to the processes with which it saw the Ahern Government grappling. Being a different political party, which had waited thirty-two years to come into power, it had both time and political circumstance at its disposal — a credit balance that it took six years to dissipate. It is surely one of the sweeter ironies of Queensland's political history in the 1980s and 1990s that, in managerial, economic and administrative matters, the Ahern Government should have been the harbinger of Goss and Labor.

Notes

1. Ahern laid these objectives down two days before becoming Premier.
2. On moving to the Health portfolio he asked to see the strategic plan which would take the department to 2000. His request was met with astonishment.
3. See Ahern's remarks to Bennett on anti-intellectualism cited in chapter 2.

CHAPTER 8

Under pressure

An examination of the Ahern Government's legislative record shows it to have been a reformist administration; but it is undeniable that it was beset by a series of political crises from the outset. There seems to have been three major causal features at work. Undoubtedly the most important was the Fitzgerald Inquiry and its damaging Report. Sensational revelations, and their subsequent developments (Dickie 1988, pp. 249–64) preoccupied the Government from its swearing in until the Fitzgerald Report was published on 3 July 1989. Ahern repeatedly affirmed that his Government would implement this unseen report "lock, stock and barrel"; nevertheless the collateral damage that the Report caused the National Party can scarcely be underestimated.

Other factors destabilising Ahern's Government flowed from the events that preceded Bjelke-Petersen's overthrow, and the electoral damage sustained by the Nationals, caused both by Fitzgerald Inquiry and by the way in which Ahern came to power. Both impacted on a further difficulty: the fact that Ahern possessed no electoral mandate for the changes he championed. In his words, he had to "recreate the Government from within" (interview 4 September 1997) and was thus under continual pressure to defend himself, his Government and its actions from both internal criticisms and external assaults. He was also under parliamentary pressure from a reinvigorated Labor frontbench led by Goss as leader and Tom Burns (Lytton), his deputy.

Leadership problems

Ahern's assumption of the premiership may have been welcomed but, despite any public enthusiasm for this "changing of the guard", significant elements within the National Party remained uneasy. Opposition arose from two sources. First was the faction of the Parliamentary National Party that saw no reason for Bjelke-Petersen's departure. Despite all members of the Parliamentary National Party (except Bjelke-Petersen) signing the Minute to the Governor supporting Ahern's election as leader (Coaldrake 1989, pp. 164–9), this was simply unity born of exigency. This faction was both temporary in nature and suspicious in character as it awaited further, and future, developments. The second group comprised the National Party rank and file who, together with loyalist National voters, would have supported Bjelke-Petersen irrespective of the findings of the Fitzgerald Inquiry. They saw their erstwhile leader as having been victimised by the Fitzgerald process, set in train and abetted by National Party "trendies". Necessarily they perceived Ahern to be a pretender who had usurped power and set aside the "rightful" leader, and used the Fitzgerald Inquiry to legitimise the successful pursuit of his political ambitions.

Adverse reaction to Ahern was not slow in coming. On 6 December 1988, one week after assuming the leadership, Ahern stood aside two high-profile Ministers, Don Lane and Russell Hinze, because both had been adversely mentioned at the Fitzgerald Inquiry. Although he suggested that, should their names be cleared, they might be reinstated, their collective rage was as palpable as it was unmasked. Both had, after all, been long-serving Ministers; and Lane and Austin, as the 1983 Liberal turncoats, had provided the Nationals with the requisite majority to govern in their own right. Lane felt that the Nationals owed him unswerving support in perpetuity and, by his own admission (interview 2 April 1993), henceforth worked to destabilise Ahern by leaking material which he had accumulated in his confidential ministerial files to the media. Lane's previous record, character and modus operandi ensured the secrecy of these operations, to which he increasingly resorted as his personal and political worlds began to fall apart. After admitting corruption to the Fitzgerald Inquiry, he sought to save himself from the full consequences of his disgrace by trying to bring down as many of his former colleagues as possible. Unsuccessful though he was in this endeavour, and while prosecution was succeeded by sentencing and subsequent imprisonment, unseating Ahern was his ultimate goal. Hinze's style was different. He had always been more comfortable in the limelight and resorted to public posturing to pursue his anti-Ahern vendetta.

It was not only Lane and Hinze who pursued the new Premier. Clearly, Bjelke-Petersen was incapable of either forgiving or forgetting, and he maintained a ceaseless barrage against his successor. On 4 January 1988, a month after his deposition, he personally lambasted Ahern, following this up on 13 February with a scornful assessment of the Government's developmental policies. Bjelke-Petersen was more than a sniper from a politically marginalised position. Journalists assigned to the state political round knew they could always obtain good political and anti-Government copy by running to Bjelke-Petersen for comment. Early in Ahern's term, much of this was motivated by by-election campaigns for the federal seat of Groom (based on Toowoomba and the Darling Downs) and for Bjelke-Petersen's former state seat of Barambah.

The first by-election was a three-cornered contest. In an amazing reversal, given his involvement in arranging the 1980 National–Labor electoral pact and his preparedness to terminate the 26-year-old coalition agreement in 1983, Bjelke-Petersen publicly supported the Liberal candidate, Bill Taylor, in preference to the National Party's David Russell QC, who later become its state president. It was a measure of Bjelke-Petersen's unrelenting hostility to both Ahern and the restyled National Party that he would actively support a Liberal for a federal seat that the Nationals had held since 1972. On 11 April 1988, the Liberals captured Groom with a 21 per cent swing against the Nationals. Never known for his modesty, Bjelke-Petersen claimed sole credit for this result, although it should be recorded that the Liberals went on to win Groom at every subsequent election.[1] This unexpected result, together with Bjelke-Petersen's continuing media profile, sent shock waves through the National Party organisation and its Government.

Media speculation was immediate on two fronts. As the journalists saw it (13 April 1988), Bjelke-Petersen was either challenging for the party presidency following Russell's trouncing, or would be expelled from the party owing to his disloyalty during the Groom by-election. Perhaps the ex-Premier was running both stories simultaneously; he continued the attack by charging that Ahern had "bungled the [leadership] job", while for good measure his wife, Senator Lady Florence Bjelke-Petersen, threatened to sit in the Senate as an Independent if expulsion was to be her husband's fate. Finally, in an all-too-characteristic display of political bluff, Bjelke-Petersen threatened that if the National Party expelled him he would form a new political party.

Although in retrospect Bjelke-Petersen's threat seems hollow, it should be remembered that he made it on the eve of the by-election for the National Party and Bjelke-Petersen heartland seat of Barambah. The National Party organisational wing evidently took him seriously, as he was not expelled; but neither did he proceed to challenge Sparkes for the presidency. He was obviously not prepared to test his strength on the conference floor lest he be humiliated. However, the threat of a Bjelke-Petersen party loomed large in party calculations. Their fear was that, however ephemeral such a party might turn out to be, there might be sufficient of his supporters in the parliamentary party to move to the crossbenches, thereby denying the Ahern Government its majority. Further, enough rank-and-file National members and voters might be induced to support whatever right wing mavericks Bjelke-Petersen preselected for future by-elections, let alone for the 1989 state election.[2] So this threat had the potential to inflict serious electoral damage on the Nationals, either by the loss of heartland seats or by preferences being directed to Liberal or minor party candidates hostile to the Nationals. It is doubtful whether Bjelke-Petersen could or would have delivered such an electoral outcome, but it was testimony to his continuing influence within the party that the National hierarchy moved to appease rather than confront him. Ahern, given his long and stormy relationship with Bjelke-Petersen, was apparently not party to this strategy, and he may well have been indifferent to it; but, given the now fraught political atmosphere, the organisation clearly felt it necessary to placate the former Premier in order to neutralise him.

Ahern and Bjelke-Petersen had been political foes since the Landsborough by-election, and the poisonous relationship between the two was intensified by Ahern's claim that, had his predecessor remained in office, Bjelke-Petersen would have used his power as Premier to terminate the Fitzgerald Inquiry. As early as 27 February 1988, Ahern had hinted at this when addressing 200 delegates at the National Party Conference. When delivering the leader's keynote address, he left them in little doubt about how things had altered. He said, "We are on a mission for truth and we are absolutely determined about it" (*Sunday Sun*, 28 February 1988, p. 7). Six weeks later he made the charge explicit, declaring that Bjelke-Petersen, had he remained as Premier, would have closed down the Fitzgerald Inquiry. Bjelke-Petersen, for his part, angrily denied the claim.

The veracity or otherwise of Ahern's accusation is impossible to ascertain now. Incontestably both men were locked in a bitter political struggle as Ahern, now in power, was determined to assert his authority and Bjelke-Petersen, although out of power, nevertheless claimed vicarious authority. Neither would yield, yet both used Fitzgerald to bolster their respective positions. As the inquiry was still in session when these claims and counterclaims were made, and because the Report does not canvass the question, Bjelke-Petersen's designs remain a matter for conjecture. It is beyond question that both continued to believe their respective versions, and that charge and countercharge exacerbated their feud.

The Barambah by-election

As stated above, it was the imminence of the Barambah by-election that occasioned this barrage of allegations. On the eve of the poll Bjelke–Petersen declared, "I'll destroy the Premier" (*Courier-Mail*, 15 April 1988, p. 11). The following day, the National Party candidate suffered a spectacular defeat at the hands of a former National, Trevor Perrett, who had defected to a far-right splinter party.

Table 8.1: Election results for Barambah, 1986 and 1988 (percentages)

Party	1986	1988	Swing
National	77.5	41.1	–36.4
Labor	22.5	17.5	–5.0
Others	–	41.4	+41.4

Perrett won 32.1 per cent of the primary vote, and received 65 per cent of Independent and 89 per cent of ALP preferences, giving him 54.1 per cent of the total vote after distribution of preferences. Shortly thereafter he rejoined the National Party, and became Minister for Primary Industries in the 1996–98 Coalition Government.[3] However the psychological damage had been done in a seat which had returned Bjelke-Petersen since 1944. On these figures, 47 per cent of Bjelke-Petersen's 1986 voters had followed their former Member and deserted the National cause in protest at Ahern's coup. Two subsequent by-elections (South Coast and Merthyr) inflicted further electoral damage on the Ahern Government, but it was the Barambah defeat that strengthened Bjelke-Petersen in his fight with Ahern and doubtless rallied his forces within the National Party.

Over the next four months, murmurings of discontent emanated from various sections of the party as Ahern's enemies manoeuvred. They focused on the leadership and the declining level of electoral support as measured by opinion polls. After the Barambah result, the media speculated as to backbench and rank-and-file anger at the stand-off between Bjelke-Petersen and Ahern, suggesting that Ahern and Gunn should "lay off Joh". Two days after the by-election (18 April), at the National Party Central Council meeting in Roma, a delegate told Ahern that he had moved the Nationals too far to the left, that compared to Bjelke-Petersen he was a weak leader, and that he was virtually unknown outside Brisbane.

Up to this point such rumblings were, for both the Government and organisation more a distraction than a matter of major concern. However, politics is frequently characterised by volatility and rumour, and a harbinger of things to come occurred on 12 May 1988 when the *Townsville Bulletin* ran a front-page story speculating on the likelihood of a leadership spill. Ahern, it conjectured, would be replaced by either Cooper or Austin. The following day Ahern supporters retaliated in the *Courier-Mail*, asserting that no such moves were in preparation. In a press release on 14 May, Austin flatly denied any challenge for the leadership. Interestingly, no such statement came from Cooper's office.

The following week (27 May), at a National Party Management

Committee meeting, Sparkes threatened to expel any party member who publicly criticised either the leadership or the party. This whip-cracking temporarily silenced internal criticism but, despite Sparkes' efforts, the publication of a Morgan Gallup Poll a week later (*Courier-Mail*, 2 June 1988) unsettled the Government. Its results gave the Nationals 28 per cent support, Labor 37 per cent and the Liberals 26 per cent. Somewhat paradoxically, Ahern was given a 63 per cent approval rating, compared to 54 per cent for Goss and 43 per cent for Innes. National support had eroded, but the Government's electoral position was not desperate. On these figures 9 per cent were either undecided or declared for a minor party. If most could be persuaded to gravitate to the Nationals (as they had in 1986) via preferential voting, the Government, protected by its zonal system, stood a good chance of victory. To capitalise on the situation, Sparkes now used these results to threaten a snap election if there was any further internal dissent.

Sparkes's authority was eroding, however. The Bjelke-Petersen loyalists blamed him as much as Ahern for their hero's fall. Thus Powell, in a calculated snub, announced on 15 July that he would host a Bjelke-Petersen testimonial dinner at Hervey Bay in his electorate of Isis; and in the run up to the South Coast by-election Hinze told the *Sydney Morning Herald* (8 August 1988), "It would take ten Aherns to equal one Bjelke-Petersen".

The South Coast by-election

In a bid to appeal to his party's traditional constituency, Ahern opened the South Coast by-election campaign, occasioned by Hinze's (enforced) retirement, with a morally simplistic speech pitched at social conservatives. It was a ploy more reminiscent of Bjelke-Petersen than of Ahern's enlightened conservatism, but it was made as much to consolidate internal party support as to appeal to right-wing voters. In the event, the Government narrowly retained the seat.

Table 8.2: Election results for South Coast, 1986 and 1988 (percentages)

Party	1986	1988	Swing
National	49.2	30.2	–19.0
Labor	31.1	23.0	–8.1
Liberals	19.7	28.6	+8.9
Others	–	18.2	+18.2

Two-fifths of the Nationals' 1986 vote deserted, as did one-quarter of Labor's support. The Liberals, Independents and minor parties were the beneficiaries. The Nationals' Judy Gamin had a narrow win over the Liberals' Bob Quinn, finishing with 50.4 per cent of the total vote. ALP preferences were decisive: incredibly, they divided 50.1 per cent National, 49.9 per cent Liberal. Although it was an extremely narrow victory, the Ahern Government had avoided another humiliation, while the Liberals were considerably buoyed by their performance. Labor, however, had been trounced, failing to capitalise on the Government's internal problems and the damage being done to the Nationals by the evidence unfolding before the Fitzgerald Inquiry.

Legal issues

Before the presentation of the Fitzgerald Report, the Government had to deal with legislation concerning criminal proceedings that arose from the Inquiry. Hitherto, when evidence before the Inquiry necessitated the preparation and laying of charges, these matters fell to a special prosecution task force but, as Attorney-General Clauson told Parliament, the complexity and volume of evidence required a permanent body to implement this process and continue it beyond the completion of both Inquiry and Report.

Thus, on 27 October 1988 the Government introduced the Special Prosecutor Bill, modelled on Commonwealth legislation passed after the Costigan Royal Commission. This Bill established a Special Prosecutor's Office, independent of Government, and subject only to general guidelines as published in the *Government Gazette*. Clauson specifically excluded issuing such guidelines for particular cases. He confirmed that Commissioner Fitzgerald both had been consulted and had recommended that, except where their tasks proved complementary, the

Special Prosecutor should operate independently of his inquiry. According to the Attorney-General, his Bill attempted to balance the rights of the accused against those afforded to potential witnesses and their evidence. He finished his second-reading speech by outlining conditions under which he would withdraw indemnities from prosecutions. This would happen when:

- the person so indemnified had committed perjury
- such a person was convicted of an offence that should have been disclosed when indemnity was applied for
- untruths had been told when applying for indemnity.

Two weeks later, and on the day that Lane confessed to corruption (9 November), the debate was resumed. Although Lane's admissions provided the non-Government parties with ammunition to attack the Government, neither the ALP nor the Liberals could take their criticisms very far. The Bill was, after all, integral to the Fitzgerald process, and hence they could hardly oppose it. Only Wells and Innes rose, and while attacking the Government on Lane's evidence, both indicated general support for the measure. Wells criticised the Bill for failing to exclude Crown privilege, and foreshadowed an amendment to clause 20 which would disallow the Government from making regulations to limit the Special Prosecutor's ability to call for documents. Innes opposed the amendment, claiming that it would put at risk future state or national cases combating organised crime. He wanted the Attorney-General to table his guidelines in Parliament, and for the Special Prosecutor to possess "exceptional forensic skills". He concluded by warning against appointments based on patronage.

In reply, Clauson claimed that clause 20 ensured that sensitive information, to be shared on an intergovernmental basis, would remain confidential. He noted that the Australian Bureau of Criminal Intelligence had, subject to such confidentiality being maintained, supplied material to the Fitzgerald Inquiry. Where documents existed and were relevant, they would be obtained by summons, and where public interest matters were raised by the Crown, precedent suggested that they would be weighted in favour of the accused. He took strong exception to allegations that the Bill was drafted to protect Ministers over accusations concerning their ministerial expenses, and confirmed that he had initiated the approach to Fitzgerald. He concluded by assuring Innes that any suggestion he made as to the Special Prosecutor's appointment would receive consideration.

When the Bill moved into committee, debate centred on clause 20. Clauson rejected Wells's amendment, arguing that the clause, as drafted, was essential to protect both evidence and witnesses at future trials. However, before the amendment was moved, he sidestepped Wells's question as to whether it would be the Attorney-General's decision to withhold certain matters in the public interest. The Liberals combined with the Government and the amendment was defeated by fifty-one votes to twenty-six.

There was now no doubt that the Ahern Government had embraced a reform agenda, and was committed to the Fitzgerald process; but the National Party organisation, together with some backbenchers, remained uneasy. At the time of the Special Prosecutor Bill debate, Fitzgerald's reaction to the unfolding revelations was largely unknown. This Bill therefore marked another stage in an all-consuming process that was to take several years to bring to finality. The Bill was essentially a legal and technical device, but one with very important implications if Lane's confession was to be taken up by the Special Prosecutor and tested in the courts. The Government, while trying to limit any associated damage, was also attempting to put appropriate processes in place — a matter of particular importance in the cases of former Supreme Court Justice Angelo Vasta and District Court Judge Eric Pratt.

Vasta and Pratt

Both Vasta and Pratt had been adversely named in evidence before the Fitzgerald Inquiry; Vasta also faced charges of perjury and tax evasion. Both were strongly identified with the Bjelke-Petersen era, as Vasta was a close friend and confidant of former Police Commissioner Lewis, and Pratt presided over the Police Complaints Tribunal. This body never once found against a police officer and it was largely discredited by civil libertarians, who saw it as a means of "whitewashing" the police force. However, because calling the probity of two judges into question was unprecedented, the Government had no institutional mechanisms at its disposal to cover this question. In one form or another these cases persisted for eight months (from October 1988 to June 1989). The Government was placed under some pressure, because once more, it had to operate in the political and legal twilight zone that existed after the Inquiry ended in December and before the presentation of the Report in July.

Parliamentary involvement began when Clauson, on 25 October 1988, made a ministerial statement, "Security of Tenure and Removal from Office of Judges". It transpired that the Government had taken advice from its senior legal adviser, Ian Callinan QC. Clauson had then written to the Chief Justice and subsequently held discussions with both the Chief Justice and Senior Puisne Judge. As a result, Vasta was stood down. Clauson ended his statement by informing the House that, at this stage, the Government awaited further developments.

The following day Goss directed his two allocated Questions Without Notice to Ahern. He tabled a letter from Vasta to Ahern expressing lack of confidence when supplying confidential material to the Premier, and requesting that the allegations against him be referred to a panel of retired judges. Goss stated that this course of action was supported by the Opposition and the Bar Association. Would the Government move in this direction? Ahern, who was doubtless expecting such a line of questioning, merely replied that the Government was monitoring all Fitzgerald developments and that the matter was under daily review.

At Question Time the next day the issue was again raised. Ahern responded by accusing Vasta of orchestrating a media campaign, and denying that the Government would respond in like fashion. More importantly, he went on to make a ministerial statement, "Mr Justice Vasta", in which he announced that a panel of three retired judges would sit as a tribunal to evaluate the case against Vasta. He affirmed that the Government had no "plan" regarding Vasta, but sought to maintain the integrity of the Bench, and thus public confidence in the judiciary while not wishing to prejudice Vasta's case. Simultaneously he tabled correspondence: Clauson to the Chief Justice; the Chief Justice and Senior Puisne Judge to Clauson; two letters from Fitzgerald to Ahern; and Ian Callinan QC's legal opinion. The next step, less than three weeks later, was to legislate for the tribunal.

On 15 November Clauson introduced the Parliamentary (Judges) Commission of Inquiry Bill. Under Standing Orders, Bills are required to lie on the Table for seven days after their introduction but in this case, the Government took urgency, seeking to pass the Bill immediately through all stages. A week earlier the Attorney-General, in another ministerial statement, "Mr Justice Vasta: Judge Pratt", had foreshadowed this move by assuring the House that the commission would have access to all relevant Fitzgerald Inquiry and Government material, that Goss and Innes had been consulted as to the tribunal's membership, and that it was required to report on Vasta's case by 30 March 1989 and on Pratt by 27 July 1989. Pratt was included in the process although a District Court judge could be removed through a "show cause" procedure. When presenting the Bill, Clauson added that this was a unique piece of legislation, which he hoped would never be repeated. The three retired judges constituting the tribunal would report to Parliament. The evidence they received would be protected and could not be used in other legal proceedings.

In "shock, horror" mode Wells, Innes, Braddy and the National's Beryce Nelson (Aspley) spoke. Wells and Innes each claimed credit on behalf of their respective parties for the Government's move. However, the debate was short and Clauson, in reply, pledged that the consultative process would continue. No serving or retired Queensland judges would be appointed to the tribunal. The Bill then passed all stages without amendment or division.

A similar procedure occurred four months later when, on 15 March 1989, Clauson took urgency on the Parliamentary (Judges) Commission of Inquiry Act Amendment Bill. This was occasioned because secrecy provisions in the Police Complaints Tribunal Act precluded Pratt from adequately briefing counsel, which could prejudice his gaining a fair hearing. Again, while both sides supported what was essentially a machinery Bill, none could forgo the inevitable political point scoring.

The Parliamentary Judges Commission of Inquiry (PJCI) sat and heard evidence. Both Vasta and Pratt were represented by counsel. In their report the PJCI found against Vasta and for Pratt. On 30 May, two months after they were required to make a determination on the Vasta case, Ahern moved a formal motion for Vasta to appear before the Bar of Parliament to answer the PJCI charges and show cause why he should not be removed from office. In his speech, Clauson canvassed such precedents as existed and asserted that the PJCI had been appointed to assist Parliament, not to pre-empt it. Innes complained that Members should have had access to the report before it was discussed in the media, while Goss claimed that the Opposition had forced the Government to delay debating report until Vasta appeared. He accused Ahern "of seeking a public execution" (*QPD* vol. 310, p. 5151) to allow him to project a "tough guy" image and demonstrate that the Government was handling corruption.

Thereafter the debate turned to details of Vasta's appearance before Parliament. Wells thought that a special sitting day devoted to the question could have been avoided, complained about the expense involved (including $3000 a day to each of the judges) and moved an amendment to remove restrictions requiring Vasta to confine his speech to the specific charges. Both Innes and Braddy supported the amendment, with Braddy claiming that seventy-five minutes was insufficient for Vasta, considering what was at stake for him. He contended that Vasta should be granted as much time as he needed, this being the case for any accused person in court or, for that matter, Ministers when introducing legislation.

Ahern countered by citing the time limit of seventy minutes in the 1956 Creighton affair while asserting that, if necessary, an extension of time could be moved. This last brought a riposte from Terry Gygar (Liberal, Stafford) that, if the time could be extended, then no time limit was necessary. He noted that, when Vasta appeared, Parliament would be operating not under standing orders but under the terms of this resolution, which would make any move for an extension of time more complicated. Austin, rather irritably, observed that Parliament was the master of its own destiny and need not be bound by the terms of any prior resolution. The amendment was put, and lost by forty-two votes to thirty-eight (two pairs).

A week later, Vasta appeared and presented his defence before the Bar of the Parliament (*QPD* vol. 310, pp. 5215–60), after which Ahern moved an "Address to His Excellency the Governor: Removal of Mr

Justice Angelo Vasta from Office". The Premier stated that he had found Vasta's explanations unconvincing, being denied by others' testimony. The PJCI had made its findings after a thorough and exhaustive examination, and Vasta could have resigned at any time before the PJCI was established. He attacked Vasta for his persistent claims of a conspiracy against him, involving Fitzgerald, Clauson and the Chief Justice. In accordance with the Fitzgerald guidelines, no findings were made as to costs, while the protection of the judiciary and maintenance of public faith and confidence in it were given paramount importance.

Eighteen other speakers participated, under the gaze of Vasta's family who were seated in the public gallery. None supported Vasta's retention in office, although qualified support came from some quarters. Of the Government speakers, Clauson made a detailed examination and refutation of Vasta's arguments, particularly regarding the Administration Appeals Tribunal (AAT), defamation and conspiracy indictments. He concluded that it was Vasta's extrajudicial activities, rather than the discharge of his judicial office, that had brought him to this situation.

Goss led for the Opposition, condemning the Government's handling of the case. According to him, Labor had forced the Government to the PJCI, and the Government had erred over the question of a time limit. Moreover, he accused Ahern of being part of the process of debauching the judiciary over the failure to appoint Douglas J to the Chief Justiceship (see chapter 3). He considered that Parliament needed more time to reflect upon Vasta's speech, the PJCI report and upon the transcripts thus produced, and moved a seven-day adjournment of the debate.

McElligott seconded the motion, suggesting that the complexity of the tax charges required expert advice rather than a rushed decision. Wells spoke after the amendment was lost (43:38, one pair), and, in a clever speech, said that those accused by Lane should not be judging Vasta who, he claimed, was the "fall guy" for the National establishment which had promoted him. He concluded that "justice rushed is justice ruined".

The last word went to Labor's Deputy Leader, Tom Burns, who, in his own inimitable way, summarised the situation thus:

> Today this Parliament heard an impressive reply of almost two and a half

> hours by Mr Justice Vasta to a unique report that identifies him as a liar, a perjurer, a tax cheat and an unreliable witness, but at the same time finds him to be a good and honest judge. That says something about the judicial system in this state. (*QPD* vol. 310, p. 5337)

No vote was taken on the motion for the Address to the Governor, nor on the consequential Hon. Angelo Vasta (Validation of Office) Bill, which validated his actions as a judge. It also asserted that he had not breached section 12 of the Supreme Court Act after taking $5000 in "consultation fees" in the 1986–87 and 1988–89 tax years from the toilet paper manufacturing company Cosco. Having thus terminated Angelo Vasta's judicial career, the House rose at 3.25 am on 8 June 1989.

It would be an overstatement to suggest that the Government was sorely wounded by the Vasta–Pratt affair. As the separation of powers enables the judiciary to operate independently of the Parliament or the executive, Ahern's Government could not be held directly responsible for these judges' alleged misconduct. Inevitably, Labor linked the Vasta case with the Douglas controversy (see chapter 3) cases to press its broader charge that both Coalition and National Governments had successfully politicised the judiciary. Innes, in debate, rejected allegations of prejudice in relation to Vasta's Italian background, thereby, probably intentionally, drawing attention to it. Innes contended that objections to Vasta's appointment flowed from his possessing no extensive practice in civil law, his comparative youth, and his lack of both experience and standing in the profession. Innes succeeded in demonstrating his snobbishness as a barrister — something he constantly engaged in when attempting to denigrate Wells for lacking professional legal experience. Nevertheless, the circumstances surrounding Vasta's appointment did raise eyebrows and provoke adverse comment. Ahern's Government, however, was not responsible for Vasta's elevation to the Bench.

Ahern's problem was that there were no substantive guidelines or recent precedents for dealing with a judge's removal. Such an event was all but unknown. Ahern has stated (interview 4 September 1997) that his overriding concern was to ensure that the processes were correct. Fitzgerald had initially raised the issue with him, as both recognised what Ahern described as "the potential for disaster" if due process was not observed. This, according to Ahern, was why he extensively consulted with the legal profession, Goss, Innes, Cabinet and the party room. Effectively he had two choices: either Vasta could somehow have been tried by his peers, or the matter could have been handed to Parliament. The latter course of action, given the circumstances of the time, would have politicised the case beyond rehabilitation, miring the Government in endless controversy. By handing the issue over to retired interstate judges, Ahern ensured that both Vasta and Pratt were judged by their peers. When Parliament unanimously accepted both verdicts, it effectively validated this process.

A final question is whether the week's adjournment, as sought by Labor and the Liberals, would have made any substantial difference. It is hard to be dogmatic because further exposure to the documentation and further time for reflection might well have confirmed Members in their initial decision to remove Vasta. Ahern alleged that Labor's caucus had divided fourteen to thirteen on the adjournment option, and he was probably correct. As he saw it, a divided Opposition sought to buy time to come to terms with the PJCI findings.

On the Hansard evidence, only a handful of Members (e.g. Menzel and Mackenroth) might have supported Vasta if a vote had been taken. After a week's elapse, even they might have deserted under their colleagues' or respective leaders' influence. Equally they could have persuaded others to their cause. But it is surely absurd to imagine that, among the seventy who did not speak, a week's delay would have brought forth a groundswell of support for Vasta.

The cases of Vasta and Pratt represented collateral damage from the Fitzgerald Inquiry. The Government had to respond, and in doing so faced only minor criticism about the level of consultation, the cost of the process and the time limit applied to Vasta's speech. In short, the Government's procedures were agreed to. No one either denigrated the processes or argued alternatives. Indeed the Opposition had urged this course on the Government and tried to claim due credit. There had to be a time scale for the PJCI to work through its brief. In Vasta's case it reported promptly, and Pratt's report was brought in two months ahead of schedule. Tactically it might have been wiser for Parliament to have heard Vasta and then, a week later, to have resumed debate as to his fate. On the other hand, its more speedy resolution prevented further delay and uncertainty, although nothing could have saved Vasta from his painful public disgrace.

Pre-election campaigning

While the Government was grappling with the issues of Vasta and Pratt it continued to wrestle with internal problems, which inevitably impacted upon the wider political arena. On 15 October, in his regular *Courier-Mail* column, state roundsman Peter Morley criticised Ahern for failing to initiate positive economic change in Queensland. Five days later, Labor attacked the economic strategy prepared for the Government by the Stanford Research Institute (see chapter 7). Ahern has since defended this report (interview 4 September 1997) as representing the first occasion on which a planning process, as distinct from a series of departmental initiatives, was prepared for Queensland. Austin, on the other hand, was so unimpressed that he quietly rewrote it to give it practical application (interview 7 July 1993).

From 2 November, the ALP ran a number of pre-campaign advertisements, highly critical of the Premier, under the slogan of "Mr Ahern, how could you?". Three mock-up photos depicted Ahern as the three wise monkeys who saw no evil, heard no evil and spoke no evil. The intention was to tie him to the corrupt excesses of the previous Government, in which he had for seven years served as a Minister. This was followed on 6 November by poor poll results showing a decline in Ahern's satisfaction ratings as Premier. More seriously, allegations followed in Parliament on 17 November that there was a spill attempt for the leadership. In all probability this was an exaggerated interpretation of a minor revolt by four of his National opponents led by Bob Katter (Flinders) who was Minister for Northern Development, Community Services and Ethnic Affairs. Always erratic, Katter later claimed, for some inexplicable reason, that he should, and could, have succeeded Bjelke-Petersen. He was abetted by Powell, Tony Burrekett (Townsville) and Menzel. Ahern brushed this plot aside as "laughable". As plotters, they did not constitute a "Gang of Four" but were nevertheless an incubus on the leadership.

As stated above, in 1989 the political New Year began on 19 January when, in a ministerial reshuffle, Leisha Harvey was replaced by Craig Sherrin. Her Health portfolio went to Ivan Gibbs, while Brian Littleproud yielded Education, Youth and Sport to Sherrin and was moved to Family Services. The original Ahern Ministry had lasted thirteen months.

Harvey stood accused of using Health Department moneys for private and party-related expenses, and of appointing relatives and someone with a criminal record to her personal staff. She was later tried, convicted and imprisoned for misusing ministerial expenses. Ahern had acted to quarantine the Government from her inept and illegal behaviour, but he was damaged in the process because he had appointed her and therefore had to accept responsibility. In the wake of these allegations, Labor gleefully released one of their polls which showed Goss leading Ahern as preferred Premier.

Better news came later in the month, with Lane's resignation from the Parliament on 30 January, thereby necessitating a by-election in Merthyr. Rightly or wrongly, Lane had come to personify all that was corrupt and abhorrent during the National Party's time in government. For many, his sobriquet "Shady Lane" was shorthand for the dark side of contemporary Queensland politics.

One week later, when the Parliamentary National Party met for the first time after the Christmas–New Year break, Ahern threatened to sack any Member who publicly criticised him. He would have needed Sparkes' concurrence for this, but resorting to such an extreme threat was evidence that options were being canvassed privately and numbers counted. There were ambivalent signals of Ahern's attitude to the Liberal Party. In an interview with journalists at the end of February he flatly ruled out any coalition, citing what he termed "irreconcilable differences" between the two parties and dismissing the Liberals as "an independent rabble". However, when pressed as to whether this meant that there could be no coalition after the 1989 election, he refused to eliminate this possibility.

Speculation about the leadership continued, with Cooper announcing on 2 March that he was not planning a challenge. At the end of March, Ahern indicated that he would not call an early election, but this brought him little respite. Within the Parliamentary National Party, his enemies were now looking for any issue on which to destabilise and overthrow him. Thus on 8 May, Powell threatened to resign from the National Party because the Government had decided to grant the Education Minister (Sherrin) discretionary powers to re-employ teachers convicted of minor drug possession charges. Despite the gross constitutional impropriety of this public intervention by a Speaker in a political issue, Powell's reactionary stand led to a party-room row, with four Members indicating strong support for his position and refusing to agree with Ahern's initiative. Leaked details of this party-room dispute resulted in speculation in the *Australian Financial Review* (10 July) that Ahern would be vulnerable "on the floor of Parliament if they [the Government] decide to push Powell out".

This was merely the latest incident in the continuing Ahern versus Powell saga. It will be recalled that they were implacable political foes from their backbench days. Powell was prepared to identify with the Bjelke-Petersen forces, while Ahern sought an alternative route to power for himself, and new directions for his party. Although Powell was now Speaker, his determination to thwart his old enemy was in no way diminished as he continued to use his influence, and such prestige as he possessed, to rally the anti-Ahern forces in the National Party. He may even have seen himself as a leader in exile, dedicated to removing the Premier in the interests of restoring the *status quo ante*. His vendetta against Ahern was played out over the next two months, with Ahern rebuking him on 15 May because, despite being Speaker, he continued to involve himself in internal party issues. Three weeks later Powell made good his threat and resigned from the National Party, and one month after that (5 July), and amid uproar in Parliament, he resigned the Speakership, flinging his wig to the floor in a fit of pique.[4] He then sat as an Independent, and in this capacity contested his seat of Isis in 1989. He won only 15 per cent of the primary vote, thereafter exiting public life.

A further charge which increased unease in the National Party was that Ahern's Government was too reformist. Ahern had always been a reformer but, in a party so steeped in the past and especially as personified by Bjelke-Petersen, Ahern faced a task of herculean proportions in attempting to take all sections of his party with him. Because they lacked the formalised factions of the ALP, National Party dissidents could only coalesce into informal and ad hoc cabals, whose numbers waxed and waned according to the particular (if ephemeral) issues that arose to excite their indignation. However, when a permanent group emerged determined to change the leadership, two consequences followed: any issue was seized upon to foment rebellion and swell their numbers, and such elements became permanently alienated from the leadership. Instead they looked both to rank and file and to organisational networks to orchestrate a groundswell of party opinion to support their allegations. They contended that the leadership was too remote, that the party was moving too far from its roots and that its policies were out of touch both with mainstream party sentiment and with traditional issues which had served it well in the past. The coded message was that Bjelke-Petersen had been the "real" leader, Ahern was merely a usurper. The Nationals could prosper only if a legitimate heir to the Bjelke-Petersen inheritance was installed as leader. In retrospect there seems little doubt that, within six months of Ahern assuming the leadership, the dissidents found their protagonist in Cooper.

Merthyr and its consequences

In the meantime, the Government had to fight the Merythr by-election, scheduled for 13 May 1989. Merthyr had traditionally been a Liberal seat. Lane had won it in 1971 at a by-election, called during Bjelke-Petersen's declaration of a State of Emergency to enable the Springbok rugby team to play fixtures in Brisbane and Toowoomba (Harris 1972). Lane, as an ex-Special Branch police officer, was the perfect Liberal candidate for such a law-and-order campaign, and in the absence of a three cornered contest he had duly won and held it as a Liberal. After winning it for the sixth time in 1983, he had switched to the Nationals and in 1986 retained it on Liberal preferences.

For political analysts, the by-election was problematic. Although Merthyr was an urban National seat, it was not one the Nationals had won in their own right in 1983 — although Lane had held it as a National, in 1986, before his disgrace. It was now an open question as to whether the Nationals would keep it, the Liberals would reclaim it, or Labor would win it by capitalising on the "Fitzgerald factor", anti-Lane sentiment and their core support concentrated in the seat's southern (New Farm) booths. Neither of the two previous by-elections offered any predictive assistance. Barambah had been lost, on the day, to a right-wing National defector who had subsequently returned. In South Coast the Government had held off a strong Liberal challenge by the narrowest of margins in the equally disgraced Hinze's former seat. Apart from the three-major party candidates, there was a large field of Others, including Fitzgerald Inquiry identity Gerry Bellino (Dickie 1988, p. 268) and the transgender gay activist, Toye de Wilde. The Liberals again preselected Santo Santoro, later Minister for Industrial Relations in the Borbidge Government. The results are shown in table 8.3.

Table 8.3. Election results for Merthyr 1986 and 1988 (percentages)

Party	1986	1989	Swing
National	32.5	15.9	–16.6
ALP	33.1	32.2	–0.9
Liberal	32.1	35.7	+3.6
Others	2.4	16.2	+13.8

These results suggested that the National Party was being repudiated in Brisbane because of the Fitzgerald revelations, but that neither of the two alternatives was reaping any immediate benefit. Labor's vote was barely static, while the Liberals, although improving on their 1986 vote to lead on first preferences, came in only 2.5 percentage points ahead of the ALP. Their tenuous position could well have been overturned by the preference distribution, as the bulk of the National and Labor voter outflow went to the plethora of Other candidates. In the event, the Liberals gained the seat courtesy of National preferences, which divided 85:15 in their favour. While the Nationals had lost nearly 60 per cent of their 1986 support, the Liberals, however narrow their victory, received a morale boost by increasing their parliamentary representation at the Nationals' expense. As in the two previous by-elections, Labor had been left on the sidelines.

Immediately after the by-election Ahern again ruled out a coalition with the Liberals, apparently feeling that Merthyr was a Liberal seat "going home". Despite the operations of some dissidents his majority was safe, and he retained the confidence of the Parliamentary National Party and the support of the National Party organisation. No further by-elections were expected before the 1989 election, but Ahern now faced clear electoral problems. He could hold Labor at bay in conservative heartland seats, but he could not stop mainstream National voters from drifting elsewhere. In Barambah they had attached themselves to a National rebel, while in South Coast and Merthyr they had gravitated to the Liberals and an array of minor-party and Independent candidates. His Government had to soldier on, having a program to enact; but the Nationals' electoral base was now crumbling, and his internal opponents knew it.

In a sign that the gathering opposition was becoming bolder, Ahern had to communicate a heavy-handed message to the backbench, via Clauson and Gunn, that he would call a snap election if the three known Vasta sympathisers crossed the floor to vote for Goss's seven-day adjournment motion. Although only Mackenroth, in the Labor Party, had offered any support to Vasta, and despite the adjournment motion gaining caucus approval by the narrowest of margins, the National leadership was clearly worried. In the event they held the line. Had they not done so Vasta would still have been removed, but the defections would have been extremely damaging. The media and opposition parties would have trumpeted such a revolt as proof that the Government was split, that Ahern's premiership was in serious contention, that the leadership had arbitrarily imposed its will on the party and that, despite dire warnings to the contrary, some backbenchers were prepared to repudiate Cabinet's position.

An intriguing question is whether Sparkes and the organisation would have supported an early poll. Lacking evidence to the contrary, one may assume that they would have had little choice; but it would not have been a comfortable alternative. Such a snap election could hardly have been fought on Vasta's alleged guilt or innocence. It would have been fought on the Government's leadership, and its competence and ability to carry through the Fitzgerald process. Six months later the election was fought on those issues, but not with Ahern as Premier and National Party leader. The result was an overwhelming rejection of the Nationals.

The Fitzgerald Report

The next matter on the Government's seemingly never-ending, crisis-ridden agenda was the long-awaited debate on the Fitzgerald Report. This was handed to Ahern on 3 July 1989 and extensively reported the following day in the local, national and international media. The parliamentary debate was set down for 6 July and 39 per cent (35) of Members spoke, comprising 16 Nationals, 14 Labor and five Liberals. Although Labor and the Liberals protested, the debate was adjourned after a division (43:34). Despite the customary motion to adjourn the debate "to the next day of sitting", Parliament never again considered the Fitzgerald Report, save through consequent legislation.

If the Fitzgerald Inquiry and subsequent report were a defining moment, in Queensland politics, the debate on the Fitzgerald Report failed to be such an event for the Queensland Parliament. The debate had been eagerly anticipated, because Parliament had been in an anomalous position during the inquiry. The evidence had been fully covered and discussed in the media but any parliamentary debate had been prevented by the Speaker, who had ruled that all Fitzgerald material was sub judice. Thus the one forum where, under privilege, Fitzgerald-related issues could have been discussed and commented upon was effectively gagged. This did not stop Fitzgerald from having numerous, wide-ranging confidential discussions with the Premier and senior Ministers, but the Parliament was excluded.

Just as the Report was long, wide-ranging and multi-targeted, so also was the debate broad and multi-themed. As might be expected, some Members pursued parochial and/or personal concerns, but most speeches resonated to the wider concerns. The speakers, naturally, did not confine themselves exclusively to any one area, most concentrating on those aspects they thought pertinent. The themes fell into five broad categories:

- praise for the Government for establishing the inquiry and for its commitment to the Report's implementation

- condemnation of the Government, which was seen as corrupt and/or incompetent
- police affairs
- electoral issues
- parliamentary reform.

Praise for Government

Ahern had repeatedly committed the Government to implementing the Report "lock, stock and barrel", and he reiterated these sentiments when introducing the debate. He said that he was proud to have been part of a Government which had established the Inquiry; that corruption was not limited to recent times and his Government had been praised by Fitzgerald. He committed the Government to three key recommendations: the Electoral and Administrative Review Commission (EARC), the Criminal Justice Commission (CJC), and parliamentary committees. (A significant omission here was any commitment to electoral reform.) As to the two commissions: "Work has commenced on a draft bill to achieve that end". This legislation would go before the next sitting of Parliament, to be called (early) on 29 August 1989. He charged that, while Goss was trying to subvert EARC by demanding a timetable for electoral reform, "I will deliver and I will deliver fully" (*QPD* vol. 312, p. 5566).

Other Government contributors lauded the report as a model for Australia. The Nationals should be re-elected because only they had the will and capacity to implement it. They claimed that corruption was worse elsewhere, and asserted that there was no linkage between corruption and the zonal system of vote weightage. Fitzgerald, in their opinion, should have concentrated on drugs and pornography.

Condemnation of the Government

While various Government Members were busily congratulating themselves on the Fitzgerald process and their commitment to reform, they were being attacked for past corrupt practices, and/or their failure to possess any credible commitment to the implementation of the report's recommendations. Thus Goss, leading for the Opposition, criticised Ahern for a brief speech lacking in specifics. He alleged that the

Premier did nothing to combat corruption during his twenty years as part of the Bjelke-Petersen Government, and had never acted on allegations of corruption raised by Goss, Casey, Kev Hooper (late ALP Member for Archerfield) or anyone else. He accused Ahern of continuing to use public money to run self-promoting Government advertising when Fitzgerald had said that the propriety of this should be examined by a Parliamentary committee, and of continuing to use taxpayer's money to fund Bjelke-Petersen's writs against Labor Members. Gunn, he alleged, had only established the inquiry to provide himself with credentials to succeed Bjelke-Petersen.

Goss accused Ahern of not being genuine about Parliamentary reform, as it had taken him twelve months to establish the PAC and then he had weakened its operations by introducing a ministerial veto. Finally, he considered the Parliamentary Pecuniary Interests Register flawed because it allowed Members to transfer their assets to their spouses without any declaration. Ahern, under Sparkes's direction, had refused to commit his Government to electoral reform before the next election, whereas Labor's timetable would ensure electoral reform by 18 November, well in time for the forthcoming election.

Other Labor speakers added that there had been no meaningful consultation in the past so Ahern could not be trusted to consult over CJC and EARC. They were convinced the Government would never deliver on electoral reform, and was not genuine in its reform agenda. All governments after 1957, they maintained, were rife with entrenched cronyism which bred corruption, and the old practices could be eradicated only by an incoming Labor Government.

Police matters

A major sub-theme raised in the debate was the question of the police force (now termed Police Service), because it was corruption originating in the Licensing Branch that had triggered the Inquiry. Gunn, who spoke after Ahern, detailed corruption in Queensland during the 1940s and 1950s. He saw problems with police culture, which had defeated reform plans during the tenure of a former Police Minister Max Hodges (Gympie) and Police Commissioner Ray Whitrod. When reforms were proposed, the Police Union would secretly go to Bjelke-

Petersen who would then veto any reform. When Gunn became Police Minister in February 1986 he had heard rumours of corruption. His suspicions were aroused over the next twelve months from anonymous tip-offs and other information. The screening of the ABC Four Corners program, "The Moonlight State", and especially ex-policeman Nigel Powell's revelations, had triggered the Inquiry. Some reforms were now in place, including the videotaping of evidence, Neighbourhood Watch, an increase in police numbers and better police housing.

Other speakers, perhaps surprisingly, only tangentiality referred to police issues, although Cooper launched into an orgy of self-congratulation over his administration of the portfolio.

Electoral issues

The theme of electoral reform was essentially a rerun of all previous parliamentary debates on the subject. National rural backbenchers, who had greatly profited from the operations of the zonal system of vote weightage, vigorously defended it, denying its link to corruption and bitterly denouncing the report and the ALP for claiming otherwise. Labor speakers presented reverse mirror-image arguments and challenged the Government's "lock, stock and barrel" commitment on this cardinal recommendation.

Parliamentary reform

The final theme to be addressed was parliamentary reform. Both Goss and Hamill raised this to attack the Government, and the two main Liberal speakers, Innes and White, also concentrated on it. Innes saw the report as challenging all parties to continue working together to implement reform by means of a committee system. He therefore wanted the Parliamentary Committee for Electoral and Administrative Review (PCEAR) chosen now, and EARC and the CJC to be established as soon as possible. He asked for all-party negotiations to choose the consultants to advise on CJC and EARC personnel. He thought that, if small groups of Members worked together, they would develop an obligation to pursue justice and fairness. He foresaw a dilemma in that, if the election cut across the parliamentary reform timetable, such reforms could be delayed for a further five months.

White reviewed some of his experiences, claiming that the Liberals had been fighting corruption from the late 1970s and citing the efforts of former Liberal Members Bruce Bishop (Surfers Paradise) and Peter White (Southport) as examples.[5] In 1983 and 1986, White claimed, Bjelke-Petersen and the Nationals had coerced business into funding the Nationals' election campaigns. Because of this, he supported the public funding of political parties for campaign purposes. He condemned the Pecuniary Interests Register as a "farce", both because of its loopholes and because of its failure to include the chairs of statutory authorities and heads of government departments. In view of Lane's allegations, all past and present Ministers should be investigated by the Australian Taxation Commissioner. He concluded by making unspecified allegations of phone tapping and a Government-inspired "dirty tricks" campaign, while at the same time criticising the report for wanting limitations placed on parliamentary privilege.

The debate was comprehensive and wide-ranging, and displayed some interesting patterns. The Government was clearly in a dilemma over electoral reform. No one had predicted that Fitzgerald would raise this issue, let alone make it a central priority of his Report. Although he did not directly advocate such reform, he recommended that EARC investigate the electoral system as its first priority. Cabinet, by way of response, hinted only that the Government would take the matter up, but not before the forthcoming election. Labor, however, produced a timetable and a plan which purported to show that it could be done by mid-November. The Liberals chose not to participate directly in this aspect of the debate, while sections of the Government backbench, especially those from rural seats, were both hostile and resentful towards the Report. For years Sparkes and the National Party organisation had defended vote weightage; and at his first press conference as Premier, Ahern had told reporters that electoral reform was not on his agenda. This issue had never been expected to form part of the Report's recommendations, so the Government possessed no contingency plans to deal with it. Ahern's dilemma over this question, and his ineffectual attempts to deal with it, proved lethal to his premiership.

The Government's claim that it could be trusted to implement Fitzgerald reforms would have been more credible if Ahern had been more specific in debate; if his senior Ministers (with the exception of Cooper) had been more forthcoming as to their own portfolio responsibilities; if Clauson had been more focused and less inaccurate; and if the backbench had displayed any appreciation of the task ahead of them. Of the eleven backbenchers who spoke, only one (Hobbs) explicitly supported any of Fitzgerald's recommendations. The others defended the zonal system, denied that the level of corruption was worse in Queensland than elsewhere, attacked the Liberals, or merely ignored the report to pursue parochial concerns. Typical was the "contribution" of Burreket, who congratulated the Townsville police for not being mentioned in the report, and proceeded to make a series of unsubstantiated allegations of corruption against the (ALP-controlled) Townsville City Council. With debate waged at this level, Ahern was clearly presiding over a backbench which did not, or could not, appreciate that the old Queensland political order, to which they owed so much, was now passing.

Significantly, no Minister addressed either electoral matters or parliamentary reform. Instead they limited themselves to self-congratulation on establishing the Inquiry, with only Gunn and Cooper deviating to discuss police issues. On the Labor side, only Braddy and Hamill extensively canvassed electoral issues, although the Hamill, together with Goss, did deal with parliamentary reform. The rest were simply vindictive, seeing the Report as the ultimate vindication for all they had criticised, and been subjected to, under the Bjelke-Petersen Government. By rehashing the past, they used the debate to settle old scores.

Had the Government ever reconvened the debate, it is doubtful whether Members would have displayed any greater depth in their understanding of the issues. Ministers might have been better briefed and more positive, especially if Ahern had insisted on this; Labor and the Liberals might, perhaps, have advocated more specific reform proposals. But Ahern had already locked the Government into the general reform process, and an election was only five months away. Ahern has claimed (interview 4 September 1997) that Fitzgerald told him he had never envisaged that electoral reform could be realised before the 1989 election but, when asked by the Premier to state this in public, Fitzgerald refused. Indeed Fitzgerald made only one brief public comment (in Melbourne) after his Report was handed to Government. The Government's position would have been greatly eased had the Report come to it midway through an electoral cycle, or even if Fitzgerald had reported, as originally scheduled, in May. As it was, the timing of the Report and its concentration on electoral matters put the Government under duress as it grappled, in a tight time frame and with a complex reform agenda, a recalcitrant backbench and an emboldened Opposition.

Notes

1. Mr Taylor announced, in October 1997, that he would not contest the next federal election. In the 1998 federal election the Liberals retained Groom despite a National challenge, as they did also in 2001.
2. In this one may see a prefiguring, in rural/National seats, of the rise of One Nation some nine years later.
3. Perrett resigned his portfolio in February 1998 after allegations of his involvement with a prostitute who had been found dead in her home. He lost Barambah to One Nation in the June 1998 state election.
4. As it happened, Powell was the last Speaker ever to wear a wig. Fouras, the Speaker during the Goss Government, refused to do so. Neil Turner, Speaker in the 1996–98 Coalition Government, did not do so — despite flying the Union Jack from the Parliamentary flagpole because, as he said, "I am responsible, through the Governor, to the Queen, for the conduct of the Parliament" [sic].
5. Both Bishop and White had lost their seats to the Nationals in 1980 as a result of the secret National–Labor electoral pact.

CHAPTER 9

Fall

The nature of political leadership

Political leadership is, at base, consensual. Political leaders must first convince their colleagues that they deserve the leadership. They must then persuade voters that they are superior to claimants from rival parties. Their leadership skills are constantly tested in Cabinet, on the floor of Parliament, in the party room, and by their interaction with both their extra-parliamentary party and all relevant interest groups. They must stamp their persona and political style upon their party and Government by way of policies, ideas and modus operandi. Simultaneously this complex process must be communicated, primarily to that section of the public which is attentive to political matters, and also to those who only intermittently and spasmodically attend to events in the political arena. The media, which carry the task of communication, not only report but comment, analyse, discuss and pontificate upon this process as it influences the parameters of public debate, and attempt to direct the political agenda.

When in power the leader personifies the collective will of both party and Government. S/he becomes their spokesperson and facilitator. The leader has to stand separately from the party, hence the pollsters ask their respondents differing questions, the one to evaluate the leader's performance, the other to discern voting intentions. A leader's credibility will often, therefore, be opinion driven. A leader lacking in public trust or confidence will inevitably be viewed by his or her colleagues as an electoral liability. No MP will willingly lose a seat so, if the leader is judged by a significant number of his or her peers to be incapable of winning the next election, moves will be undertaken against the incumbent. If they cannot save the Government, Members will seek to save themselves.

A Premier (or Prime Minister) does, however, possess an array of resources to buttress his or her position. These include:

- control of the Cabinet agenda
- the ability to:
  - appoint and dismiss Ministers
  - deploy patronage to advance or retard one's colleagues' careers
  - set policy
  - persuade party conferences to endorse the leader's ideas, policies and actions
  - play the symbolic and public relations relevant role of first citizen of the state (or nation)
  - accumulate relevant knowledge
  - be briefed with information unavailable to either colleagues or rivals (whether the latter be within or without the party)
  - exercise formal and informal influence across the whole range of governmental activity.

All such resources become available to leaders upon attaining office; paradoxically, however, none can necessarily be relied upon should the balance of numbers within the party shift decisively against the incumbent. Such is the case when a leader is overthrown by internal revolt while the party is in Government; ironically, this was the fate of both Bjelke-Petersen and Ahern.

While each case is different, there appear to be several prerequisites for the mounting of a successful coup. Obviously there has to be a leadership aspirant whose claims are both credible and recognised within the party, often through occupancy of a ministerial position. Additionally, such a challenger requires good interpersonal skills in order to win the loyalty and trust of significant others, and may possess new, interesting and/or novel ideas incorporating a vision for the party's reconstruction or rehabilitation. The challenger must be in possession of a solid power base outside the parliamentary party, whether in the organisational hierarchy or in local branches, while also enjoying popular recognition within the electorate, perhaps owing to publicly approved actions taken elsewhere in the public arena.

Conversely, for the aspirant to succeed, there must be some perception that the incumbent has serious deficiencies of a magnitude that s/he is incapable of addressing. These may be in the realm of policy, style, parliamentary or electoral performance, public trust or credibility. The proximity of an election, or other similar test of political will or resolve, is the final prerequisite for focusing the party's collective will and purpose, ensuring that the leadership question becomes dominant over all other considerations.

Hence the two-edged sword of political leadership: just as the media may personalise politics, so too do the political parties, whether they be in or out of office. The Hawke Government, as well as those of Bjelke-Petersen and Goss, are but three recent examples. When a parliamentary party, and its organisation, believes the leader to be its most important electoral asset, it will elevate this individual above all political considerations.[1] When leadership becomes all-important for achieving power, great expectations are thereby created of the leadership. If these expectations are not fulfilled, or are realised contrary to popular expectations, the result will be popular disenchantment and, concomitantly, electoral punishment.

Ahern had not faced the electorate as Premier and, after the Fitzgerald Report was presented, electoral speculation increasingly dominated Queensland politics as the Government was now perceived to be in crisis mode. Not only had the report totally discredited the Bjelke-Petersen Government and its practices, but the zonal system — the National Party's electoral bulwark — was under notice. Cabinet now faced an acute dilemma. Ahern had repeatedly promised to implement the report, "lock, stock and barrel", but could not have known that the report's highest priority would be the electoral system. The National backbench was now susceptible to revolt. Some had resented the leadership change when Ahern replaced Bjelke-Petersen; others were fearful that the Report's recommendations would cost the Government office and thereby terminate their career aspirations; yet others were afraid of losing their seats. These fears were not mutually exclusive. The fear factor, however expressed, necessarily emerged as a powerful motivation to seek a scapegoat. By now the leader had become the obvious candidate.

As a result of his consensual leadership style and his non-threatening demeanour, Ahern was seen by his backbench enemies as weak and indecisive. He personified the antithesis of the aggressive, confrontational style of political leadership. The practitioners and would-be supporters of the confrontational political and leadership mode forever contrasted him unfavourably with the leadership of Bjelke-Petersen. For them, Ahern's alleged indecisiveness became an electoral cost not to be borne by their party. Additionally the "ultras" blamed him, as they had over his chairing of the Education Select Committee, for shifting to more progressive policies. As his legislative record demonstrates (see chapter 6), Ahern personified the progressive conservative leader. It was inevitable that he would alienate those reactionaries in the National Party who yearned for a return to the verities of the Bjelke-Petersen era. And, by his full commitment to the Fitzgerald Inquiry, Report and subsequent processes, he became an anathema to those in the Parliamentary National Party and organisation who could not, or would not, recognise that a cleansing process was necessary if the public's faith was to be restored to those political institutions that previous National party Ministers had systematically plundered and despoiled.

Referendum and EARC

For the second half of 1989, Queensland politics was dominated by the Fitzgerald Report and the Government's attempts to come to terms with, and implement its major recommendations. It was in this context that the Parliamentary National Party was forced to consider the leadership issue.

If the Fitzgerald Report had come down in May, as originally expected, the Government would have had seven months to investigate the electoral system and redraw the boundaries before 2 December election. It would have been a tight schedule, but could have been done. With the report down in July, there were only five months and Ahern was certain this gave insufficient time to establish EARC, staff and resource it and give it all the time it needed to conduct a thorough examination of the electoral system. He therefore decided to hold a referendum on whether to extend the current (forty-fifth) Parliament's term by six months to enable EARC to do its work on the electoral system, so that in July 1990 the election would be held according to EARC's recommendations, including new boundaries. Cabinet decided to introduce the legislation to facilitate this, together with the Bill to establish EARC, when the House resumed in the first week of August.

Ahern, knowing that his Government would be severely criticised for this tactic, went on the attack. In opening the debate he observed that, although the EARC Bill had been introduced, it would be impossible to have it passed, the Commission established, its personnel appointed, its investigations concluded, its submissions examined, its recommendations finalised and any alterations made to both the boundaries and rolls before the current Parliament was due to expire, on or before 8 January 1990. The proposed legislation would extend Parliament until 8 July 1990 unless it was sooner dissolved. If dissolution did not occur before 25 May 1990, the Governor would be obliged to issue the writs for an election to be held on 7 July 1990. Ahern asserted that this Bill was "an ironclad guarantee of electoral reform" (*QPD* vol. 313, p. 31), locking both Labor and the Liberals into this process. If there was a "Yes" vote, there would be an election on new boundaries on or before 7 July 1990. If a "No" vote was returned, no such election could occur until 1992.

He then charged that the opposition parties were "frauds, hypocrites and phonies". He condemned the ALP on the grounds that it had previously circulated a petition calling for electoral reform and had now reneged. Goss had appeared on the media, in conformity with a three-party agreement that all sides would abide by EARC's electoral recommendations, but, less than twenty-four hours later, his party's faction "heavies" had forced him to back down. Now he would state only that Labor would support EARC if its findings on electoral reform coincided with ALP policy. For his part, Liberal leader Angus Innes was "the Uriah Heep of the electorate of Sherwood". He did not want electoral reform until 1992 because both the Liberals and

Labor were determined to create confusion and misunderstanding among voters. Hyperbole and perhaps desperation were now driving Ahern.

Despite these complaints, the debate on the referendum bill was limited to Goss, Wells, Terry Gygar (Liberal, Stafford) and Clauson. Goss charged that the debate was a sham because the Government knew the referendum would fail. According to Goss, Ahern had broached the idea at the recent National Party Conference but it was leaked to the media; Ahern then panicked, and conference stampeded him into adopting this course of action because the Government possessed no other tactic to resolve its current dilemma over electoral reform. From the time of the Fitzgerald Report, both Labor's and academic opinion was that electoral reform could occur before the 1989 election. Because of poor opinion poll results, the Government had procrastinated, now proposing to extend Parliament's life so that it could regroup. In 1977 the Coalition Government of the time had organised its redistribution in five months; thus, if this Government had the resolve, it could do likewise. With variations, this theme was elaborated upon by the two other opposition party speakers, earning them a short, abusive reply from Clauson. The Bill then passed its second reading by forty-four votes to thirty-five.

It all turned out to be, in Shakespeare's words, "much ado about nothing". A month later (6 September) Ahern was forced to introduce the Constitution (Cancellation of Referendum) Bill to a Parliament that knew his Government was in a state of collapse, as his backbench was now in near open revolt. In a short speech, and without elaboration, he announced the Government's change of mind and stated that this Bill would do as its title suggested.[2]

The major debate of that sitting week in August, however, was undoubtedly the Electoral and Administrative Review Commission (EARC) Bill. In retrospect one is struck by the pervasive air of unreality; the debate was yoked to the referendum proposal, with both issues hopelessly enmeshed. Further, the only aspect of the legislation addressed by the debate was that pertaining to electoral affairs, with each side claiming electoral virtue for itself and accusing its opponents of perfidy. The ALP had now scented victory, realising that Ahern was under strong pressure from the Cooper faction.

In his second-reading speech Ahern reiterated his commitment to Fitzgerald reforms and claimed that only a National Party Government could be trusted to implement this process in full. EARC would consist of five commissioners, and national advertisements were now ready for placement. For the sake of continuity, the initial appointments would be staggered. The first task of EARC would be to investigate the electoral and zonal systems and report by 31 March 1990 so that an election could be held before 8 July on its proposed new boundaries and zones (if any). If the referendum proposed for 14 October was passed, EARC was to report on the zones by 12 December 1989. If the referendum failed, then its investigations would cease, pending an election by 8 January 1990. He concluded by assuring the House that this draft bill, if passed, would lie on the table for public consideration.

Ahern may have been sincere in his desire for consultation, but his Government's political and time constraints precluded this. Cabinet lost its nerve and, seven and a half hours later, Austin took urgency on the Bill so debate was brought on immediately and it was debated across two days, 9 and 10 August. The Government put up four other speakers, Labor nine and the Liberals three.

Curiously, the Government contented itself with four backbenchers, whose brief appeared to be to attack Labor (state and/or federal) and defend the zonal system. Innes, for the Liberals, again attacked the lack of consultation, further claiming that the referendum was a ploy for the Government to buy time, and criticised the fact that the Bill specified eighty-nine seats. He reminded the House that the Liberals had, in 1985, opposed raising the number of seats from eighty-two to eighty-nine.

Three themes dominated Labor's speeches: the consultative procedures, electoral reform and "cronyism". As to the first, Goss cited the Opposition's lack of trust in the Government, stemming from the appointment of the Vasta–Pratt commissioners. Dean Wells (Murrumba) predicted that a similar procedure to that for Vasta and Pratt would be employed, namely a ten-minute warning beforehand.

As electoral reform was central to the EARC Bill, this received detailed attention. Goss also questioned both why the legislation tied EARC to eighty-nine seats and contained fourteen references to the zonal system. He thought this indicated a lack of commitment to reform, especially should the referendum be defeated. He further alleged that Sparkes was confident that EARC would retain the zonal system and, if the referendum was defeated, the Nationals would then claim that the zonal system was not an issue for voters.

The Fitzgerald Inquiry had revealed networks of corruption throughout public life in Queensland, and the EARC Bill gave legislative expression to the central concerns of the Fitzgerald Report. The ALP therefore raised the matter of cronyism to damage the Government, specifically arguing that appointments to EARC would be no different from those for other Government statutory authorities and QANGOs. Thus Tom Burns alleged that Sparkes dominated Ahern through Wendy Armstrong, a theme embroidered upon by Terry Mackenroth (Chatsworth), who predicted that the Government would stack EARC with "stooges" (*QPD* vol. 313, p. 164).

Ahern did not reply extensively to the debate, limiting himself to reiterating that it was impossible to have a comprehensive, Fitzgerald-inspired EARC boundary and zonal system review between 9 August and the next election. This was why the Government had requested a six-month extension of office to achieve this goal. The Bill was read a second time, and passed by forty-three votes to thirty-eight with the Liberals voting with Labor. However, this version of the EARC legislation was aborted, its fate being effectively sealed when the Government reneged on the referendum. A second Bill was put to the Parliament by the Cooper Government and formed the legislative basis for EARC and its subsequent activities.

While the conjoining of EARC and the proposed referendum illustrated both the confusion in Government ranks and the inability of sections of the National Party to come to terms with the new order, it was the quintessentially parochial issue of daylight saving that triggered Ahern's fall.

Renewed pressure

Once the House rose from considering these Bills, Ahern fell under near-constant pressure. A parliamentary sitting week scheduled for the end of August was cancelled, probably to avoid open revolt in the Parliamentary National Party over daylight saving. After first rejecting calls to experiment with daylight saving, the Government responded to pressure from the business lobby and South-East Queensland opinion, by deciding to trial it over the forthcoming summer. On 25 August it was reported that the National Party Management Committee had "grilled" Ahern over the decision — a sure sign that the party was divided. The balance of opinion within the National Party was opposed to daylight saving because its senior officials, who wielded power within the organisation, were overwhelmingly from rural areas. They were joined by National Members representing northern and western Queensland electorates. But those in the Parliamentary National Party who represented South-East Queensland and urban seats were, if not publicly in favour, very much at the mercy of pressure from business and urban interests. So also were Ahern and his senior lieutenants, given the intimate and ongoing links forged between the Government and business community — networks dating both from the Bjelke-Petersen era and Ahern's time as Minister for Industry, Small Business and Technology (see above).

After this "grilling", matters came to a head as both sides utilised the media to bolster their support and argue their case. Over the weekend of 26–27 August, speculation was rife that Ahern "was just hanging on" (*Courier-Mail*, 26 August 1989). The following day, 27 August, the three key plotters, Russell Cooper, Paul Clauson and Bob Katter resigned from Cabinet,[3] citing "lack of leadership". Ahern responded by vowing to fight off any leadership challenge. This eventuated 24 hours later when, in the party room, Cooper moved a leadership spill. Ahern defeated him twenty-six to twenty-one, thus buying time. Immediately after this win (largely attributable to Austin, who did Ahern's numbers), Ahern blamed Bjelke-Petersen for fomenting the revolt, and stripped him of his package of retirement benefits.

Although Ahern had won, it was a Pyrrhic victory. As Bill Hayden had found in 1983 (and in an experience yet to befall Bob Hawke), the only way to win a leadership contest is decisively and comprehensively. A narrow win makes no converts, and only allows the opposition time to regroup, work on the waverers and await a more propitious opportunity. Ahern's margin of five was far too narrow. Had only three of his supporters changed, he would have lost. Paradoxically, a challenger can afford the narrowest of wins as s/he can then consolidate, using the prestige and patronage the office brings. For career reasons former opponents of the new order tend to swing over, leaving the previous incumbent isolated, surrounded by an ever-dwindling band of loyalists.

While Ahern was doubtless correct in discerning the hand of Bjelke-Petersen in the Cooper challenge, and while sections of the media were wont to depict Cooper as a "Joh clone" because of his rural background, lack of sympathy for the Fitzgerald process[4] and right-wing social views, the danger to Ahern was more substantial than Bjelke-Petersen's baleful urgings from the sidelines. Rather, this threat lay within the Parliamentary National Party where pro-Bjelke-Petersen sentiment was only one element. Other factors were opposition to his policy direction and leadership style, confusion over the Fitzgerald Report's targeting of the electoral system, and daylight saving. Thus while Ahern's actions towards Bjelke-Petersen were designed to show leadership strength towards an implacable foe, they further incited his internal enemies; while outsiders, who were ignorant of the details, tended to view his actions as petty and needlessly vindictive.

When Ahern announced the cancellation of the referendum on 30 August speculation concerning a new challenge commenced immediately, fuelled by another statement from Cooper strongly critical of the leadership. On 31 August Ahern announced his third (and final) Ministry, which lasted a mere twenty-six days. Tony Fitzgerald (Lockyer) was brought into Justice, Huan Fraser (Springwood) went to Industry, Small Business and Technology and Administrative Services, while Tom Gilmour (Atherton) received Community Services, Ethnic Affairs and Northern Development. There were some consequent reallocations, but the changes were merely cosmetic. No one believed that Cooper would let the matter rest after his narrow defeat, and his next challenge was expected sooner rather than later. Ahern's only hope was to hold the line until he called the 1989 election. This event would rally the party, focusing its collective efforts on a fight for survival. In this event,

Ahern's best tactic to silence his internal critics would have been to mount a strong campaign around the implementation of Fitzgerald reforms. If the Nationals won, either in their own right or by re-forming the coalition, a new government under his leadership would necessarily be locked into the Fitzgerald process.

In reality, while such considerations inspired the Government's reversal over the referendum proposal, it now appeared weak and indecisive. Ahern's best, and perhaps only, option was to call an early election immediately after Cooper's first defeat. This had been threatened by Sparkes on 2 June 1988 after an early flurry of leadership speculation, and although Ahern had ruled out an election then, he was not bound to that decision now. In any event, an election in September would have been only three months ahead of schedule. It would have stifled opposition from within the organisation, and capitalised on widespread public support for Ahern rather than Cooper as Premier.[5]

Undoubtedly this would have been a high-risk strategy, with the National Party now severely divided over Fitzgerald and daylight saving. Whether or not Sparkes could have vetoed this option is difficult to determine. However, given that two years earlier he could not prevent the "Joh for PM" movement, by the late 1980s his power to block a determined Premier might have been more apparent than real. In the time lapse between the two Cooper challenges, he appears to have become convinced, or to have convinced himself, that Cooper was the preferred option, allegedly because Cooper would be more successful in holding National heartland seats.[6] If this indeed was the basis of Sparkes's reasoning, then the 1989 election was already lost.

By the end of August Ahern had faced down the Cooper challenge but had won the support of only 55 per cent of the Parliamentary National Party. The whole party was now divided over any number of issues, including daylight saving, the Fitzgerald Report, the electoral system and, of course, the leadership. Parliament, on 5 September, resumed for the last time under Ahern's premiership. In an event that had been widely expected, Goss immediately moved a Want of Confidence motion in the Premier and Treasurer, with a speech designed to highlight the obvious disarray in Government ranks.

According to Goss, instability in Government needed to be resolved by Parliament and not by Sparkes, who could support whoever he pleased for the leadership. The EARC Bill had passed through Parliament, the Government now said that EARC's powers should be "severely qualified" (*QPD* vol. 313, p. 305). Thus, he said, the first Fitzgerald reform had been "sold out". The Government's inquiry into trade union corruption was "shonky" because its first choice as commissioner, Rob O'Regan QC, had withdrawn. Any corrupt union official would be prosecuted by an ALP government. The referendum "shambles" had occurred because Sparkes opposed electoral reform, therefore the election had to be held on zonal boundaries. The Government had stacked the Queensland Investment Development Corporation (QIDC) board because, despite aiming for rural representation, it had appointed five members based in Brisbane or South-East Queensland. Finally if the Government had nothing to hide, as it claimed, why did it not produce ministerial expenses and cash advance accounts?

Ahern replied by delineating the hardship caused by the nationwide airline pilots' strike that was taking place, and the federal government's "inaction" in response to it. Queensland's economy was the strongest it had been in years, with unemployment declining and 150 000 new jobs created. Labor, he predicted, would wind up the trade union inquiry to protect its union friends. The Government had received legal opinion from senior counsel (a Mr Finnis), to the effect that it had to ensure EARC did not become a Star Chamber with inquisitorial powers, thereby destroying the integrity of public service advice to Ministers. He denied the existence of a QIDC loan scandal and said that the issue of ministerial expenses was being handled by professionals, not by politicians. These two speeches established the parameters of the debate, with later contributions trading charge and countercharge across the Chamber as the parties moved into campaign mode.

Innes and Sir William Knox (Nundah) spoke for the Liberals. Innes acknowledged the criticism of the Government, but would not support the No Confidence notion. He claimed that Labor was negotiating with disgruntled Nationals; that it was necessary to bring down a state budget before the election to ensure proper financial planning for 1990;

and, with great originality, he attacked Labor for having trade union affiliates.

Five further speakers rose for Labor. Their dominant theme was the Government's imminent demise. Burns analysed the Ahern–Cooper contest by pointing out that Ahern had twenty-six votes, twenty from Cabinet, the Speaker, the Chairman of Committees and six backbenchers; now eleven Liberals would keep him in power. Clauson, on television, had described Ahern as "dopey"; but that applied to Clauson himself, as neither he nor Cooper could obtain the required numbers. Ahern's enemies were Cooper, Clauson, Katter, Yvonne Chapman, Max Menzel and Leisha Harvey.

Bob Gibbs (Wolston) openly jeered at the Nationals and Liberals, correctly predicting that at the 1989 election, the Liberals would lose Redcliffe, Ashgrove, Nundah, Mt Isa, Yeronga and Stafford. The Liberals, according to him, supported the Government only because they needed National preferences in Brisbane seats.

But it was Paul Braddy (Rockhampton) who made the most telling point of the debate. He pointed out that most backbenchers ignored the Premier when he rose to speak, no National speakers either praised or defended Ahern, and few even bothered to join the debate.

Braddy was correct in that, of the five other Nationals, only three backbenchers spoke. Of the two Ministers who rose, Vince Lester made a rambling speech about economic development in Queensland, while Austin alone directly supported Ahern. He claimed that ALP policy would prevent it from supporting EARC's establishment and that of the CJC.[7] With some credibility, he attacked Labor for wanting to expedite the Fitzgerald legislation when the Government wanted to ensure sufficient time for full consideration. He was, however, deflected by the following exchange:

> Hamill: Are you running for leader now, Brian?
>
> Austin: No, I am not. Members of the media should get that clear: no, I am not. (*QPD* vol. 313, p. 331)

Under standing orders, this motion was treated as a discussion rather than a debate, and hence no vote was taken. However, had one been permitted, the Liberals would have supported the Government, which they did when Ahern then moved a Motion Without Notice to debate the airline pilots' dispute. Leave was granted (57:29), thereby allowing the conservative parties the opportunity to outdo each other in attacking the Commonwealth, and seeking to implicate the Queensland ALP in their campaign against the Hawke Government.

Daylight saving

The last legislative matter to which the Ahern Government turned its attention was the Daylight Saving Bill, notable because it is one of the few issues to split all parties along regional lines. (It has never seriously been revisited since the Goss Government held a referendum on daylight saving in 1992, declaring that it would be bound by the result. The referendum was defeated.)

On 6 September Ahern introduced the Bill, noting that he had announced on 21 August that daylight saving would be trialled for the 1989–90 summer to give Queensland uniformity with New South Wales and Victoria. Daylight saving had previously been trialled in Queensland from 31 October 1971 to 27 February 1972, and this legislation was therefore based on the 1971 Act. Because daylight saving was problematic for northern and western Queensland, a representative task force would be established to consider submissions from community organisations and report to the Government at the end of the trial period. The Government would then make a decision on the future of daylight saving.

For the Opposition, Goss supported the legislation, seeing recreational benefits for South-East Queensland and also for those involved in the media, business, banking and financial industries. The disadvantages were for people, in northern and western Queensland, particularly those with children. He observed that it was typical of the Government that daylight saving was introduced in a tortuous and incompetent fashion. First, there was controversy over whether it should be introduced. Then the Government leaked information that it would hold a trial. Next Sparkes had lobbied Cabinet, which subsequently went cool on the idea, but finally moved to introduce it when market research showed that the trial enjoyed wide public support.

Gygar, for the Liberals, spoke fulsomely and with hyperbole, extolling the benefits daylight saving would bring. According to him, Brisbane Lord Mayor Sallyanne Atkinson and Angus Innes had led the campaign for the trial, and should now receive the credit for its introduction.

Four further speakers, all from north Queensland, participated and demonstrated their problems with the issue. Keith De Lacy, as Shadow Treasurer, acknowledged daylight saving's economic benefits but, as Member for Cairns, was conscious that lifestyles in Far North Queensland would suffer. Cairns, while nearly 500 km west of Brisbane, is also west of Charleville; so what is appropriate for the state's south-east does not necessarily apply to its far north. Peter Beard gave another geography lesson, observing that Townsville is due north of Augathella, but Mt Isa is another 960 kilometres to the west. His electorate of Mt Isa is closer to Adelaide than to Brisbane, so Mt Isa should be on South Australian time. Smith had reservations about daylight saving for Townsville, but rejected the argument of two time zones because of the sparseness of the population in the non-daylight-saving zone. Vince Lester summed up the general sentiment of these speakers by stating that, while he personally was against daylight saving, he would support both the trial and the subsequent consideration of all resulting options. The Bill was read a second time without division and immediately proceeded through its committee and third-reading stages.

The daylight saving legislation had papered over the cracks in the Parliamentary National Party while Parliament was sitting. The provision for a task force, while consonant with Ahern's general consultative style, was a sop to National Party backbench and organisational hostility that the Government had even raised the question. His internal enemies could now promote this initiative as displaying further evidence that the Premier was out of step with party policy and sentiment, that he was continuing to take the party further from its heartland issues, that he was too much influenced by urban and South-East Queensland interests, and that he was an ideological Trojan Horse within his party. But they could not, with any credibility, attack his National Party provenance or his rural credentials.

Pressure on Ahern continued to mount, however. On 7 September he alleged that a newspaper vendetta was being waged against him. On

9 September senior Nationals participated in a telephone conference over the leadership. On 10 September the *Sunday Mail* featured an article extolling Ahern's fifty achievements as Premier; but by 20 September Cooper's supporters claimed to have gained the numbers, and successfully overthrew him on 25 September.

The National Party leadership was thus fought out over an extended period, and in a variety of political theatres. Instability had begun with the political demise of Bjelke-Petersen, which by December 1987 had become a necessity rather than option for the National Party. Bjelke-Petersen, Lane and Hinze represented a formidable trio of opponents in Ahern's early days, although Austin proved to be a loyal and effective lieutenant.

It is somewhat unclear why support coalesced around Cooper, who was a relative newcomer and had made no political impact until promoted by Ahern. He was a grazier and graingrower, whose background was, for the National Party, as orthodox as it was unremarkable. Perhaps, as with Ahern before him, he entered Parliament determined to take over the leadership, and hence was prepared to take the necessary political risks to attain his goal. Possibly his typical and unexceptional background gave him particular intra-party appeal when contrasted with the policy innovations and consultative leadership style that characterised his predecessor. Ahern now believes that the most damaging attack he sustained within the party was that put about by Cooper's supporters: that "you cannot trust Ahern to control Fitzgerald" (interview 4 September 1997). If true, this charge amply demonstrates the air of unreality which had descended upon the National Party after the Fitzgerald Inquiry and Report.

By the last part of 1989 the Nationals effectively had two choices. They could follow Ahern down the "lock, stock and barrel" path, taking over the Fitzgerald agenda and, in making it their own, expiate their past by carving out a future characterised by a cleansing of the political processes. Alternatively, they could adopt a minimalist approach, taking as much from Fitzgerald as was electorally expedient, relying on the zonal system, a rampant law-and-order campaign couched in flamboyantly exaggerated anti-Labor rhetoric,[8] thereby reverting to the old political devices of the Bjelke-Petersen era. The second option was predicated on the belief that such a traditional approach would sustain them in power, if necessary in coalition with the Liberals, who were now more than ready to escape their political wilderness. Nine weeks before the 1989 election the National Party chose this second alternative. In all probability they would have lost the 1989 election under Ahern's leadership,[9] but they might thereby have experienced a more dignified exit from power. However, nobility in defeat was never an ambition of the Queensland National Party.

Notes

1. Bob Hawke believed that he possessed a special rapport with the voting public, the more so when he won the 1990 federal election. When twice challenged by Paul Keating for the leadership, publicly this was his chief (perhaps sole) justification for attempting to withstand the challenge. After 1986, Bjelke-Petersen was utterly convinced that no one else could lead the Nationals, and indeed the nation; hence his ill-starred quest for the Prime Ministership, the prelude to his overthrow. One is thereby drawn irresistibly to the aphorism of the Ancient Greeks that those whom the gods wish to destroy, they first make mad. Goss, while not replaced until after the 1995 election, faced a series of semi-related electoral revolts which brought his Government to its knees. When the ALP lost the Mundingburra re-election in 1996 it accepted the inevitable, gave way to the Coalition and Goss stepped down (as had his predecessor, Nev Warburton, after the 1986 election). At the time Goss's perceived arrogance and distance from popular concerns was widely blamed for this reversal in his Government's fortunes. All three leaders had run highly personalised election campaigns during their periods of incumbency. Thus did asset turn to liability.
2. It fell to Cooper, the day after he overthrew Ahern (26 September), to complete the referendum's funeral rites. Wells saw it as a historic occasion, being the only time when a referendum was both called and cancelled. It represented a waste of money for no purpose. The Government's incompetence was thus proven, while Cabinet was now full of Cooper cronies who had been, "paid back for dumping Ahern" (*QPD* vol. 313, p. 734). Innes, as usual, claimed all virtue for the Liberals, maintaining that they were the only party to have seen through the referendum by consistently opposing it. Cooper placed the blame on the opposition parties for "denying Queenslanders the opportunity to have the next election fought on new boundaries" (*QPD* vol. 313, p. 734). He maintained that his Government was left with no other choice but to withdraw the legislation.

3. Katter, ranked eleventh in the Ministry, held the portfolios of Community Services and Ethnic Affairs; Clauson (thirteenth) held Justice, Attorney-General and Corrective Services while Cooper (sixteenth) was now Minister for Administrative Services, Emergency Services and Police.
4. Cooper declared during the 1989 election campaign that, with passage of EARC and CJC legislation, the Fitzgerald process was finished. His attitude towards the CJC when back in Government (following the Memorandum of Understanding he concluded with the Police Union, and his role in the debacle of the Carruthers and Connolly–Ryan Inquiries), demonstrated his less-than-wholehearted support for the post-Fitzgerald process.
5. The day before Ahern was overthrown (24 September) an ANOP poll showed that two-thirds of National voters preferred Ahern to Cooper. Similarly, on 5 October *Queensland Country Life* published a poll it had commissioned, which revealed that in National heartland a strong majority preferred Ahern to Cooper. Significantly, 67 per cent said that Sparkes "had too much power".
6. On 21 September (four days before the successful challenge) Sparkes threatened to resign as National President if Cooper was defeated. In the first challenge he refrained from publicly supporting either candidate.
7. This specious claim brought an interjection from Hamill, "Are you hallucinating again?" (*QPD* p. 313, p. 329).
8. Cooper claimed during the 1989 campaign that, should Labor be elected, homosexuality would be legalised and Queensland would be flooded with thousands of gays and lesbians. Apparently, prior to the advent of the Goss Government, no such persons existed in Queensland.
9. Ahern has claimed (interview 4 September 1997) that he commissioned an exit poll on election day, 2 December 1989, which showed that, had he remained Premier, the Nationals would have won sufficient seats to re-form Government in coalition with the Liberals. In the absence of any methodological details or examination of the results, this claim is impossible to verify. However, given the magnitude and extent of the swing to Labor (Reynolds 1990), such a claim should be treated with scepticism.

CHAPTER 10

Aftermath and assessment

In 1989 Mike Ahern won his ninth election victory in Landsborough, although Labor won Government with a nineteen-seat majority (Reynolds 1990).[1] However, Ahern was not widely expected to serve his full parliamentary term. It is customary in the National Party for a leadership ballot to be held immediately after an election. When the party went into Opposition, Ahern challenged Cooper for the leadership and lost, such an outcome turned his thoughts towards an early retirement. He took his seat in the forty-sixth Parliament as an Opposition backbencher, a position he had never before occupied.

He was now forty-eight and had been a Member for twenty-one years. After his re-election he took his family on a touring holiday of New Zealand and, with them, considered his options. In 1990 Labor confidently expected to be at least a two-term Government, and while Ahern's internal opponents were no longer pursuing him, their latent hostility could easily be reactivated should he seek office within the Parliamentary National Party. Cooper, while not particularly popular among his colleagues, was not widely blamed for the Nationals' first electoral defeat since 1955. Besides, as the leadership ballot demonstrated, those who sought Cooper's replacement were unlikely to turn to Ahern, with any future challenge being more likely to originate from Cooper's ambitious deputy, Rob Borbidge (Surfers Paradise), another younger National promoted by Ahern.[2]

Ahern's relative youthfulness, the longevity of his parliamentary service, his credentials as a competent, innovative, hard-working Minister and Premier, together with his being untainted by corruption or scandal ensured that he could expect a successful career after politics should he so choose. He had little to gain from waiting on the Opposition backbench for a National revival under the leadership of others. Should that occur, the most he could realistically expect would be a Cabinet post or, perhaps, the Speakership. Having been Premier, such positions could be viewed only as meagre consolation prizes, and even then, by no means assured.

Over the holiday period he made up his mind; but before retirement, he was presented with one final political opportunity. Keith De Lacy, the new Treasurer, acting from bravado born of inexperience, conducted a journalists' lock-up so they could examine confidential Treasury papers. These purported to show that, owing to the financial policies of the previous Government, Queensland's budgetary position was a great deal worse than either Labor or the public had been led to believe. When, in the first session of the 1990 Parliament, the matter came on for debate, Ahern made what many considered to be one of his finest parliamentary speeches. So effectively did he defend his record as Treasurer, and the fiscal policies of his Government, that De Lacy's case was demolished; the Goss Government never revisited allegations that it had inherited an unsound and unstable economy. Ahern had thus been presented with a satisfactory ending to his political career.

He resigned his seat on 16 May 1990, and thereafter played no further role in state politics. It was a supreme irony, given the events that had surrounded the 1968 Landsborough by-election (see chapter 1), that the 1990 Landsborough by-election should be won by the Liberals in the person of Joan Sheldon. In the subsequent EARC redistribution Landsborough disappeared, being divided between Caloundra and Nicklin. The latter, comprising the rural section of Landsborough, had been named (aptly from Ahern's viewpoint) for his predecessor and former mentor.

After leaving Parliament, Ahern commenced a successful business career. He maintained the interest acquired during his ministerial days in technology and satellite communication by establishing his own firm, Space Transportations Systems. His career had spanned a remarkable period in Queensland politics.

Even as late as the mid-1980s, the *ancien régime* of which he was a part seemed to be indestructible, yet it was abruptly terminated by the Fitzgerald Inquiry and Report. While Ahern had advocated reform within the political context of his times, it was well beyond the efforts of any single individual to bring about such wholesale political change, however strategically placed that individual might have been. For twelve years Ahern was marginalised, relegated to observer status, as others demonstrably less capable than himself had their careers promoted at his expense.

When Ahern finally forced his advancement in the teeth of Bjelke-Petersen's hostility, he was either preoccupied with running a large, complex department (DPI), or bringing a new one into being and establishing its credentials and credibility. When at Health, although his tenure was relatively short-lived, he nevertheless displayed an ability to face critical issues (such as HIV-AIDS) in a non-judgmental, professional manner. It was argued by his political opponents that, during his seven years in Cabinet, he should have been more aware of the excesses and corruption that were features of National Party rule; but he was not one of the "heavy players". Indeed, given the longstanding hostility towards him from the clique that then controlled the Government, it would be stretching credulity to imagine that he would be either admitted to their circle or briefed as to their activities. While the doctrine of collective responsibility bound him to Cabinet's decisions and actions, the Fitzgerald Inquiry made clear that ministerial corruption was an individual matter, and not one that involved the Cabinet as a whole. While the tendering processes were corrupt, these decisions were made outside the Cabinet room and presented to Cabinet for ratification as a *fait accompli*. So enmeshed and entangled had party, bureaucratic and governmental processes become that only a "root and branch" inquiry of the Fitzgerald type was able to disaggregate the situation and advocate new institutional procedures to ensure that there was no repetition.[3]

Ahern was not cleared by the Fitzgerald process, because he was never under suspicion. His personal probity was never impugned, while his "lock, stock and barrel" commitment effectively locked in his Government and party to the reform process — to the discomfort of some and the hostility of others. His, however, was a doomed agenda. Even without the internal revolt against him, by July 1989 the electorate was increasingly single-minded in its determination to sweep the Nationals from power. No plans harboured by the Ahern Government to complete the process would have turned aside this electoral current. When such a tide is rising, individuals are inevitably overwhelmed. Had Ahern fought the 1989 election as Premier, he might perhaps have abated the impact of this tide, but it is very unlikely that he could have stemmed it.

The publication of the Fitzgerald Report had effectively sealed the Nationals' fate. Although Labor had performed poorly in the three by-elections held during Ahern's term, none was held after May 1989, so there were no electoral contests with the Fitzgerald Report as their backdrop. After June, it would not have mattered when the general election was held; the result (though not its magnitude) was largely a foregone conclusion. One could argue that it would have been better for Ahern not to have led his party to defeat although, given his personal record, his reputation would have survived anyway.

A final observation is warranted as to the charge that Ahern was a weak leader presiding over an indecisive Government; that he was incapable of asserting strength through leadership and moving his Government in a firm direction. In part, this criticism has already been answered, by contrasting Ahern's decision-making style with that of his predecessor. Almost twenty years of authoritarian rule, which frequently invoked the full coercive powers of the state, had created a particular political climate in which this approach was accepted as the inevitable, and perhaps appropriate, way to make decisions. The National Party organisation had, through its propaganda, equated Bjelke-Petersen with that populist distinctiveness held to characterise Queensland politics. A shift to a more consensual and inclusive mode of decision-taking was bound to take time to become established, let alone accepted. Such a time span was denied Ahern. Austin's forthright and at times confronting approach marked some continuity with the previous regime, but a reformist agenda characterised by consultation with interested parties was a development that many in Government had great difficulty in accepting.

That having been said, the Government was under extreme pressure as the National Party era drew inexorably to its close. The Government did not — perhaps could not — discipline its backbench, because it failed to communicate to them the necessity to act upon new strategies and formulate new behaviour patterns. Simultaneously it needlessly opened itself to accusations of hesitancy and incompetence over important issues such as the abortive referendum and the trial of daylight saving. The reform process became too protracted over the establishment of the Public Accounts and Public Works Committees, and the Pecuniary Interests Register was piecemeal in both coverage and application. Other attempts to appeal to the Government's traditional constituency by continuing with previous initiatives, such as sending Geoff Muntz (later jailed for ministerial fraud) to Brazil to fight the federal government's attempt to list the North Queensland rainforests on the World Heritage Register,[4] not only failed, as predicted, but also undermined the Government's reform credentials.

Efforts to deflect attention, such as the trade union inquiry, were seen for what they were: desperate and ineffective attempts to shift scrutiny from corrupt practices associated with the Government. In similar vein was the attempt to capitalise on the airline pilots' strike. This was a federal issue, beyond the control of state authorities, let alone of the Queensland ALP, then in opposition. As the Ahern Government operated in a state of near-continual crisis, beset by internal and external pressures, it was inevitable that at times it would stumble and underperform. On the credit side was the successful implementation of its reform agenda and its embrace of the Fitzgerald process.

Finally, terminal paralysis came from this Government's inability to grapple with electoral reform. It is true that this was an unexpected collateral issue arising from the Fitzgerald Inquiry; but because Ahern had, at the start of his premiership, set himself against any such initiative, he had no contingency plans when it dominated the report. But if such basic reform was never to be contemplated, how could any part of his reform program achieve full credibility? Fitzgerald was surely correct to perceive that an unjust and weighted electoral system tainted every aspect of Government activity. The flaw in the Ahern Government lay, not in alleged deficiencies concerning its decision-making processes, but rather in its failure to undertake electoral reform. By 1989, with or without the Fitzgerald Report, this had become a necessity that could be neither postponed nor denied.

Notes

1. In 1986 the result in Landsborough had been: National 50.0 per cent, Labor 32.8 per cent and Liberal 17.3 per cent. After the distribution of Liberal preferences, Ahern won 61.6 per cent of the final vote. In 1989, the Nationals polled 39.5 per cent (-10.5), Labor 40.0 per cent (+7.3), Liberals 17.0 per cent (-0.3) and Independent 3.5 per cent. On the final count Ahern won 55.9 per cent (-5.7).
2. Implicated in December 1991 by the CJC's so-called Travel Rorts Affair, Cooper voluntarily stepped aside for Borbidge.
3. Ahern (interview 11 May 1998) noted that he opened all Cabinet documents for scrutiny by the Fitzgerald Inquiry, which had an officer in the Cabinet records room "trawling for two months" as to whether there was any corporate complicity in corruption. Ahern claims that this was the first (only?) time any Government had afforded such cooperation to a Commission of Inquiry. By contrast, the Lawrence Government supplied the "WA Inc" Royal Commission with documents on request. The difference is that, by inspecting the documents, the Fitzgerald Inquiry could identify the ones it wanted. Lacking such information, the West Australian investigators could not.
4. For a critical assessment of this decision see Richardson (1994, pp. 228–9). Richardson mistakenly attributes this despatch of Muntz and others to Bjelke-Petersen, apparently unaware that, in 1988, Ahern was Queensland Premier.

Bibliography

Aitkin, D. 1982, *Stability and Change in Australian Politics*, 2nd edn. Canberra: ANU Press.

Barclay, G. St.J. 1968, "Political Chronicle: Queensland", *Australian Journal of Politics and History*, XIV (2).

Beattie, P.D. 1990, *In the Arena*. Brisbane: Boolarong.

Bennett, L.D. 1991, A Vision of Excellence. The Political Career of Michael John Ahern (unpublished BA Hons Thesis, University of New England).

Charlton, P. 1983, *State of Mind. Why Queensland Is Different*. North Ryde: Methuen Hayes.

Chittick, G.K. and Reynolds P.L. 1992, "The Ahern Government: The Quest for Legitimacy", Paper read to 34th Annual Australasian Political Studies Conference, Australian National University, Canberra.

Coaldrake, P.O. 1989, *Working the System. Government in Queensland*. Brisbane: University of Queensland Press.

Cribb, M.N.B. 1979, "Political Chronicle: Queensland", *Australian Journal of Politics and History*, 25(2).

Cribb, M.N.B. 1981, "Political Chronicle: Queensland", *Australian Journal of Politics and History*, 27(1).

Cribb, M.N.B. 1982, "Political Chronicle: Queensland", *Australian Journal of Politics and History*, 28(2).

Cribb, M.N.B. 1991a, "Political Chronicle: Queensland", *Australian Journal of Politics and History*, 37(1).

Cribb, M.N.B. 1991b, "The National Party" in Whip, R. and Hughes, C.A. (eds), *Political Crossroads. The 1989 Queensland Election*. Brisbane: University of Queensland Press.

Cribb, M.N.B. and P.J. Boyce (eds) 1980, *Politics in Queensland 1977 and Beyond*. Brisbane: University of Queensland Press.

Davis, G. 1995, *A Government of Routines. Executive Coordination in an Australian State*. Melbourne: MacMillan.

Dickie, P. 1988, *The Road to Fitzgerald and Beyond*. Brisbane: University of Queensland Press.

Fitzgerald, R. 1984, *From 1915 to the Early 1980s. A History of Queensland*. Brisbane: University of Queensland Press.

Fitzgerald, R. and Thorton, H. 1989, *Labor in Queensland from the 1880s to 1988*. Brisbane: University of Queensland Press.

Fitzgerald Report, see *Report of a Commission of Inquiry …*

Gowers, A. and Scott, R. 1979, *Fundamentals and Fundamentalists: A Case Study of Education and Policy Making in Queensland*. Australasian Political Studies Association Monograph 22, Flinders University.

Hamill, D.J. and Reynolds, P. L. 1983, *Three Cornered Contests in South East Queensland State Seats*. Occasional Monograph No. 1, Department of Government, The University of Queensland.

Harris, H. 1972, *Political Football — The Springbok Tour of Australia, 1971*. Melbourne: Gold Star.

Hogan, M. 1987, *The Sectarian Strand: Religion in Australian History*. Ringwood: Penguin.

Hughes, C.A. (1969), *Images and Issues. The Queensland State Elections of 1963 and 1969*. Brisbane: University of Queensland Press.

Hughes, C.A. 1980, *The Government of Queensland*. Brisbane: University of Queensland Press.

Humble, W.J. 1984, The Retail Shop Leases Dispute in Queensland — David Against Goliath — A Case Study in Public Policy Formation. Unpublished M.Pub.Ad. Thesis, Department of Government, The University of Queensland.

Kelly, S. and Reynolds, P.L. 1992, *The 1991 Queensland Re-Distribution*. Occasional Monograph No. 2, Department of Government, The University of Queensland.

McKenzie, R.T. and Silver, A. (1968), *Angels in Marble: Working Class Conservatism in Urban England*. London: Heinemann.

Moroney, T.F. 1997, The Rise and Fall of the Queensland Parliamentary Service Commission: A Study of Parliamentary Independence versus Executive Government Control. Unpublished M.Pub.Ad. Thesis, Department of Government, The University of Queensland.

Miller, J and Koch, T. 1983, *Joh's KO*. Brisbane: Boolarong.

Murphy, D., Joyce, R. and Cribb, M. (eds) 1990, *The Premiers of Queensland*, 2nd edn. Brisbane: University of Queensland Press.

Nordlinger, E. 1967, *The Working Class Tories*. London: McGribben and Kee.

Overacker, L. 1968, *Australian Parties in a Changing Society*. Melbourne: F.W. Cheshire.

Queensland Parliamentary Debates (Hansard): abbreviated in the text as *QPD*.

Queensland Parliamentary Handbook 1991.

Report of the Select Committee on Education in Queensland, 1980. Queensland Legislative Assembly.

Report of a Commission of Inquiry Pursuant to Orders in Council, 1989 (Fitzgerald Report). Queensland Government.

Reynolds, P.L. 1974, *The Democratic Labor Party*. Brisbane: Jacaranda Press.

Reynolds, P.L. 1986, "Queensland Politics, The Rise and Rise of Populism", *Social Alternatives*, 5(3).

Reynolds, P.L. 1988, "Three cornered contests in Brisbane and South East Queensland federal electorates: 1974–1987", Paper read to 28th Annual Conference Australasian Political Studies Association, University of New England, Armidale.

Reynolds, P.L. 1990, "The 1989 Queensland State Election: The end of an era", *Australian Journal of Politics and History*, 36(1).

Reynolds, P.L. 1994, "The changing composition of the Queensland State Parliament, 1929–1992", *Legislative Studies*, 8(2).

Richardson, G. 1994, *Whatever It Takes*. Sydney: Bantam.

Scott, A. and Scott, R. 1980, "Reform and reaction in the Deep North: Education and policy-making in Queensland" in Wirt, F. and Harman, G. (eds), *The Education Policy at State Level: An Australian–United States Comparative Study*. Canberra: ERDC.

Shannon, A. 1991, "Jack Ahern. Horseman, cattleman, dairyman and National Party stalwart" in *Twentieth Century Profiles*, vol. 11. Brisbane: Boolarong.

Shaw, G. (ed.) 1988, *Mood of '85. The People's Response*. Australian Studies Centre, The University of Queensland.

Stevens, B. and Wanna, J. 1993, *The Goss Government: Promise and Performance of Labor in Queensland*. Melbourne: Macmillan.

Swan, W. 1983, "Queensland: Labor's Graveyard?" in Parkin, A. and Warhurst, J. (eds), *Machine Politics in the Australian Labor Party*. Sydney: George Allen and Unwin.

Walker, J. 1995, *Goss. A Political Biography*. Brisbane: University of Queensland Press.

Walter, J. 1990, "Johannes Bjelke-Petersen. The populist autocrat" in Murphy, D., Joyce, R. and Cribb, M.N.B. (eds), *The Premiers of Queensland*, 2nd edn. Brisbane: University of Queensland Press.

Whip, R. and Hughes, C.A. (eds) 1991, *Political Crossroads. The 1989 Queensland Election*. Brisbane: University of Queensland Press.

Interviews conducted with:

Hon. M.J. Ahern (8 September 1993; 7 April 1994; 14 September 1994; 4 September 1997; 11 May 1998; 24 January 2000)

B.J. Austin (7 July 1993)
Late M.N.B. Cribb (24 March 1993)
W. D'Arcy (13 September 1993)
D.K. Ford (6 March 1993)
H.D. Fraser (24 January 2000)
T. Koch (1 September 1994)
Late D. Lane (2 April 1993)
T. White (7 May 1993; 15 October 1993)

Index